Illustrated SuperCalc 5

Jerry Yancey

Wordware Publishing, Inc.

Library of Congress Cataloging-in-Publication Data

Yancey, Jerry
Illustrated SuperCalc 5 / by Jerry Yancey.
p. cm.
ISBN 1-55622-154-1
1. SuperCalc 5 (Computer program). 2. Business — Data processing.
3. Electronic spreadsheets. I. Title.
HF5548.4.S85Y36 1989
005.369— dc20 89-25012
CIP

1506 Capital Avenue
Plano, Texas 75074

Printed in the United States of America

ISBN 1-55622-154-1
10 9 8 7 6 5 4 3 2 1
9002

All inquiries for volume purchases of this book should be addressed to Wordware Publishing, Inc., at the above address. Telephone inquiries may be made by calling:

(214) 423-0090

Contents

Contents (Cont.)

Recommended Learning Sequence

Recommended Learning Sequence (Cont.)

Module 1
ABOUT THIS BOOK

INTRODUCTION

This book introduces you to Computer Associates' program, SuperCalc 5™, an advanced multipurpose electronic spreadsheet. It describes how the spreadsheet, graphics, and database capabilities of SuperCalc 5 are used in the office or home. Detailed information on each command enables you to easily manipulate, organize, and display data of all types.

This book is written for all users. It is a self-teaching text for beginners who want to learn SuperCalc 5 on their own. It is a quick reference to SuperCalc 5 commands for intermediate and advanced users. Also, it is a text for the classroom instructor to use in teaching both fundamentals and advanced applications of SuperCalc 5.

Although SuperCalc 5 is a sophisticated software package that permits you to create, customize, and link spreadsheets, its command structure is easy to understand and to use. Once you begin to use SuperCalc 5 and see the ease of creating your own spreadsheets, you'll begin to see even greater versatility. All this may appear overwhelming to the inexperienced computer user, but this book demonstrates that SuperCalc 5 is easy to learn and use.

All of the capabilities of SuperCalc 5 are exercised by commands presented in a series of menus. Most SuperCalc 5 commands, when selected, will respond with another command menu or a prompt for information about the operation you want to execute. Once the command has all the data it needs to do its job for you, it is quickly done. In this book, commands are explained in detail, and an example of the operation performed by each command is given.

An important time-saving feature of SuperCalc 5 is the use of spreadsheet templates, analagous to "form letters." Not only can you buy these preprogrammed templates for a wide variety of special applications, you can create your own.

"Seeing is believing," so to prove to yourself how easy SuperCalc 5 is to use, you may want to turn to Module 3 right now and go through the sample session. In Module 3 you set up a simple spreadsheet, perform calculations, and graph your spreadsheet. Going through these operations, you encounter SuperCalc 5 commands. At first they may not be clear, but after continued use their function becomes apparent. Do not become frustrated if everything is not immediately apparent, as time and practice will make you an experienced SuperCalc 5 user.

ORGANIZATION

This book is organized in short, easy-to-read modules. Each module, except for Modules 1 through 3, contains a description and application of a command or limited number of commands. An example and step-by-step procedure (typical operation) for use of the command is also included in the module.

The first three modules introduce you to this book and SuperCalc 5. This module, Module 1, provides information about the book and the equipment you need. Module 2 is an overview of SuperCalc 5. General information and descriptions are given. Included in Module 2 are characteristics of SuperCalc 5 which are common to all commands. Module 3 includes a sample session to get you started.

Modules 4 through 35 describe and illustrate the SuperCalc 5 commands. They are arranged in alphabetical order by command name for ease of reference. However, to use this book as a learning or teaching tool you should read the modules in the order listed in the Recommended Learning Sequence at the front of the book. It lists the command modules in simple-to-complex order, so that as you progress, you build on what you have previously mastered. Each module contains three sections: Description, Applications, and Typical Operation. The description section describes the command, the applications section gives uses of the command, and the typical operation section provides illustrations of using the command.

Appendix A provides a listing of terms and definitions. Most are in reference to SuperCalc 5, although many of them are general to all computers and computer programs.

Appendix B contains a listing of functions contained in SuperCalc 5's programming. Included are arithmetic functions, financial functions, and other useful calculating tools.

Appendix C discusses the compatibility of SuperCalc, SuperCalc 2, SuperCalc 3, SuperCalc 4, and the subject of this book, SuperCalc 5.

Appendix D describes configuring the SuperCalc 5 program for your particular computer system. The diskettes you received in your SuperCalc 5 package must be installed on your system before you can use SuperCalc 5. This appendix explains how to do that.

Appendix E is provided for either classroom or self-teaching environments. If you are a classroom instructor, you might include these exercises in student assignments or examinations. If you are learning SuperCalc 5 on your own, use these exercises to check your understanding of each of the SuperCalc 5 commands. If you can answer the questions successfully, then you are ready to move on to the next module in the recommended learning sequence.

HARDWARE AND SOFTWARE REQUIREMENTS

SuperCalc 5 operates on most personal computer systems. Check your documentation to verify that you have the correct version for both your computer and the operating system you are using.

SuperCalc 5 requires a minimum of 512K of RAM, one floppy disk drive (3 1/2" or 5 1/4" DSDD), and a hard disk drive. However, 640K of RAM is recommended for normal operations. If you work with large or linked spreadsheets, expanded memory is recommended. SuperCalc 5 will support up to 32 megabytes of expanded memory.

A printing device is necessary if you want printouts of your spreadsheets and graphs. If your dot matrix printer is capable of printing in compressed print, you can print 132-character-wide spreadsheets on 8 1/2 x 11" paper. SuperCalc 5 also supports plotters for multi-color output of your graphics.

WHAT YOU SHOULD KNOW

You should be familiar with your computer and its keyboard and the commands available on your operating system which allow you to list your directories, format a disk, and copy, rename, or delete files. If you can do these things, you're ready to use SuperCalc 5!

Module 2
SUPERCALC 5 OVERVIEW

INTRODUCTION

This module introduces you to SuperCalc 5 and the world of electronic spreadsheets. As suggested by the name, the electronic spreadsheet is equivalent to an accountant's worksheet, but your computer performs the calculations for you.

THE ELECTRONIC SPREADSHEET

A spreadsheet is a computer workspace consisting of rows and columns. Entries are made at the intersection of a row and column, called a *cell.* Cells may contain words (text), numbers (numeric values), or formulas. Formulas instruct SuperCalc 5 to perform an operation on or between cell entries.

The border of the SuperCalc 5 screen display identifies each row and column. Follow a row number to the right and a column number downward to find a cell. Cells are designated by their column letter followed by their row number. For example, the designation of the cell located at the intersection of column G and row 15 is G15. As you move into rows or columns which are not initially on your display, SuperCalc 5 scrolls your display to present that portion of your spreadsheet. A portion of the SuperCalc 5 spreadsheet looks like the following illustration.

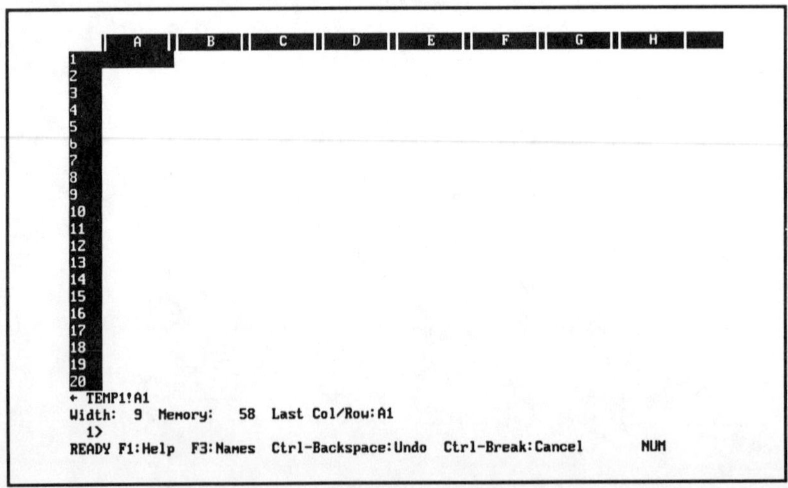

Although you can only display 20 rows at a time, there are 9999 rows in SuperCalc 5's spreadsheet. There are 254 columns, labeled A through IT, which initially have space for 9 characters each. The top and left borders of the spreadsheet indicate the current cell selection by highlighting the column location on the top border and the row location on the left border. You have the option to turn the highlighter on or off. The current cell location of the spreadsheet cursor on your spreadsheet is called the active cell. The row containing the active cell is the active row, and the column containing the active cell is the active column.

CELL RANGES The term "range" is a cell group specification. You are asked to enter various cell ranges by most of SuperCalc 5's commands. The following table provides an explanation of ranges and examples.

Table 2-1. SUPERCALC 5 RANGE DESCRIPTION

Range	Description	Examples
Cell	A single spreadsheet location designated by a column letter followed by a row number.	A8, B3, BK254
Column	Cells in a vertical line designated by a letter or pair of letters from A through IT.	A, J, DY, IA
Partial Column	A consecutive group of cells in a single column indicated by separating the beginning and ending cells with a colon.	D8:D29, CR12:CR357
Column Range	A consecutive group of columns indicated by separating beginning and ending columns with a colon.	A:F, AS:HV
Row	Cells in a horizontal line designated by a number from 1 through 2000.	1, 15, 1648
Partial Row	A consecutive group of cells in a single row indicated by separating beginning and ending cells with a colon.	C8:J8, Z12:HA12
Row Range	A consecutive group of rows indicated by separating beginning and ending rows with a colon.	1:3, 21:88, 251:1739
Block	A rectangular area of cells designated by separating upper left and lower right cells with a colon.	B9:H15, AS258:CX912

CELL ENTRIES A cell may contain text, repeating text, a numeric constant, or a formula. You may specify a cell's content characteristics without affecting the actual contents of the cell.

Text SuperCalc 5 will handle a text string containing a maximum of 115 characters. Any text entry is assumed to have a preceding quote mark ("). However, you need not begin your text entry with a quote mark unless your text begins with a character reserved by SuperCalc 5 (=!;&/ or ?).

Numerical A cell containing a numeric value as a constant may have its contents displayed in either the integer, general, exponential, or money format. Values can have up to 16 significant digits, a decimal point, and a value sign, which is optional. Exponential numbers may contain up to 16 significant digits, a decimal point, a value sign, and an exponent between positive and negative 63. Values containing more than 16 digits will have their extreme right digits changed to zeros.

Formulas SuperCalc 5 accepts mathematical expressions, created with or without using SuperCalc 5's available functions as formulas, and you may enter a formula containing up to 116 characters in a cell. Formulas begin with a numeric constant, a mathematical function, a special function, a cell reference, a calendar function, or a textual constant. After you have completed your entry and the formula is entered into the spreadsheet, SuperCalc 5 automatically performs the calculation instructions of the formula, and the *result* is displayed on your screen. The formula is kept in spreadsheet memory until you edit or remove it. Also, the formula calculation result of one cell may be written to another cell by entering the origin cell's designator in the destination cell.

OPERATING MODES

SuperCalc 5 has three types of modes: program, macro, and keyboard. Program modes are for spreadsheet operations. Macro modes allow you to construct or use macros. Keyboard modes perform special functions when activated. Refer to Table 2-2 for a list of the modes and a brief description of the function of each. Mode indicators appear on the help line of the dialog panel to show the active mode. Supercalc 5 always begins in the Ready mode, waiting to respond to your first action.

Table 2-2. SUPERCALC 5 MODES

Mode	Mode Type	Function
Audit	Program	Options in this mode allow you to find, locate, and replace data, optimize memory usage, and detect errors.
Edit	Program	Edit data located in the current active cell.
Entry	Program	Enter new data in the active cell.
File	Program	This mode is entered when a filename entry is required.
Input	Program	Data can only be entered in a certain range, as the Restrict command is active.
Menu	Program	A menu is being displayed.
Name	Program	The Named Range Directory is being displayed.
Point	Program	This mode is entered when a range entry is required.
Ready	Program	The program is waiting for a data entry or command.
Sheet	Program	The Open Spreadsheet directory is being displayed.
Wrap	Program	The word-wrap function has been selected to enter data.
Macro	Macro	A macro is executing.
Step	Macro	Macro single-step mode is on.
Astep	Macro	Single-step mode is occurring automatically. (Autostep mode)
Learn	Macro	Keyboard entries are being stored in the learn range.
Direct	Macro	Macro commands can be entered directly during a learn session.
F8 To Resume	Macro	Pessing F8 terminates keyboard input and resumes macro execution.

Table 2-2. SUPERCALC 5 MODES (Cont.)

Mode	Mode Type	Function
Return To Resume	Macro	Pressing Enter terminates keyboard input and resumes macro execution.
(F8)Step L:# Line#/ Cell Contents	Macro	Pressing F8 single-steps a macro, where L:# is the level number in a sequence of nested macros, followed by the macro name, line number or cell, and content of the command sequence currently executing.
CAPS	Keyboard	Letters are typed in upper case only.
NUM	Keyboard	Enables numeric keypad at right end of keyboard.
SCROLL	Keyboard	Locks cell cursor in place.
TAB,BTAB	Keyboard	Moves cursor to first (TAB) or last (BTAB) cell in a series of occupied cells.
END	Keyboard	Used in combination with other keys, moves cursor to bottom right cell of active spreadsheet or to last occupied cell or edge of active spreadsheet.

COMMANDS

The Command menu of SuperCalc 5 contains a very versatile and powerful set of commands that enable you to build and manipulate a spreadsheet quickly and easily. To display the Command menu, simply type / (slash mark). The Command menu is displayed and you select the operation needed to accomplish your job. Other command-like functions are available in SuperCalc 5, and they are listed in Table 2-3. Note that you may type a question mark (?) or press F1 anytime to receive HELP from SuperCalc 5.

Table 2-3. COMMAND FUNCTIONS

Type	Instruction	Description
? or F1	Answer Key	Type a ? whenever you need instructional assistance. This key provides information at any time, at any command level.
/	Slash Command	Type a / to access any of SuperCalc 5's operational commands. Use the Backspace key to "back out of" a command.
=	GoTo	Type an = followed by any cell designator and press Enter to move your spreadsheet cursor directly to the cell specified. If the cell you specified is not currently displayed on your screen, then the cell specified becomes the new upper left cell of your display. If no cell designator is entered, then your Active Cell becomes the new upper left corner cell of your display.
!	Recalculate	Type an ! to instruct SuperCalc 5 to recalculate your spreadsheet formulas. Use this key anytime you wish to update your calculated values.
;	Switch	When using the WINDOW command's Windows split screen ability, type a ; (semicolon) to move your spreadsheet cursor from one window to the other.
&	Resume Execute	Type an & (ampersand) to resume a halted EXECUTE file. An & entered in an EXECUTE file pauses its operation, letting you make any needed entries. Type an & to continue your EXECUTE file.

Press F1 or type a ? anytime for help, and the general help Answer Screen is displayed, as shown in the following illustration.

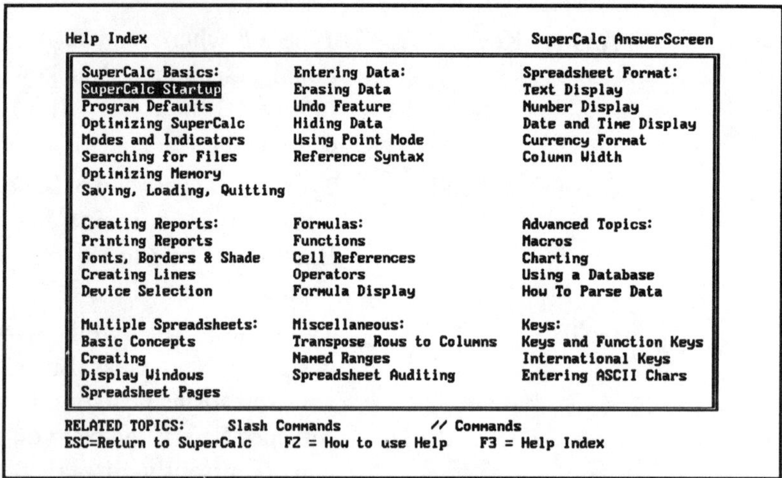

Press F1 or type a ? after typing a /, and an Answer Screen is displayed that briefly explains each of SuperCalc 5's commands. The command Answer Screen is shown in the following illustration.

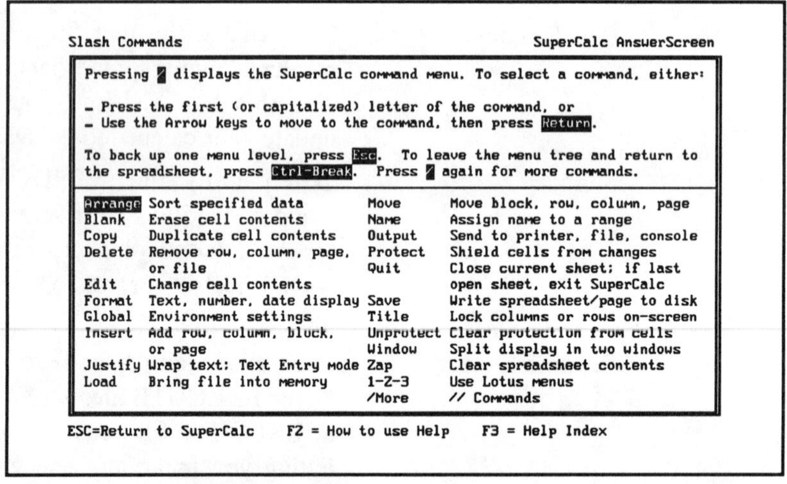

Press any key to return to your spreadsheet.

CURSORS

Two SuperCalc 5 cursors are displayed on your screen. The spreadsheet cursor and the edit cursor are both always displayed, but only one cursor at a time is active. Move either of these cursors with your arrow keys or control key "cursor diamond." To use the control key cursor diamond, press your Ctrl key and one of the letters E (up), X (down), S (left), or D (right) simultaneously. Some computers may require setting the Num Lock key to use the arrow keys.

SPREADSHEET CURSOR The spreadsheet cursor is always located in the active cell, and its display size automatically adjusts to the formatted cell's size (cell's display character width). This cursor is active or inactive dependent on the current operating mode. It's locked in the active cell whenever you are in the Entry mode or in a command sequence. It's activated, and you can move to any spreadsheet cell, when you are in the Ready mode. As you move the spreadsheet cursor about the spreadsheet, the address of the active cell and the last direction your spreadsheet cursor moved are displayed on the dialog panel below the spreadsheet.

EDIT CURSOR The edit cursor appears on the next-to-last line of the dialog panel, called the entry line. The cursor position advances to the right as you type an entry or as you enter options to a command. Use either the Backspace or Left Arrow to back out of command options.

The arrow, Tab, Esc, Enter, Ctrl-Z, Ctrl-C, and F2 keys each have a special meaning on the entry line. These keys let you edit or enter the contents of the entry line. Press Left and Right Arrow keys to move the edit cursor left and right, respectively, without changing the contents of this line. Press Down Arrow to delete the character at the current cursor position. Press Up Arrow to insert a blank character at the current cursor position.

Pressing Tab moves the edit cursor to the beginning or end of the Data Entry line, depending on its current position. If the cursor is within or at the end of the line, it moves to the beginning of the line. If it is at the beginning of the line, it moves to the end of the line.

Pressing Esc writes the active cell's reference designator to the entry line.

Pressing Enter writes the contents of the entry line to the active cell.

Pressing Ctrl-Z, Ctrl-C, or F2 erases the contents of the entry line.

DIALOG PANEL

Below the spreadsheet display are four lines which make up the dialog panel. These lines contain information, prompts, and the entry line for text and data. For purposes of explanation, each line is given a name, and they are listed here in the top-to-bottom order of their appearance on the dialog panel (that is, the help line is at the bottom of your display).

Status line
Prompt line
Entry line
Help line

A brief explanation of the contents of each line is contained in the following paragraphs.

STATUS LINE The first line in the dialog panel shows you the current filename, the cell where the cursor is located, displays commands or options, and displays error or advisory messages when a problem occurs. As shown in the following example, the first item on the line indicates the direction of travel that the cursor took to arrive at the current cell. If Enter is pressed at the end of an entry, the cursor will move in the direction of the arrow. The second item is the current filename. If no file is loaded, TEMP1 will be shown until you load a named file. The next item of information is the address of the current cell. The address shown is the location of the cursor in the current spreadsheet. The next displayed item is entry level format options for the current cell if any are contained in the cell. This item will not be displayed unless the Format command has been used to set a format at the Entry level. The next item indicates if the current cell is protected or not. A P indicates that the cell contents are protected, and a blank space indicates an unprotected cell. The next item indicates the type of data contained in the current cell. The data can be text, repeating text, control text, or formulas including numbers and functions. Immediately after the text type of the cell, the first few characters of the cell contents are displayed. Text entries are preceded by a quotation mark.

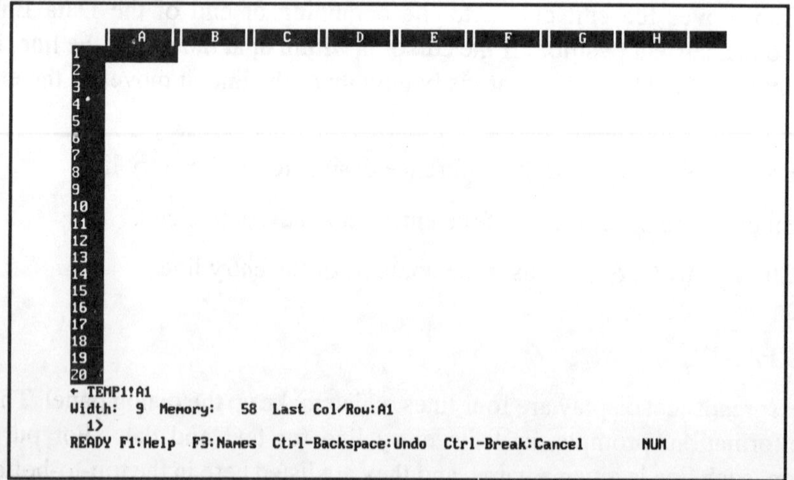

PROMPT LINE The second line in the dialog panel is the prompt line. This line lists the options available at each level of the Command menu. When not in the command mode, three pieces of information are displayed on the line. The first item is the width of the current cell. The next item is the amount of working memory (RAM) available in your computer. The number shown is the number of kilobytes of RAM remaining. This number decreases as you add to your spreadsheet. The last item on this line shows you the size of your active spreadsheet. The size is determined by the last column and last row containing data.

ENTRY LINE The third line in the dialog panel is the entry line. This line displays the data you enter. You enter or edit data, formulas, command or option selections, cell ranges, and name entries (filenames, range names, and macro names).

HELP LINE The fourth line of the dialog panel is the help line. This line displays the current mode, help messages, and reminders. In the previous example, the spreadsheet is in the Ready mode, and several function reminders are displayed. When the Command menu is displayed, a help message is displayed on this line, giving a short description of the current option which is highlighted on the command options menu.

When more information is needed than is provided on the help line, you can view the AnswerScreen by pressing F1.

Module 3
A SAMPLE SUPERCALC 5 SPREADSHEET

DESCRIPTION

This module takes you through the steps of building a simple SuperCalc 5 spreadsheet so you can get used to the operation of SuperCalc 5. Follow the steps listed in this module to build a budget management spreadsheet and see how easy it is to enter text, values, commands, and make calculations.

> **NOTE**
> SuperCalc 5 must be installed on the hard disk drive in your system before proceeding. Refer to Appendix D for the installation procedure. After you have installed SuperCalc 5 on your hard drive, store the diskettes in a safe place so they are available should you need them again.

STARTING SUPERCALC 5

To start SuperCalc 5, begin at the DOS prompt for your hard drive and follow these steps:

1. Type **CD\CALC** and press **Enter** to change the current directory to the SuperCalc directory.
2. Type **SC5** and press **Enter**. SuperCalc 5's copyright screen appears on your display.
3. Press any key and a blank spreadsheet appears on your screen. SuperCalc 5 is ready for you to enter the world of electronic spreadsheets.

BUILDING A SPREADSHEET

You are now ready to build your first spreadsheet.

1. Begin your spreadsheet by typing **BUDGET MANAGER**. Notice that as you enter the characters, SuperCalc 5 puts them on the entry line and your display looks like this:

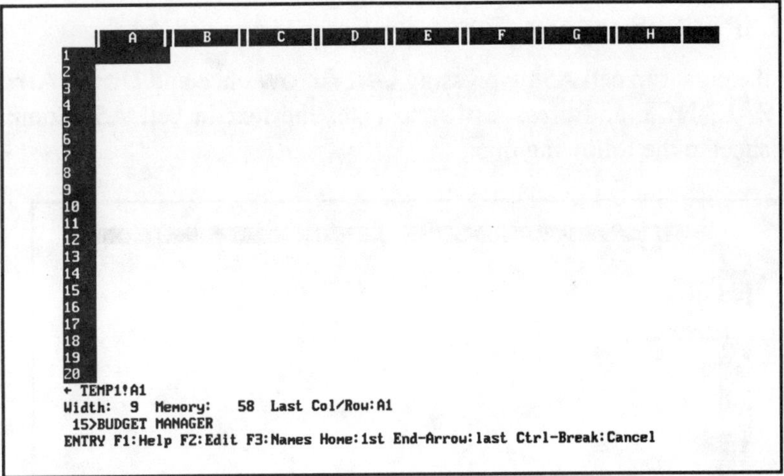

2. Press **Enter** and SuperCalc 5 moves the information on the entry line to the cell where the spreadsheet cursor is currently located (the active cell). It's that easy! Your spreadsheet now looks like this:

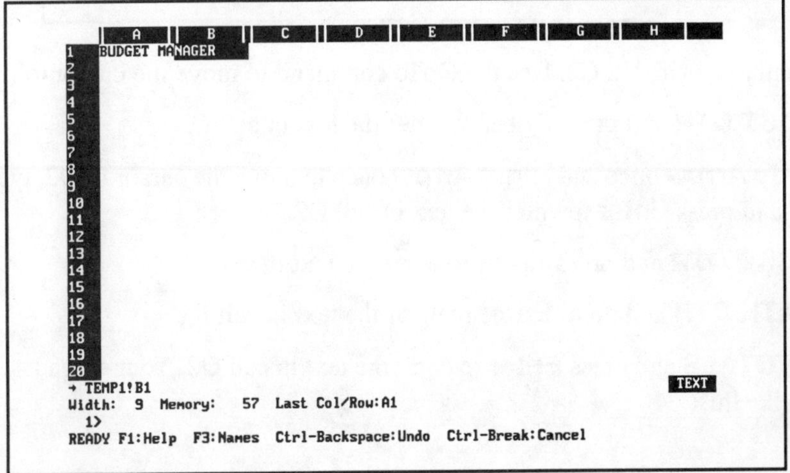

3. Type = **A3** and press **Enter** to move the spreadsheet cursor to cell A3. (The = key is SuperCalc 5's GoTo command.) Type **INCOME** and press **Enter**. Notice that your spreadsheet cursor moved to cell B3. SuperCalc 5 automatically advances the spreadsheet cursor in the direction you last moved it. Using the GoTo command does not change the last movement direction. Use the GoTo command now to move the cursor to cell A4 by typing = **A4** and pressing **Enter**.

4. Type **EXPENSES** and press **Enter** to enter the text in cell A4.
5. Move the cursor to cell A5 by pressing **Left Arrow** once and **Down Arrow** once. Type **BALANCE** and press **Enter** to enter the text in cell A5. Compare your spreadsheet to the following one:

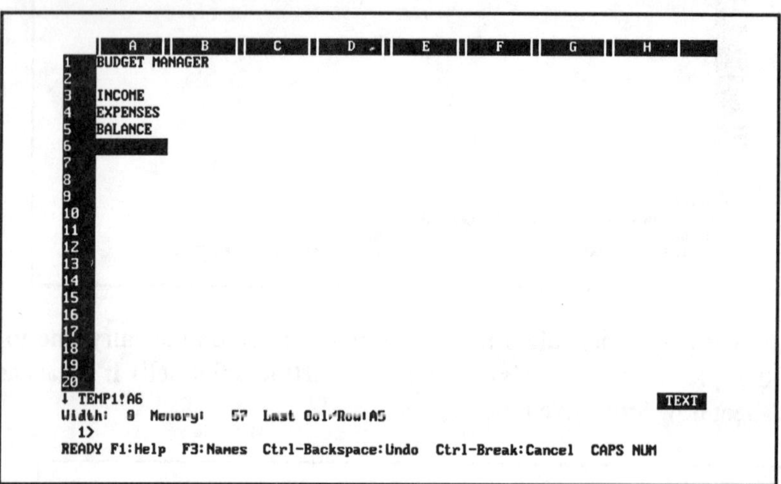

Your next entry goes in cell C2. Use the GoTo command to move the cursor to that cell.

6. Type **1ST QTR** and press **Enter** to enter the text in cell C2.
7. Press **Up Arrow** once and **Right Arrow** once to move the cursor to D2, type **2ND QTR**, and press **Enter** to enter the text in cell D2.
8. Type **3RD QTR** and press **Enter** to enter the text in cell E2.
9. Type **4TH QTR** and press **Enter** to enter the text in cell F2.
10. Type **TOTALS** and press **Enter** to enter the text in cell G2. Your spreadsheet now looks like this:

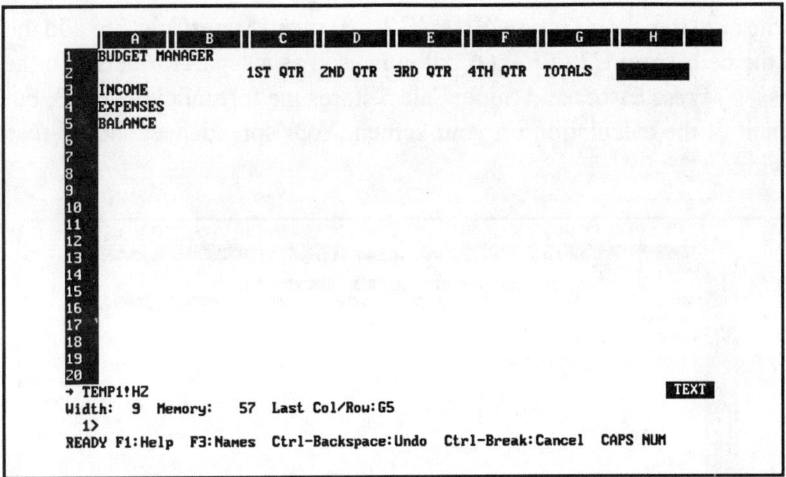

11. Now you are ready to enter numbers in your spreadsheet. Type **= C3** and press **Enter**.

12. Type **6000** and press **Enter** to enter the number in cell C3, representing an income of 6000 dollars for the first quarter.

13. Type **6000** and press **Enter** for each of the remaining quarters and compare your spreadsheet to the following one.

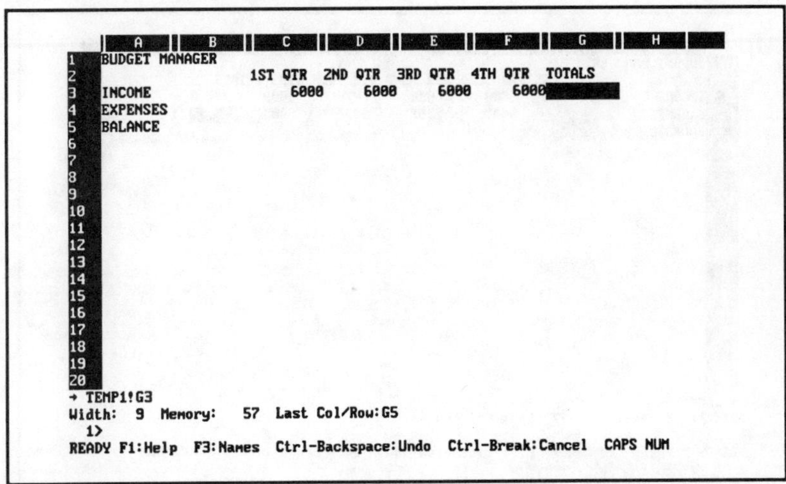

The total for the four quarters is the sum of the values in cells C3, D3, E3, and F3. By placing a simple formula in cell G3, you instruct SuperCalc 5 to add the values in these cells and place the total in cell G3.

14. With the cursor in cell G3, type **SUM(C3:F3)** to tell SuperCalc 5 to add the contents of all the cells from C3 to F3. (A colon is used as a separator between the two cell addresses.) Press **Enter** and SuperCalc 5 stores the formula in cell G3, but displays the result of the calculation on your screen. Your spreadsheet should resemble the following:

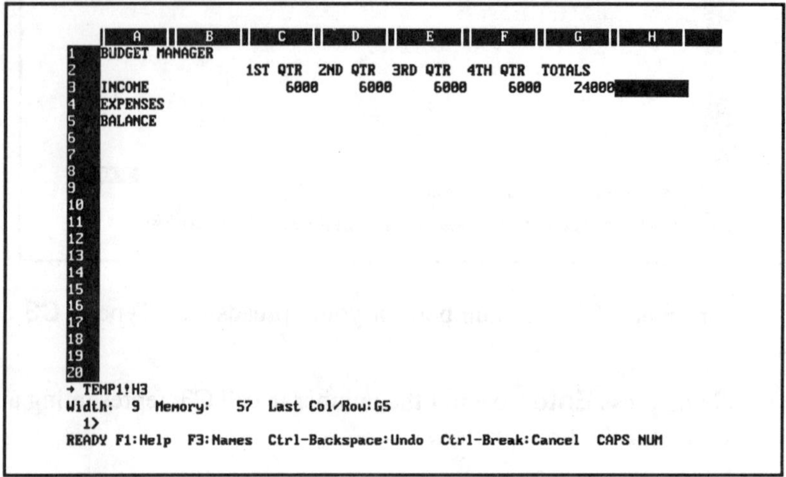

15. Type the values for expenses as shown on the following display:

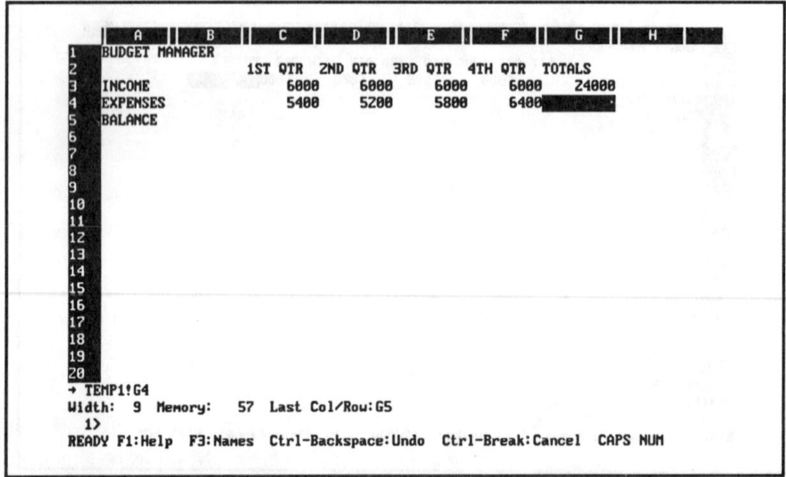

16. In cell G4, type the formula **SUM(C4:F4)** and press **Enter**. The sum of the expenses is now displayed in cell G4.

17. Move the cursor to cell C5, type **C3–C4**, and press **Enter**. This enters the formula for calculating the difference between Income and Expenses for the first quarter.

18. With the cursor in cell D5, type **D3–D4** and press **Enter**. In cells E5, F5, and G5, enter the formulas **E3–E4**, **F3–F4**, and **G3–G4**, pressing **Enter** after each entry. Your example spreadsheet is now completed.

19. Change the Income and Expenses values to see that SuperCalc 5 recalculates TOTALS and BALANCE for you after new data is entered.

20. After experimenting with other Income and Expense values, return to the original values. Compare your spreadsheet to the following:

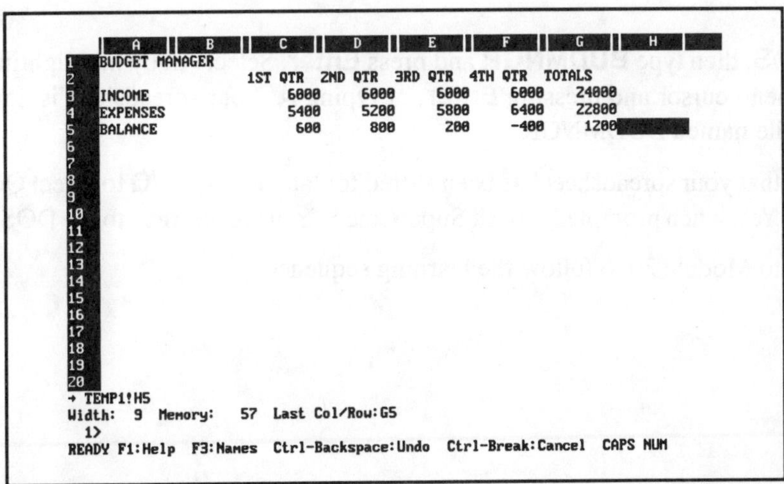

GRAPHING A SPREADSHEET

To continue this sample session, let's graph your spreadsheet now.

21. Type //**G** to access SuperCalc 5's graphing feature, the Graphics command.

22. Type **T** and SuperCalc 5 prompts you to select the type of graph you are creating.

23. Type **L** to select a line graph and press **Enter**.

24. Type **D** and you are prompted to enter the range of data you are graphing.

25. Type **C4:F4** and press **Enter** to graph your expenses.

26. Press **Backspace** and SuperCalc 5 prompts you to enter more graphing information.

27. To put a title on your graph, type **L** and press **Enter**. Select the Titles option by typing **T**. This brings up the Title Definition menu, which will be explained in a later module. Type **EXPENSES** and press **Backspace**, and type **Q** to return to the main options menu.

28. Select the View option by typing **V** and pressing **Enter** to display your graph.

29. After viewing your graph, press any key to return to your spreadsheet.

SAVING AND EXITING

This spreadsheet is used in other modules, so you should name a file in which you want to store it.

30. Type **/S**, then type **BUDMNGR** and press **Enter**. Select All by highlighting it with the menu cursor and pressing **Enter**, or typing **A**. Your spreadsheet is now stored in a file named BUDMNGR.

31. Now that your spreadsheet has been stored for later use, type **/Q** to select Quit. Type **Y** for Yes, when prompted, to exit SuperCalc 5. You are returned to the DOS prompt.

32. Turn to Module 20 to follow the learning sequence.

Module 4
1-2-3

DESCRIPTION

The 1-2-3 command gives you the capability to execute Lotus 1-2-3 command sequences from within SuperCalc 5. Each 1-2-3 command is complete with all options, so you can make good use of your Lotus expertise while operating SuperCalc 5.

After a 1-2-3 command has been executed, you are returned to the SuperCalc 5 spreadsheet. If desired, you can activate a Lotus compatibility mode by using the Global command. While the Lotus compatibility mode is activated, all commands are interpreted through the 1-2-3 menus. Return to the standard SuperCalc menus by using the Lotus Worksheet command.

APPLICATIONS

The 1-2-3 command allows you to accomplish tasks with SuperCalc that produce a result known to you from experience with Lotus. In addition, you can use 1-2-3 to work with imported files created with Lotus.

TYPICAL OPERATION

To use the 1-2-3 command, follow the steps listed here, beginning with the spreadsheet in the Ready mode.

1. Type **/1-2-3**. The following screen appears.

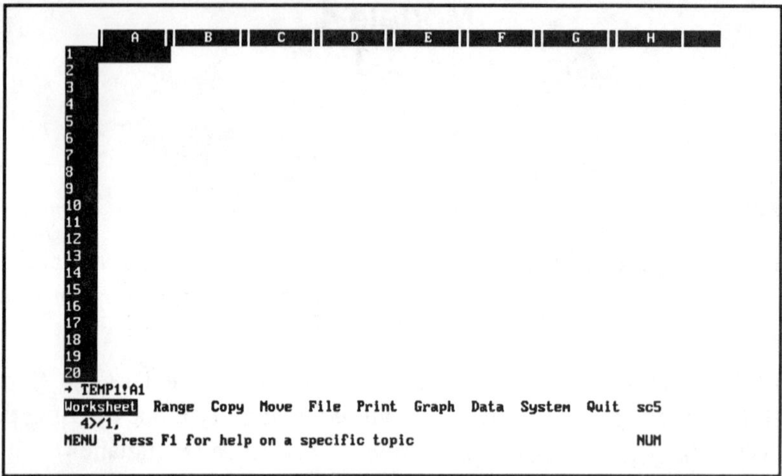

2. Notice that all the commands on the menu are from Lotus 1-2-3. Select a command and press **Enter**, and options for the command selection appear. Once completed, your command selection is interpreted by SuperCalc, and the sequence executed.

3. If you have a problem with a 1-2-3 command and need some help, press **F1** and the following screen appears.

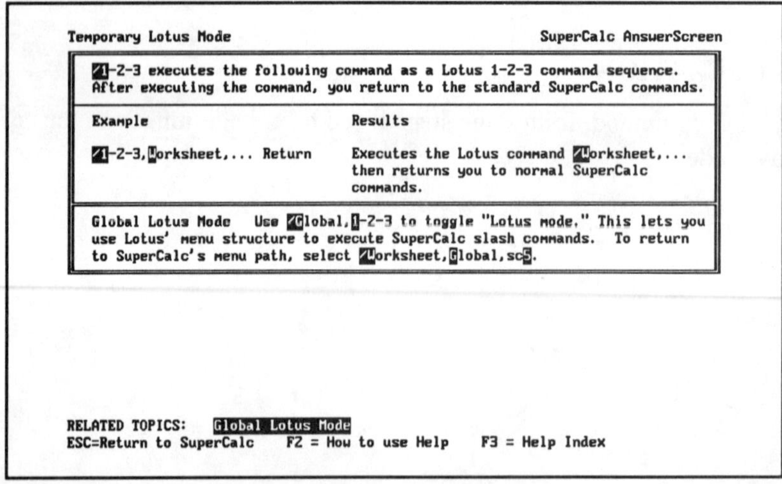

4. Press **Esc** to return to the spreadsheet.

5. Turn to Module 9 to continue the learning sequence.

Module 5
ADD-IN

DESCRIPTION

The Add-in command allows programs and functions from other sources to be used with SuperCalc 5. A list of the programs and functions is created, containing the name, drive, directory, and filename, and the options settings for each. The Add-in options are Attach, Detach, Invoke, Zap, and Quit. A description of each is contained in the following paragraphs.

ATTACH This option attaches a program or function to SuperCalc 5. Select Attach and you are prompted to enter the identifier data fo the program or function, then select from another options menu. You can select from None or 1 - 0. 1 - 0 assigns a function key (F1-F10) to an add-in, allowing you to invoke the Add-in by pressing Shift plus the function key. None assigns no function key to the Add-in. None can be used for attaching an Add-in function, as it is invoked automatically when used in a formula. After specifying a filename and assigning a function key, you can designate one attached program to be invoked automatically when you start SuperCalc 5. After assigning a function key to a filename, you are prompted to select Yes or No to automatically invoke that particular program. Add-in functions may not be automatically invoked.

DETACH This option deletes programs or functions from the Add-in list. You can select from the list or enter directly the name of any program or function you are removing. Once you select a file for deletion and execute the command, the file is removed from the Add-in list and is no longer available for use by SuperCalc 5.

INVOKE This option executes the program or function selected. You are prompted for the name and can select it from the Add-in list or enter it directly.

ZAP This option deletes all Add-in programs and functions from memory. The Add-in list is cleared, and the functions and programs are no longer available for use. You are prompted to select Yes or No after you have selected Zap, to verify that you are serious about removing all Add-ins.

QUIT This option is very straightforward. Select this option, and you are returned to the spreadsheet in the Ready mode.

APPLICATIONS

Add-in allows you to execute programs and functions at the stroke of a single key from within SuperCalc 5. Repetitious entries, calculations, or many other tasks can be reduced to using a function key. You can automatically invoke a program at start-up to bring up a partially built spreadsheet. Your creativity can do many things with the Add-in command.

TYPICAL OPERATION

To use the Add-in command, follow the steps listed here, beginning with the spreadsheet in the Ready mode.

1. Type // and select Add-in. Press **Enter** and the following screen appears.

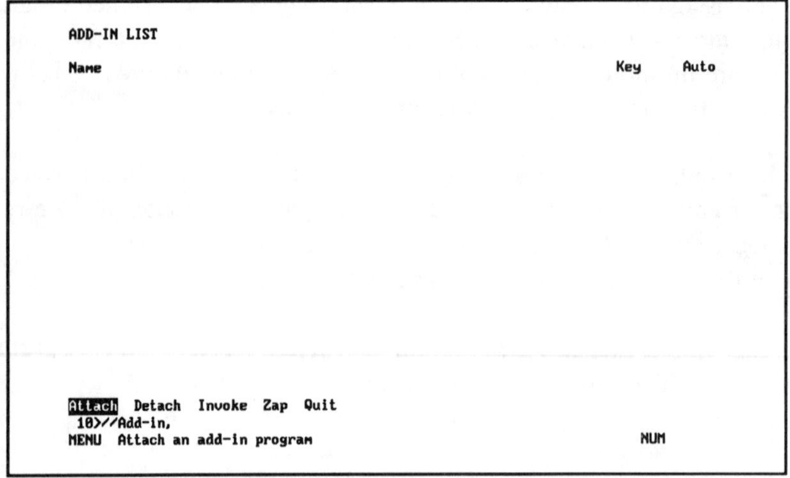

2. You are prompted to select an option from the menu which includes Attach, Detach, Invoke, Zap, and Quit. Select Attach and press **Enter**. The following screen appears.

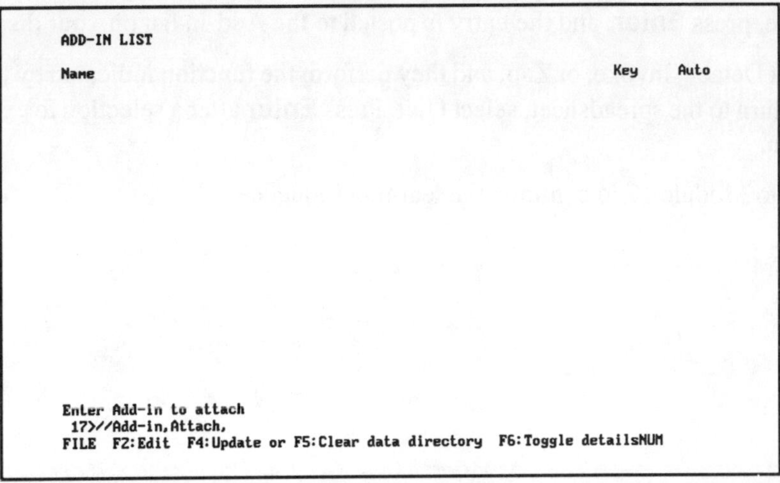

3. You are prompted to enter the directory and filename for the program or function you are putting on the Add-in list. After your entry is made, press **Enter**. The following screen appears.

```
FILE LIST
Directory displayed is C:\CALC
Data directory is C:\CALC

*.ADS

<DIRECTORIES>

Select <DIRECTORIES> to list subdirectories     12500992 bytes free
 17>//Add-in,Attach,
FILE  F2:Edit  F4:Update or F5:Clear data directory  F6:Toggle details
```

4. You are now prompted to select a function key to assign to your entry. After your selection has been made, press **Enter**. The next screen prompts you to select Yes or No to automatically invoke this program when SuperCalc 5 is loaded. After your choice, press **Enter**, and the entry is posted to the Add-in list on your display.
5. Select Detach, Invoke, or Zap, and they perform the function indicated by the name. To return to the spreadsheet, select Quit. Press **Enter** after a selection to execute the option.
6. Turn to Module 17 to continue the learning sequence.

Module 6
ARRANGE

DESCRIPTION

The Arrange command is used to sort a group of cells. The sort is performed in ascending or descending order, and up to three sort keys are allowed. Sorting with a column as a key arranges the rows in your spreadsheet, and a row key arranges the columns.

The data you work with is not always confined to letters and numbers. Therefore, SuperCalc 5 groups and sorts special characters as well as letters and numbers. When SuperCalc 5 encounters special characters as well as letters and numbers in a sort, it groups them in the following order.

For ascending sorts:

space (blank cell)
punctuation
aAbBcC......zZ
0.........9

For descending sorts:

ZzYyXx.......Aa
punctuation
space (blank cell)
9........0

The Arrange command performs a stable sort, meaning that when two items in a sort field are equal, the order in which they appeared is not changed.

When you use the Arrange command, you are offered three options, Block, Column, or Row. Each option is described in the following paragraphs.

BLOCK Selection of the block sort allows you to sort an entire spreadsheet or any part of it that you wish. You define up to three sort keys and choose ascending or descending order for your sort. You sort by row or column and choose whether or not to adjust formulas in your spreadsheet according to the sorted data. One caution, however, about sorting and formulas. The integrity of a formula is retained after a sort only if all the records (rows) contain references only to that row, i.e., A1 + B1 in row 1.

Once you select the Block option, you are prompted to select from an options menu containing Go, 1stkey, 2ndkey, 3rdkey, Options, Zap, and Quit. A brief description of each follows.

Go The Go option executes the sort after you have entered your instructions.

1stkey This option is for entry of your primary sort key. After your entry, you are prompted to select Ascending or Descending by the next option menu to indicate the direction of your sort.

2ndkey This option is for entry of your secondary sort key. You are also prompted by the next option menu to select Acsending or Descending.

3rdkey This option is for entry of your third sort key. Again, the next option menu prompts you to select Ascending or Descending.

Options The Options selection allows you to choose whether you are sorting by row or column in the block which you are sorting, or to adjust formulas when the sort is done. Select Column-wise from the options menu, and you can select Yes or No from the next option menu. Select Yes, and your sort is down the column. The rows are sorted according to your instructions. Select No, and the sort is across the rows. The columns are sorted according to your instructions. Select Adjust from the options menu, and you are prompted to select Yes or No by the next option menu. Select Yes, and formulas involved in your sort are adjusted for their new location. Select No, and formulas are not adjusted.

Zap The Zap option clears all sort key ranges and the block range.

Quit The Quit option returns you to the spreadsheet in the Ready mode.

COLUMN The Column option sorts any column you choose, arranging it in ascending or descending order, with or without formula adjustment. When you select the Column option, you are prompted to enter the column you are sorting.

If you are sorting the entire column, press Enter and the column is immediately sorted in ascending order, with no formula adjustment. If you are sorting a part of the column, enter the range of the column you are sorting. You are then prompted by an options menu to select Ascending or Descending. Another options menu then prompts you to select Adjust or No-adjust. After your instructions have been entered, press Enter to execute the sort.

ROW The Row option sorts any row you choose, arranging it in ascending or descending order, with or without formula adjustment. When you select the Row option, you are prompted to enter the column you are sorting. If you are sorting the entire row, press Enter and the row is immediately sorted in ascending order, with no formula adjustment. If you are sorting a part of the row, enter the range of the row you are sorting. You are then prompted by an options menu to select Ascending or Descending. Another options menu then prompts you to select Adjust or No-adjust. After your instructions have been entered, press Enter to execute the sort.

APPLICATIONS

The Arrange command is used to sort into alphabetical or numerical order such items as names, dates, ZIP codes, or check numbers. For effective use of the Arrange command, some thought must be given to the desired result so that entries can be made that yield the desired result. If you sort on dates where the year is significant, you might enter the dates in the form YY/MM/DD. An alternative would be to use a separate column for the year and do a multi-level sort.

TYPICAL OPERATION

To illustrate the use of the Arrange command, the example spreadsheet is sorted by the Arrange command and the results of the sort operations are shown. Begin with the spreadsheet in the Ready mode, and follow the listed steps.

1. Type **/L EXAMPLE1.SC5** and press **Enter**. Then type **R**. The file is loaded.
2. Type **/A**. The following screen is displayed.

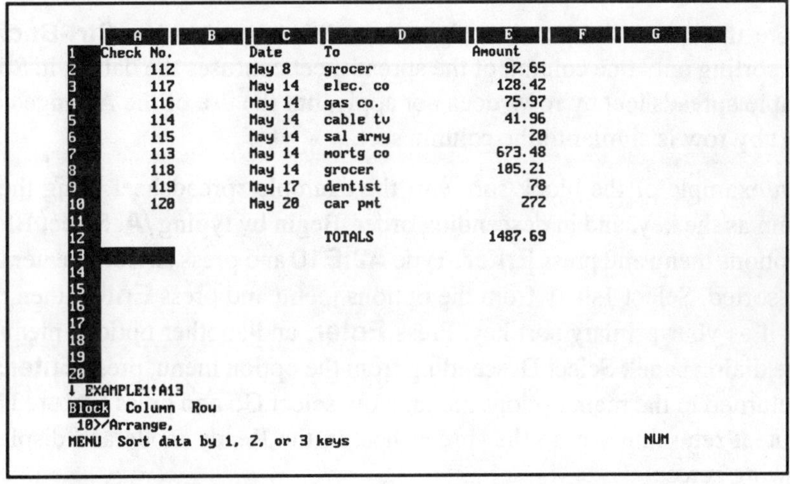

3. Notice the check numbers are not in sequence. To sort them in ascending order by check number, select Column, press **Enter**, type **A**, and press **Enter**. The column is automatically sorted in ascending order with no adjustment. The following screen appears.

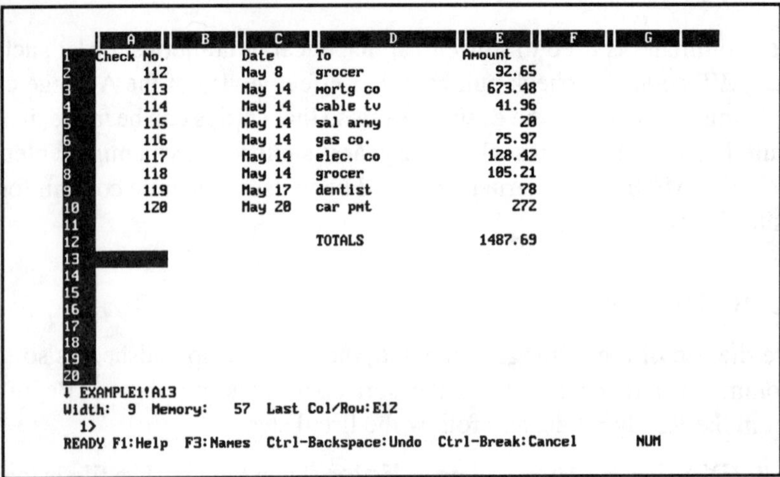

The spreadsheet is sorted according to your instructions, and you are returned to the spreadsheet in the Ready mode.

4. Restore the spreadsheet to its original condition by pressing **Ctrl-Backspace**, since sorting only one column of the spreadsheet confuses the data in it. Sorting the example spreadsheet by rows does not apply, but the use of the Arrange command to sort by row is similar to the column sort.

5. As an example of the block sort, sort the example spreadsheet using the amount column as the key, and in descending order. Begin by typing **/A**. Select Block from the options menu and press **Enter**. Type **A2:E10** and press **Enter** to enter the range to be sorted. Select 1stkey from the options menu and press **Enter**, then type **E** to enter it as your primary sort key. Press **Enter**, and another options menu appears on the dialog panel. Select Descending from the option menu, press **Enter**, and you are returned to the main options menu. Now select Go and press **Enter**. The sort is executed, returning you to the spreadsheet in the Ready mode and displaying the following screen.

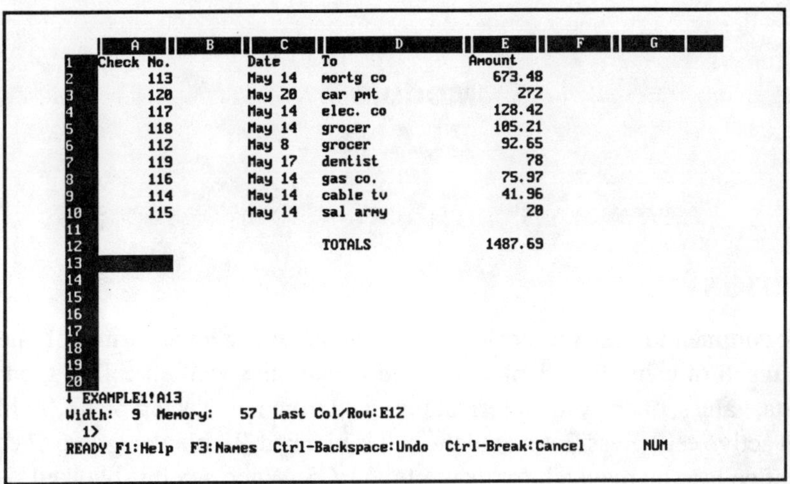

6. There is no need to save the spreadsheet. Type **/Z** then **Y** to clear the spreadsheet.

7. Turn to Module 7 to continue the learning sequence.

Module 7
BLANK

DESCRIPTION

The Blank command is used to erase the content and entry level format of one or more cells. The result of using the Blank command is that the specified cell or group of cells has any data, values, or entry level format removed from it and is left blank. To blank only the current active cell, press Enter, and the cell is blanked. To blank a group of cells, enter the range of cells to be blanked, for example, A1:C5. When a cell is blanked, SuperCalc 5 erases only the cell's data and values contents, unless you specifically indicate that any format information in the cell is also to be erased. However, only entry level format data can be removed by the Blank command. Formats entered at the Row, Column, or Global levels are unaffected by the Blank command. If a blanked cell is part of a formula, it will be interpreted by the formula as having a value of 0. Options available when using the Blank command are All and Contents, selected after a range is entered.

ALL This option erases all data in the unprotected cell or range of cells, including entry format data.

CONTENTS This option erases only the contents of the cell, but the entry level formatting is left intact.

APPLICATIONS

Empty cells in a spreadsheet are sometimes handy for use as a scratch pad while creating a spreadsheet. When you have completed the spreadsheet, the Blank command is useful in eliminating clutter and unnecessary display on your spreadsheet without affecting the integrity of the calculations in your spreadsheet. Also, as you refine and make changes to your spreadsheet, blanking cells will allow you to maintain the format of your spreadsheet and avoid the juggling of rows and columns to reflect changes.

TYPICAL OPERATION

To illustrate the Blank command, the spreadsheet created in Module 20 is used. Examples of blanking cells, rows, and columns are given and results shown. Follow the steps listed here, beginning with your spreadsheet in the Ready mode.

1. Load the example spreadsheet by typing **/L EXAMPLE1.SC5** and press **Enter.** Then type **R** and **/B** to display the following screen.

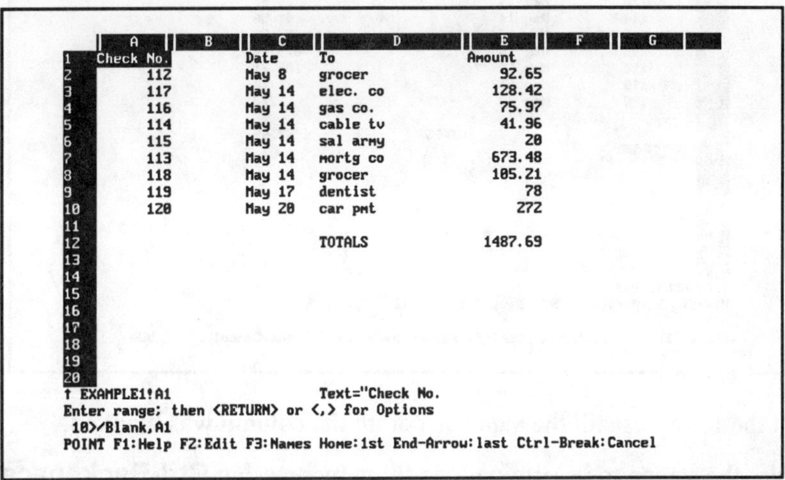

2. You are prompted to enter the range of cells to blank. To blank only the current active cell, simply press **Enter**, and the cell is blanked. If you are blanking a range of cells, enter the range to be blanked, then press **Enter**. The cells specified are blanked, and you are returned to the spreadsheet in the Ready mode.

3. Both of these blanking actions remove only data and values from the specifed cell or cells. To also remove any format data in a cell, type a comma (,) after you have entered the cell address or cell range.

4. You are prompted to select All or Contents. Select All, and data, values, and format are removed from the cell. Select Contents, and only the data and values are blanked.

5. To blank the column labeled "TO" in the example spreadsheet, type **/B**. Then type **D1:D10** and press **Enter** to display the following screen.

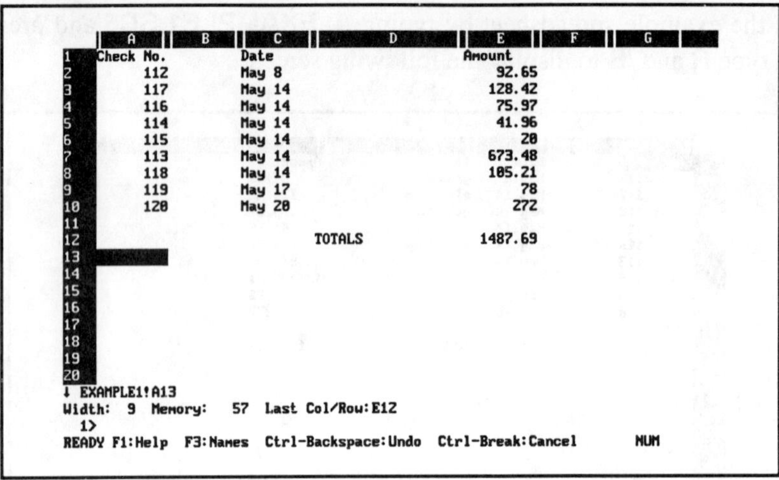

	A	B	C	D	E
1	Check No.		Date		Amount
2	112		May 8		92.65
3	117		May 14		128.42
4	116		May 14		75.97
5	114		May 14		41.96
6	115		May 14		20
7	113		May 14		673.48
8	118		May 14		105.21
9	119		May 17		78
10	120		May 20		272
11					
12				TOTALS	1487.69

EXAMPLE1!A13
Width: 9 Memory: 57 Last Col/Row:E12
1>
READY F1:Help F3:Names Ctrl-Backspace:Undo Ctrl-Break:Cancel NUM

Notice that the format is still the same as before the column was blanked.

6. Restore the screen to its original condition by pressing **Ctrl-Backspace.**
7. To blank a row, type **/B**. Then type **A6:E6** and press **Enter** and your screen displays a spreadsheet as follows.

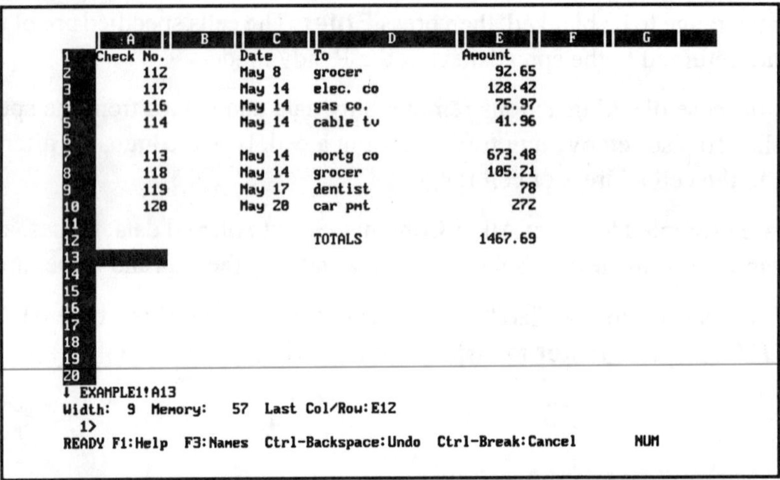

	A	B	C	D	E
1	Check No.		Date	To	Amount
2	112		May 8	grocer	92.65
3	117		May 14	elec. co	128.42
4	116		May 14	gas co.	75.97
5	114		May 14	cable tv	41.96
6					
7	113		May 14	mortg co	673.48
8	118		May 14	grocer	105.21
9	119		May 17	dentist	78
10	120		May 20	car pmt	272
11					
12				TOTALS	1467.69

EXAMPLE1!A13
Width: 9 Memory: 57 Last Col/Row:E12
1>
READY F1:Help F3:Names Ctrl-Backspace:Undo Ctrl-Break:Cancel NUM

As after each blanking operation, you are returned to the spreadsheet in the Ready mode. It is not necessary to save the spreadsheet, since it is already in a file. However, before you clear the spreadsheet, you might use it to work with the Blank command a bit.

8. Type **/Z** then **Y** to clear the spreadsheet.
9. Turn to Module 34 to continue the learning sequence.

Module 8
COPY

DESCRIPTION

The Copy command duplicates the contents of a cell or group of cells in a specified cell or group of cells. In addition, options are available that adjust formulas for their new location; perform add, subtract, multiply, or divide operations on the contents of the destination cell or cells with the contents of the source cell or cells; and transpose column and row notations of the source location. To use the Copy command, with the spreadsheet in the Ready mode type /C. The dialog panel looks like this:

```
→ TEMP1!A1
From? <Enter Range>
  9>/Copy,A1
POINT F1:Help F2:Edit F3:Names Home:1st End-Arrow:last Ctrl-Break:Cancel
```

You are prompted to enter the range of cells to copy. Type the range designation for a single cell, a row of cells, a coloumn of cells, or a block of cells and press Enter. The following screen appears.

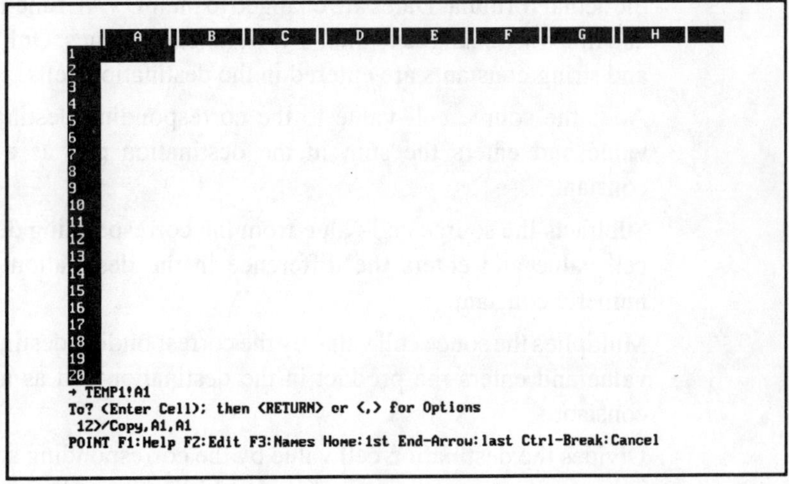

You are now prompted to enter the destination for the cell or cells you are copying. SuperCalc 5 copies the specified cell or cells into the location that you specify, according to the following rules. If more than one row is copied, the first row of the source is the first row of the new location.

Copying more than one column is similar. The leftmost column of the source is copied into the leftmost column of the destination. In a block copy, the upper left cell of the source will be copied into the upper left cell of the destination. For example, copying the block B4:D12 to E7 makes E7 the upper left cell of the destination.

After you make your destination entry, you can press Enter to execute the command, or type a comma (,) for Options. The following dialog panel appears if you choose Options.

```
→ TEMP1!A1
No-adjust  Ask  Values  +  -  *  /  Transpose
 13>/Copy,A1,A1,
MENU  Copy cell references without adjusting to new location
```

The options displayed allow you to make choices about various changes to the copied cells in their new location. Each option is explained in the following paragraphs.

No-adjust	Copies cell contents exactly, no adjustment to formulas.
Ask	Prompts you to enter formula adjustment for each cell copied. The entry line contains the formula, and the prompt line displays the source cell.
Values	Evaluates formulas in source cells and copies their value only, not the actual formula. Dates are changed to their DVAL function value, and times are changed to their TVAL function values. Only numeric and string constants are entered in the destination cells.
+	Adds the source cell value to the corresponding destination cell value and enters the sum in the destination cell as a numeric constant.
–	Subtracts the source cell value from the corresponding destination cell value and enters the difference in the destination cell as a numeric constant.
*	Multiplies the souce cell value by the corresponding destination cell value and enters the product in the destination cell as a numeric constant.
/	Divides the destination cell value by the corresponding source cell value and enters the quotient in the destination cell as a numeric constant.

Transpose	Copies a block or row range and transposes the rows and columns in the new location. Formulas are automatically adjusted. You cannot transpose a full column into a row, as a full column is larger than a full row.

After selection of one of the options, press Enter to execute the copy of the data you designated.

APPLICATIONS

The Copy command is useful in duplicating cells or groups of cells that contain identical values or data. In large spreadsheets, recurring data is often required; using the Copy command is a time-saving method for creating such a spreadsheet.

TYPICAL OPERATION

To illustrate the use of the Copy command, make use of the example spreadsheet created in Module 20. Follow the listed steps, beginning with the spreadsheet in the Ready mode.

1. Type **/L EXAMPLE1.SC5** and press **Enter**. Then type **R**.
2. Type **/C**.
3. To copy from one cell to another, enter the cell location **E10**. Press **Enter**, and you are prompted to enter the destination cell of your copy operation.
4. Type **G10** press **Enter**, and the copy is automatically done with no adjustment or other optional task accomplished. You are returned to the spreadsheet in the Ready mode and the following screen appears.

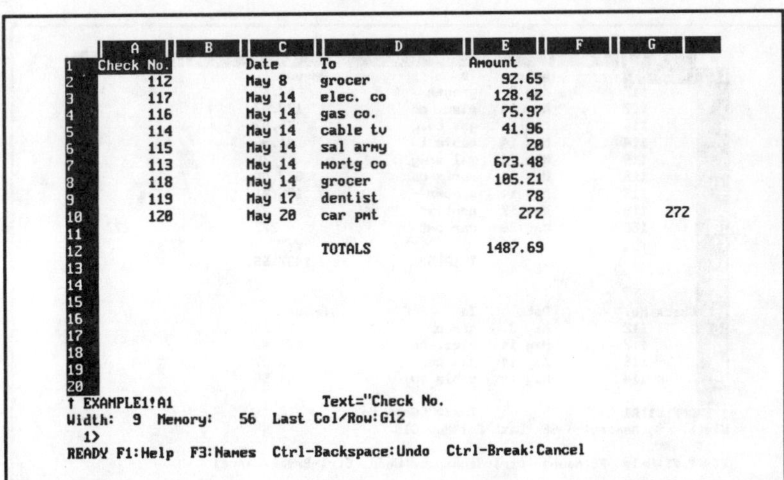

	A	B	C	D	E	F	G
1	Check No.		Date	To	Amount		
2	112		May 8	grocer	92.65		
3	117		May 14	elec. co	128.42		
4	116		May 14	gas co.	75.97		
5	114		May 14	cable tv	41.96		
6	115		May 14	sal army	20		
7	113		May 14	mortg co	673.48		
8	118		May 14	grocer	105.21		
9	119		May 17	dentist	78		
10	120		May 20	car pmt	272		272
11							
12				TOTALS	1487.69		
13							
14							
15							
16							
17							
18							
19							
20							

↑ EXAMPLE1!A1 Text="Check No.
Width: 9 Memory: 56 Last Col/Row:G12
1>
READY F1:Help F3:Names Ctrl-Backspace:Undo Ctrl-Break:Cancel

Copying a row, column, or partial row or column is similar to copying a cell. The only difference is that you must specify a range instead of a single cell when prompted for the "From" and "To" entries.

5. Copy a row or column or part of either by typing **/C** and the source range **A1:A5**. Press **Enter** and type your destination **C15:C19**. Press **Enter** again and your copying is done. The following screen apprears.

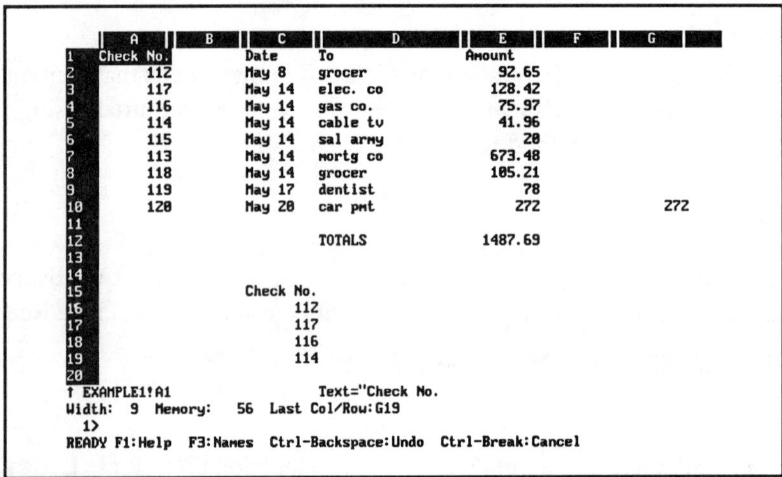

6. Copy a block by following the same procedure, specifying a block instead of a row or column when prompted for a range. Type **/C A1:E5** and press **Enter**; then type **A15:E19** and press **Enter** to complete the copy operation. The following screen is displayed.

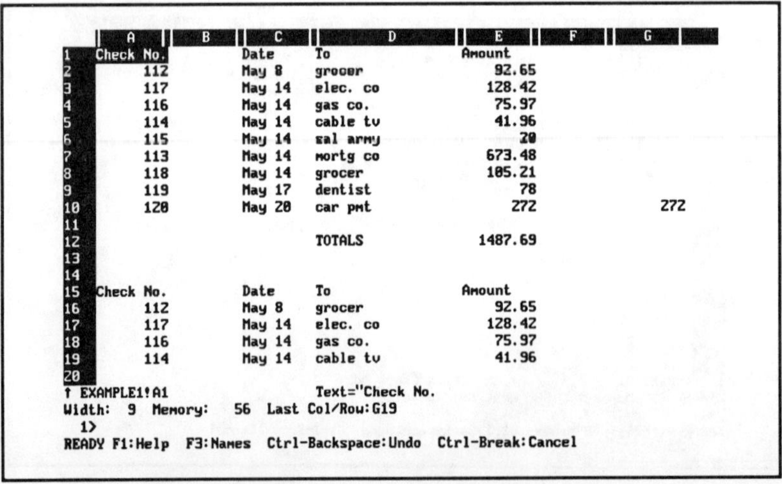

When copying, you can use the options to perform operations on the data or values in the cells to be copied. Use the options by typing a comma (,) after entering the source and/or destination for your copy. Use the options to adjust formulas, copy only values to the new location, perform arithmetic operations, and transpose rows and columns. Each option is explained in the description section of this module. Try using these options to become familiar with them.

7. Type **/Z** then **Y** to clear the spreadsheet.
8. Turn to Module 22 to continue the learning sequence.

Module 9
DATA

DESCRIPTION

The Data command contains options and functions that locate and analyze data. The options can help you to search data for selected items, and the function then can analyze selected data in different ways. Options for the Data command are listed here.

Quit	Remain
Input	Delete
Criterion	Analysis
Output	Block
Find	Matrix
Extract	Parse
Unique	Table
Select	

Each of these options are described in the following paragraphs.

QUIT This option returns you to the spreadsheet in the Ready mode.

INPUT This option prompts you for a range of cells that you are searching or analyzing. You must specify a range of cells before you use the options Find, Extract, Select, Unique, or Delete.

CRITERION This option selects the range of cells where selection criteria data are stored. You must define a criterion range and enter your criteria in the range before you use the options Find, Extract, Select, Unique, or Delete.

OUTPUT This option selects the range of cells in which the data requested by options Extract, Unique, or Select are to be placed. The selected range must be large enough for all the data requested, or an error message is displayed.

FIND This option searches the data range specified by the Input option for the values entered by the Criterion option. The Input and Criterion ranges must be defined before you use Find. As records are found that match the criterion data, they are highlighted on your display. You can use the Down, Up, Left, or Right Arrow keys to view the cells around the matched cell.

EXTRACT This option copies the rquested data from the input range to the output range. The original records are left intact. Only text and values (no formulas) are copied. Any data in the output range will be blanked before copying the requested data to the range. The Input, Criterion, and Output ranges must have been defined before using Extract.

UNIQUE This option works similarly to the Extract option, but does not copy every matched record if some of the records are identical. For example, if the name Smith appeared more than once in the matched records, only the first record that matched would be copied to the output range. The Input, Criterion, and Output ranges must have been defincd bcfore using Unique.

SELECT This option allows you to go through the records that met your criteria, and select any of the data to copy to the output range. As records are found to meet your criteria, they are highlighted, and you are given the option of accepting or rejecting any of the data in that record. You can move around the fields in the record by using the arrow keys. The Input, Output, and Criterion ranges must have been selected before using the Select option.

REMAIN This option allows you to keep the spreadsheet cursor in its current position when you terminate the Data command and return to the spreadsheet. Therefore, you can leave the cursor on a record you requested in order to edit. If the Data command is terminated without this option, the cursor is moved back to the cell that it was in when the Data command was invoked.

DELETE This option deletes the records in the input range which match your criteria. You are prompted to verify each record as it is identified before it is deleted. The options given you are Yes, No, Remaining, Down Arrow, Up Arrow, and Enter. Yes deletes the record, and No retains it. Remaining deletes the current record and all those that follow. Down Arrow moves to the next record, and Up Arrow moves to the previous one. The Enter key quits the Delete option.

ANALYSIS This option lets you select various data analysis functions to perform on the input data. Options are Analysis, Block, Matrix, Parse, and Table. A brief description of each is given in the following paragraphs.

Analysis gives you the choice of seeing the frequency distribution or doing a regression analysis on the input data. Options are Distribution and Analysis. Select Distribution and you are prompted to enter the input range of the values to be analyzed, and the bin range, or test values, that the input values are tested against. After the test, your screen displays the results. Select Analysis and you have several options. They are listed here with a short description of the function of each.

Go	Executes the regression analysis.
X-Range	Contains all columns of independent variables, up to 87.
Y-Range	Contains the columns of dependent variables. The X and Y ranges must have same number of rows.
Output	Identifies the range where the output of the analysis is put.
Fit	Genertes coefficients for a linear, quadratic, or cubic equation. The fit is computed as linear for regressions having more than one independent variable.
Intercept	Instructs SuperCalc 5 how to arrive at the Y-intercept. Calculate uses X=0 to calculate an estimated Y-intercept. Zero sets the Y-intercept value at 0.
Zap	Clears all remebered regression ranges. Type a hyphen (-) to clear individual ranges.
Quit	Returns you to the spreadsheet in the Ready mode.

BLOCK This option generates a range of numbers or date/time groups. When you first select Block, you are prompted to enter the range for the output. Then you have four options before generating a list: Number, Growth, Date, and Order. The following list contains the options and a brief description of each.

Number fills the specified range with a progression of numbers according to the following formula:

new value = Previous value + step

You are prompted to enter the start value, step value (can be positive or negative), and stop value. These entries must be done for the Number, Growth, and Date options.

Growth fills the specified range with a progression of numbers according to the following formula:

new value = previous value(1 + step)

After entering the Start, Step, and Stop values, this geometric series of numbers is generated for you.

Date fills the specified range with a series of date groups. Day, Week, and Month options each give you the Start, Step, and Stop options. Set the Step of the option you want the series to advance between each date. Order fills the range downward by columns or across by row. You are prompted to select Column or Row. Select Column to fill down each column, or select Row to fill across each row.

MATRIX This option performs several different operations on a matrix. Multiplication, inversion, and solution of simultaneous equations can be done. These operations can be performed on matrix arrays of up to 90 columns by 90 rows. Simultaneous equations can have up to 90 variables. Options for Matrix are Multiply, Invert, and Solve. The options are explained in the following paragraphs.

Multiply performs multiplication of a matrix. You are prompted to enter three ranges: the range of the multiplicand; the range of the multiplier; and the range where the result is placed. Range 1 must have the same number of columns as there are rows in Range 2.

Invert does an inversion of a matrix if it can be inverted. You are prompted to input two ranges, the input range (range to be inverted) and the output range. The output range must be as large or larger than the input range. To be invertible, the matrix must have as many rows as it does columns, and the determinant cannot be zero. Maximum size for a matrix that can be inverted is 90 columns by 90 rows.

Solve finds the solution to a set of n equations with n unknowns. You are prompted to specify two ranges: the input range, containing the variable coefficients and equivalent values (the equations); and the output range, where the solutions will be placed. For a solution to be reached, the determinant of the variable coefficients cannot be zero.

PARSE This option breaks out a set of fields from a line of text. Options for the Parse command are Go, Create, Edit, Input, Output, Zap, and Quit. A description of each is contained in the following paragraphs.

Go executes the Parse command.

Create inserts a line above the data to be parsed and puts an estimated format line in the new row. You must create a format line for each different arrangement of data to be parsed. These symbols are used in format lines.

"	First character of a text field
V	First character of a value field
D	First character of a date field
T	First character of a time field
S	Skip the character below during parsing (must be entered manually by editing)
>	Continuation character of a current field type.
*	Don't Care - ignore if blank, otherwise treat as part of current field definition

The length of a data field in a format line cannot be less than the first character symbol and the number of continuation symbols, and the length of a data field cannot be greater than the first character symbol plus the continuation characters and don't care characters. Also the data field must be the same type as the first character symbol in the format line. *V* cannot be used for a date field, " cannot be used for a value field, and *D* cannot be used for a text field.

Edit displays the format line, and you can edit it. Input specifies the range of data to be parsed. The range can be a column or partial column.

Output prompts you to enter the range where the parsed data is to be written after parsing.

Zap clears the input and output ranges.

Quit returns you to the spreadsheet in the Ready mode.

TABLE This option tests different values in formulas and displays the results. "What-if" analyses can be done and chart data prepared. One- and two-variable formulas can be evaluated. Options are Table 1, Table 2, and Zap. Each is described in the following paragraphs.

Table 1 tests formulas by varying one value. You enter a row of test formulas and a column of values to be used in the test formulas. You then specify a table range large enough to hold the width of the formula row and the depth of the values column. You also designate an input cell to hold each value during evaluation.

Table 2 tests a single formula with two variables. The formula is entered in the upper left corner of the table range. Values for the first variable are entered in the column below the formula. Values for the second variable are entered to the right of the formula at the top of each table column. Two input cells must be designated to hold the variables during evaluation. Test results are written at the intersection of the row and column variable value pair.

Zap clears the range and input cell specifications.

APPLICATIONS

With the Data command, you can search a range of cells containing data records for items you designate, then copy or delete those records. You can analyze data distribution or do a regression analysis on data. You can generate numbers and dates, and multiply or invert matrices. You can also solve sets of simultaneous equations and generate test result tables from evaluation of one- or two-variable formulas. Parsing of data can also be done, and to your specifications.

TYPICAL OPERATION

To make use of the Data command, follow the steps listed here. Begin with the spreadsheet in the Ready mode.

1. Type **//D**. The following screen appears.

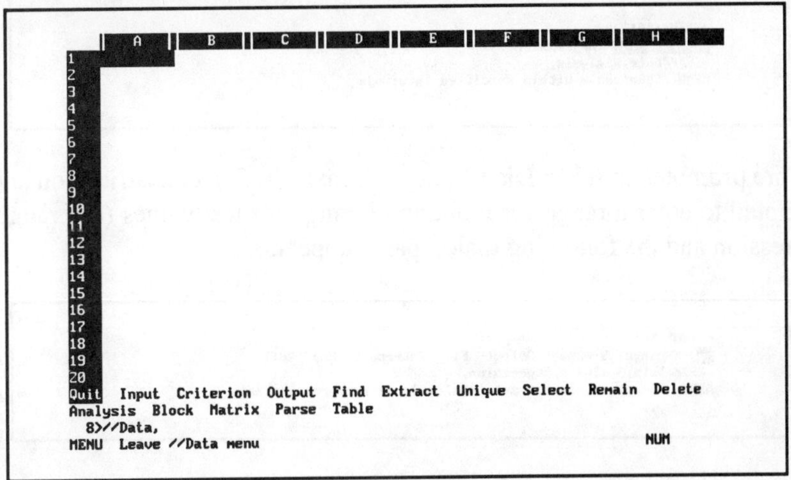

You are prompted to select one of the options from the menu. Select Input to enter the range of data you are searching. Select Criterion to enter the range where you are entering your selection criteria. Select Output to enter the range where you are writing the data you found in your search. Select Find to move the cursor about the display to view the data that was found in your search. Extract and Unique copy requested data from the input to the output file. Select allows you to move about the records that your search found and copy selected data to the output file. You are prompted to verify your choice. Remain holds the cursor in the same spot on the screen when you terminate the Data command and return to the spreadsheet.

2. Select Delete, and the following dialog panel appears.

```
→ TEMP1!A2
Delete? Y(es), N(o) or R(emaining), Next record ↓ or ↑ , Cancel <RETURN>
  14>//Data,Delete
MENU  Delete records that meet the criteria                    NUM
```

You are prompted to verify the deletion of each record, or to delete all the remaining records. Select Yes to delete the current record, No to return to review of the records. Remaining deletes the current record and all the records following.

3. Return to the main options menu and select Analysis. The following panel appears.

```
→ TEMP1!A1
Distribution  Regression
 17>//Data,Analysis,
MENU  Count data within specified intervals
```

4. You are prompted to select Distribution or Analysis. Select Distribution and you are prompted to enter a range for input and a range for test values (bin range). Select Regression and the following dialog panel appears.

```
→ TEMP1!A1
Go  X-range  Y-range  Output  Fit  Intercept  Zap  Quit
 28>//Data,Analysis,Regression,
MENU  Accept regression settings; calculate regression data
```

You are prompted to make choices from the menu. Use the Help line to make your choice for the option you need.

5. Return to the main options menu and select Block. Enter the range of the block you are working with and press **Enter**. The following dialog panel appears.

```
→ TEMP1!A1
Number  Growth  Date  Order
 28>//Data,Block,a1:b2,
MENU  Generate a linear progression of numbers
```

You are prompted to select from the options menu. Select Number or Growth and you are prompted for the Start, Step, and Stop values of number series to be generated. Select Date and you are prompted to select Day, Week, or Month. Each of these options also prompt you for Start, Step, and Stop values. Select Order from the Block options menu and you are prompted for a choice between Column and Row. Your choice determines the direction of fill of the range of the block.

6. Return to the main options menu and select Matrix. The following panel appears.

```
→ TEMP1!A1
Multiply  Invert  Solve
 15>//Data,Matrix,
MENU  Multiply one matrix by another
```

You are prompted to select whether you want to Multiply, Invert, or Solve. Make either choice and you are prompted to input ranges.

7. Return to the main options menu and select Parse. The following panel appears.

```
→ TEMP1!A1
Go  Create  Edit  Input  Output  Zap  Quit
 14>//Data,Parse,
MENU  Start parse of specified range
```

You are prompted to select an option. Your first selection should be Input, then Output, to select the range you will parse and where you will put the parsed data. Next, select Create to put your format line together. Choose Edit next if you need to make changes to the format line. Go executes the Parse command, Zap clears the ranges, and Quit returns you to the spreadsheet in the Ready mode.

8. Return to the main options menu and select Table. The following panel appears.

```
→ TEMP1!A1
1  2  Zap
 14>//Data,Table,
MENU  Show effects of varying one value in a formula
```

You are prompted to choose Table 1, Table 2, or Zap. Choose Table 1 and you are prompted to enter formulas, values, and a range to contain the table you are generating. Then you specify a cell to hold a value while evaluating the formula. Choose Table 2 and you are prompted to enter a single formula, two sets of values, a range for a table, and two cells to hold a value from each set while the formulas are being evaluated. Select Zap to clear the range and cell selections.

9. Select Quit to return to the spreadsheet.
10. Turn to Module 16 to continue the learning sequence.

Module 10
DELETE

DESCRIPTION

The Delete command removes rows, columns, blocks or pages from your spreadsheet. It can also remove files from your disk. For file deletions, you are prompted for confirmation. Once you have deleted any row, column, block, or page, you cannot access it again. However, if Undo is enabled, you can restore the deleted area by pressing Ctrl-Backspace if you do so before any other action is taken. Before deleting any large amount of data, you should save your spreadsheet in case of an inadvertent error. All of the Delete options will adjust formulas as appropriate. To use the Delete command from the Ready mode, type /D. The following screen appears.

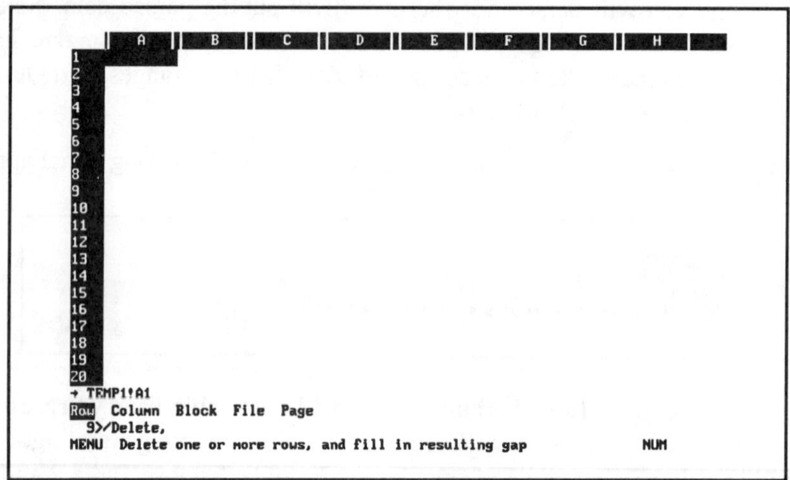

You are prompted to select whether you will delete a row, column, block, file, or page. A brief description of each option is contained in the following paragraphs.

ROW, COLUMN Select row or column and you will be prompted to enter the range of the spreadsheet you are deleting. After entering a row or column for deletion, press Enter. The specified cell or cells are deleted, and you are returned to the spreadsheet in the Ready mode.

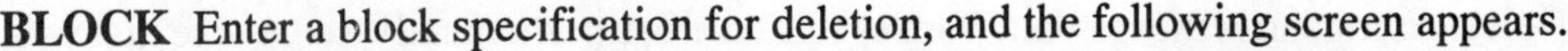

BLOCK Enter a block specification for deletion, and the following screen appears.

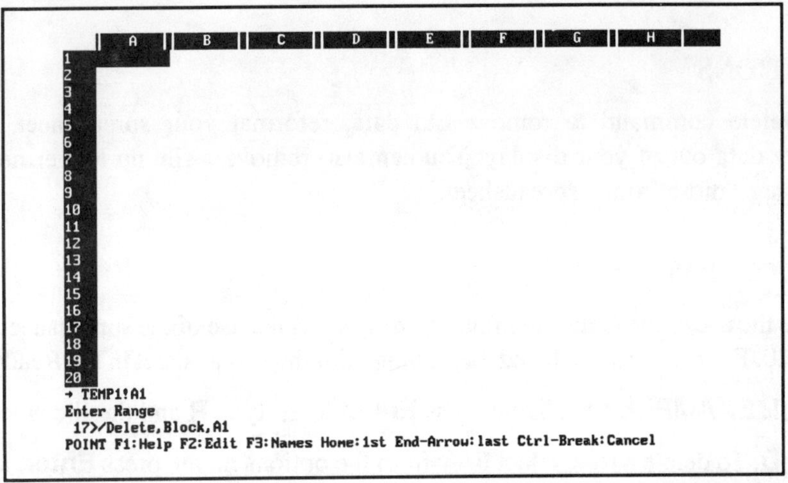

After entering the range to be deleted and pressing Enter, you are prompted to select Up or Left. The Up option prompts you to select between moving the data below the specified range, up to fill in your spreadsheet after the deletion is done, or no movement of data; the Left option prompts you to select between moving the data to the right of the specified range, to the left to fill in your spreadsheet, or no movement of data. After selecting options, press Enter. The specified block is deleted and you are returned to the spreadsheet in the Ready mode.

FILE Select File from the options and you will be prompted to enter a file you are deleting from the current or specified drive/directory. You will be prompted to confirm your file deletion by selecting Yes or No. Select Yes and press Enter, and the deletion is done, returning you the spreadsheet in the Ready mode.

PAGE The Page option deletes a page or pages from your spreadsheet. Your prompt is to specify the page(s) to delete. After your entry, you are again prompted to confirm your page deletion by selecting Yes or No. Select Yes, press Enter, and your deletion is carried out. You are returned to the spreadsheet in the Ready mode.

When using the Delete command, there are three special cases that you need to be aware of. First, formulas that reference cells that no longer exist will cause an ERROR. You should consider the impact of deletions on your formulas before carrying out your actions. Next, if a deleted row, column, or block contains a protected cell, an error message results and the Delete command is not executed. Check for protected cells before deleting large areas of data. Also, absolute cell references such as A1 are adjusted.

The Delete command removes data from specified areas permanently, so be sure that you are accomplishing what you really want before saying good-bye to your data.

APPLICATIONS

Use the Delete command to remove old data, reformat your spreadsheet, or take unnecessary data out of your display. You can also remove a file no longer needed or delete a page or more from a spreadsheet.

TYPICAL OPERATION

To illustrate the use of the Delete command, we again make use of the spreadsheet created in Module 20. Follow the steps listed, beginning with the spreadsheet in the Ready mode.

1. Type **/L EXAMPLE1.SC5** and press **Enter**. Then type **R** and the file is loaded.
2. Type **/D**. To delete a row, select Row from the options menu, press **Enter**, and type **10**. Press **Enter** and the following screen appears.

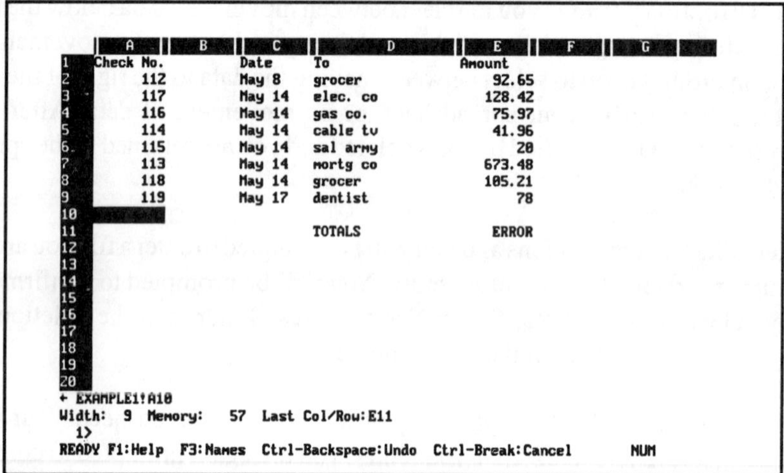

3. Restore the spreadsheet by pressing **Ctrl-Backspace**.
4. To delete a column, type **/D** and select Column from the options menu. Type **B** and press **Enter**. The following screen appears.

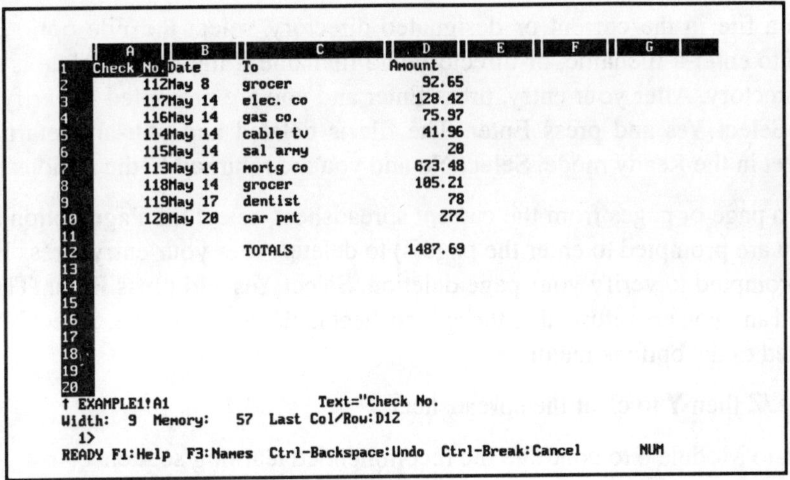

5. Press **Ctrl-Backspace** to restore the spreadsheet to its original state.
6. To delete a block of cells, type **/D** and select Block from the options menu.
7. Type the range of the block to delete, **A5:B10**.
8. Press **Enter** and select from the displayed options. Select Up to move data up to fill in where data has been deleted from a row. Select Left to move data to the left to fill in where data has been deleted from a column. For this example, select Up, press **Enter**, and the following screen appears.

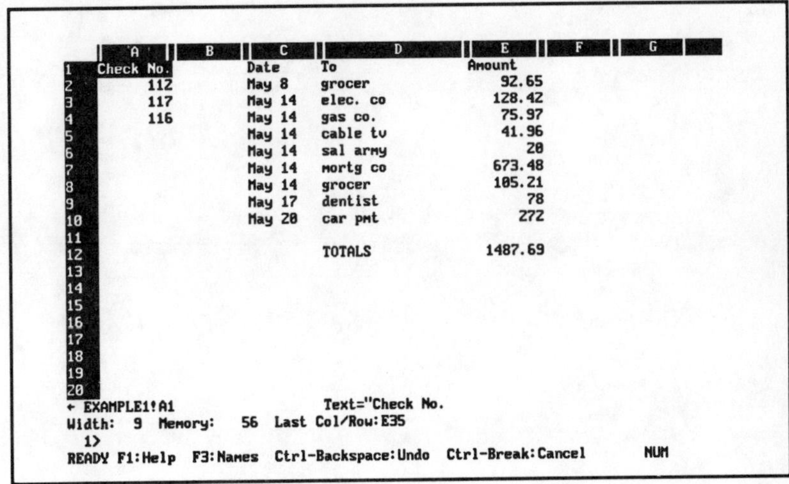

To delete a file in the current or designated directory, select the File option. You are prompted to enter a filename, or directory and filename if the file to delete is not in the current directory. After your entry, press Enter and you are prompted to verify your file deletion. Select Yes and press Enter. The file is deleted and you are returned to the spreadsheet in the Ready mode. Select No and you are returned to the options menu.

To delete a page or pages from the current spreadsheet, select the Page option and press Enter. You are prompted to enter the page(s) to delete. After your entry, press Enter, and you are prompted to verify your page deletion. Select Yes and press Enter. The page(s) are deleted and you are returned to the spreadsheet in the Ready mode. Select No and you are returned to the options menu.

9. Type **/Z** then **Y** to clear the spreadsheet.
10. Turn to Module 6 to continue the recommended learning sequence.

Module 11
EDIT

DESCRIPTION

The Edit command allows you to change the contents of a cell, then place the revised data back in the original cell or any other cell. Any cell in any spreadsheet in memory can be edited, but the destination cell must be in the current spreadsheet. The default destination is the current cell.

The Edit command copies the contents of the source cell to the entry line, where it is edited, as allowed by the data entry rules. If Edit is selected and Enter is pressed without entering a cell address, the current cell becomes the source cell. Or, press F2 to begin editing the current cell immediately.

To edit a cell in another spreadsheet, use the SuperCalc 5 extended sheetname! cell notation. For example, to edit cell B3 of the spreadsheet MANUAL.TXT, type /, E, MANUAL.TXT!B3 and press Enter.

After editing a cell, press Enter to return the data to the current cell. You can edit data in a protected cell and place it in another cell, but you cannot return edited data to a protected cell.

APPLICATIONS

You can edit data and return it to the source or edit from a source and return it to another cell. You can also edit a cell in any spreadsheet in memory. Edit allows you to correct errors, make one-cell changes, or make a change to a cell in another spreadsheet without leaving the current spreadsheet.

TYPICAL OPERATION

To illustrate the use of the Edit command, follow the steps listed here. Begin with the spreadsheet in the Ready mode.

1. Load the example spreadsheet that was created in Module 20 by typing **/L EXAMPLE1.SC5**. Then press **Enter** and type **R**.

2. Type **/E** to display the following screen.

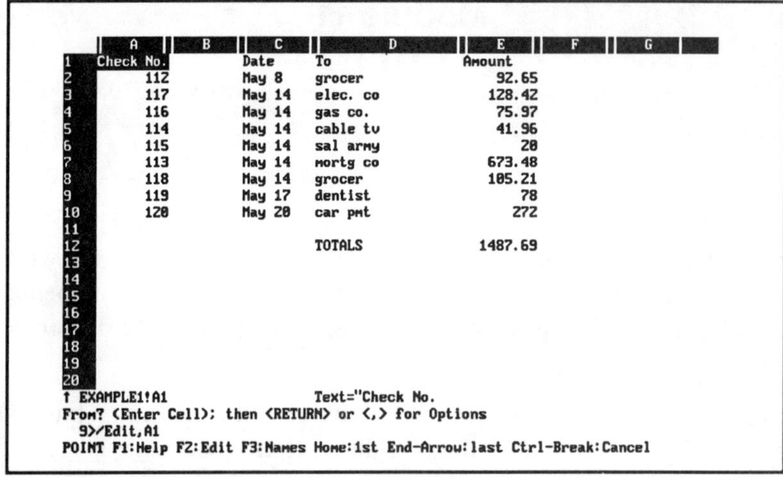

3. You are prompted to enter the source cell. Type **D6** and press **Enter**. Unless you have moved the spreadsheet cursor to the source cell, you must now enter it as your target cell by typing a comma (,) and **D6**. Otherwise, your revised data is placed in the current cell (i.e., where the cursor is currently located).

4. Press **Enter** again and make a change by typing **salvation army**. Press **Enter** and the revised data is placed in the cell, and you are returned to the spreadsheet in the Ready mode. Your screen appears as shown in the following illustration.

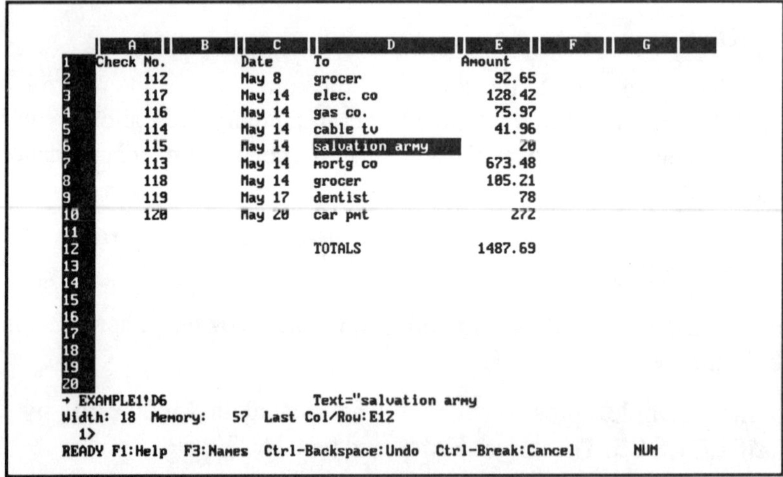

5. As another example, type **/E** and a cell to edit such as **D12**.
6. Type a comma (,) and the target cell for your revised data such as **D14**.
7. Press **Enter** and edit the cell by typing **MONTH TOTAL**.
8. Press **Enter** and the edited data is placed in the target cell, and you are returned to the spreadsheet in the Ready mode. Compare your spreadsheet to the following one.

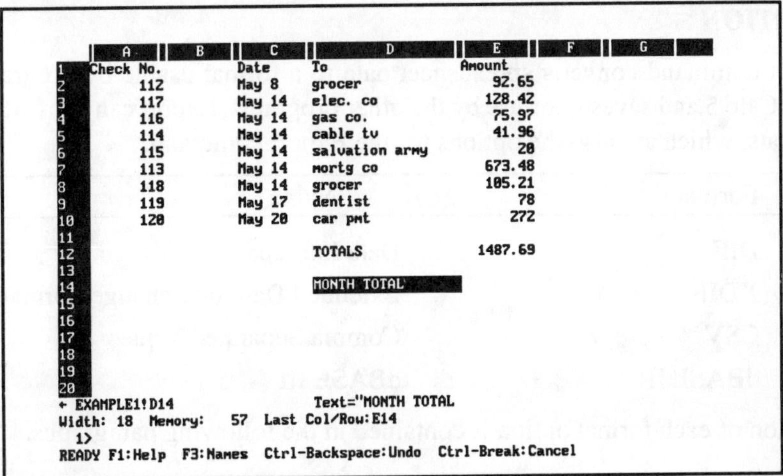

9. To edit a cell in another spreadsheet, type **/E EXAMPLE!B4** and press **Enter**. The data displayed on your entry line is from the file EXAMPLE.SC5, cell B4. Now edit the data and note the change. Return the data to the source cell. You can check the editing by loading EXAMPLE.SC5 and seeing for yourself.
10. Type **/Z** then **Y** to clear the spreadsheet.
11. Turn to Module 8 to continue the learning sequence.

Module 12
EXPORT

DESCRIPTION

The Export command converts spreadsheet data to a format usable by programs other than SuperCalc 5 and saves it for use by the other programs. Export can convert data into these formats, which are also the options for the Export command.

Format	Name
DIF	Data Interchange Format
XDIF	Extended Data Interchange Format
CSV	Comma Separated Values
dBASE III	dBASE III

A description of each format option is contained in the following paragraphs.

DIF The DIF (data interchange format) is a widely used format that can contain only values, not formulas or display formats. Many programs can use data in the DIF format. Selecting the DIF option gives you two ways to convert spreadsheet data, Colwise and Rowwise. Colwise makes each column a record, and Rowwise makes each row a record. Options for both are All and Part. All converts the entire file to DIF and stores it, and Part converts and stores only that part of the file you specify. A file converted to DIF by SuperCalc is automatically given the .dif extension.

XDIF XDIF (extended data interchange format) is a variation of the DIF standard. XDIF can contain SuperCalc formulas and display formats. Some programs can interpret the data in this format, while some ignore the formula and display formats and read only the values. The options for conversion into XDIF are All, Values, and Part. All converts the entire file and stores it. Values converts the entire file, but formula calculations are done and only the values are converted. Part allows you to choose a section of a file to convert. After entering a part of a file to export, you can choose All or Values for the partial file. All converts the entire partial file; Values does also, but formulas are not exported, only the calculated values. Any file converted to the XDIF format is automatically given the .sdi extension.

CSV The CSV (comma separated values) format makes each line (or row) a record, and each cell within the record is separated by a comma. This format does not contain formulas or display formats. Only calculated values are exported. Options for the CSV format are All and Part. All converts the entire file, then stores it, and Part allows you to select a partial file to export. Any file converted to the CSV format is automatically given the .CSV extension.

dBASE The dBASE format converts spreadsheets into dBASE III files. Each column becomes a field, and each row becomes a record, with the exception of the first row, which becomes field names. Options for the dBASE format are All and Part. All converts an entire file; Part allows you to select any part of a file for conversion.

For files that are usable by earlier versions of SuperCalc and Lotus 1-2-3, simply use the Save command.

APPLICATIONS

The Export command provides the means to move data from SuperCalc to other programs to take advantadge of their design function. Word processors, accounting, tax, and other programs may have particular functions you wish to make use of to manipulate the data in your spreadsheet.

TYPICAL OPERATION

To use the Export command, follow the steps listed here, beginning with the spreadsheet in the Ready mode.

1. Type //, select Export from the options menu, and press **Enter**. The following dialog panel appears.

```
→ TEMP1!A1
XDIF  DIF  CSV  dBase
 10>//Export,
MENU  SDI file format                                NUM
```

2. Select the file format into which you are converting a file for export. Press **Enter**; you are prompted to enter a filename. Type the filename and press **Enter**. The following dialog panel appears only if the file already exists.

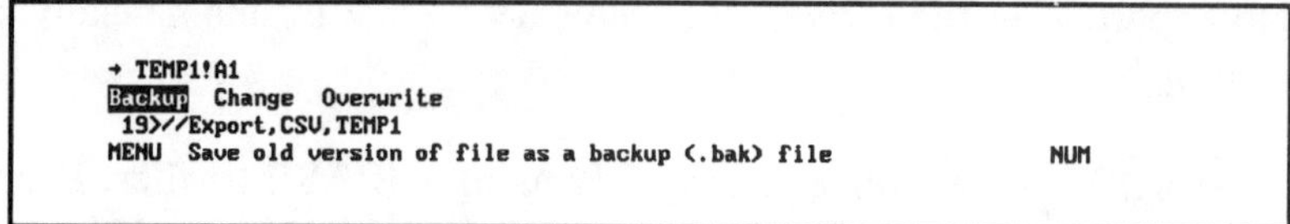

3. You are prompted to select Backup, Change, or Overwrite. A prudent selection would be Backup to avoid losing the original when converting the file. Make the selection and press **Enter**. The following dialog panel appears if your file format selection was CSV or dBASE.

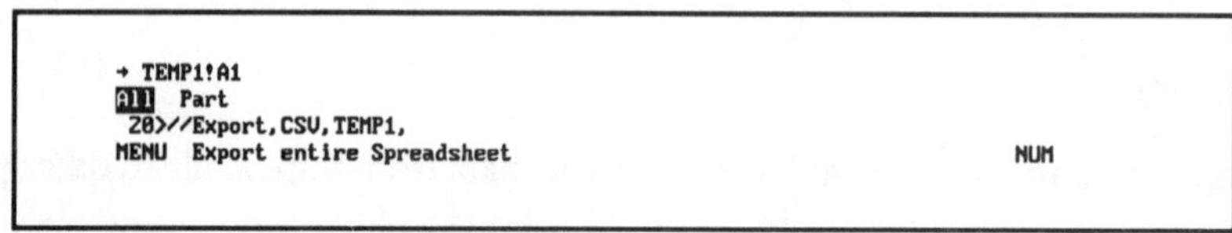

   You are prompted to select whether you will convert All or Part of the file.

4. Select All, press **Enter**, and the complete file is converted and stored according to your instructions. Select Part, and you are prompted to specify the part of the file that you are converting. After your entry, press **Enter** and the partial file is converted and stored. After either selection is completed, you are returned to the spreadsheet in the Ready mode.

5. When XDIF is selected as your export format, the following dialog panel appears after an option from the Backup-Change-Overwrite menu has been selected.

```
→ TEMP1!A1
All Values Part
21>//Export,XDIF,TEMP1,
MENU Export all of spreadsheet including formulas          NUM
```

The options for this format are All, Values, and Part. Select All and the entire file is converted and stored. Select Values and the entire spreadsheet is converted, but cells with formulas are exported as calculated values only. Formulas are not exported. Select Part and you are prompted to enter the range of the spreadsheet you are exporting, and after your selection, you must make a further selection from two options, All or Values. Select All and you are prompted to enter the range of data that you are exporting from the file, then the specified data is converted and stored. Select Values and you are prompted to specify the data you are exporting, and the data is converted except for formulas. Only the calculated values are exported. After your selections have been made, and the Export command executed, you are returned to the spreadsheet in the Ready mode.

6. When the DIF format is selected, the following dialog panel appears after an option from the Backup-Change-Overwrite menu has been selected.

7. The options for DIF are Colwise and Rowwise. In DIF, columns or rows are converted to records. One or the other can be made records, but not both. After you select the record orientation, the same dialog panel appears for either choice. It is shown in the following illustration.

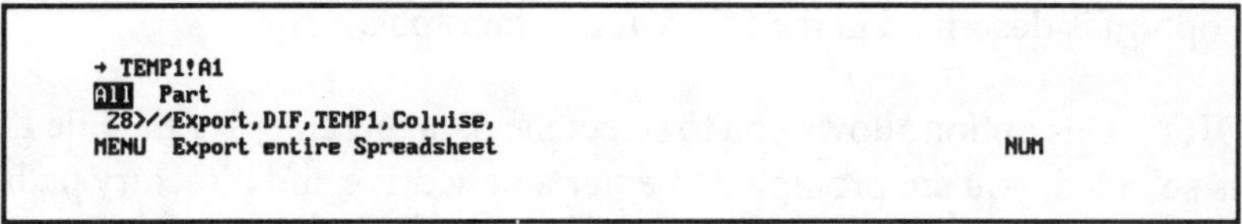

8. Again, the options are All and Part. All exports the entire file, and Part prompts you for the range of the part of the file you are exporting. After you have typed your entries, and entered them, you are returned to the spreadsheet in the Ready mode.

9. Turn to Module 4 to continue the recommended learning sequence.

Module 13
FILE

DESCRIPTION

The File command allows you to select the default data directory for the File List, display the File List, and select new directory paths for file searching. When you are in the File mode (a command is activated requiring a filename input), you can display the files in the default directory by pressing F3. The files are also displayed when you try to load or import a file that cannot be found. While viewing the File List, you can change the data directory by pressing F4.

When the File command is selected, you are presented three options: Directory, List, and Path. Each option is described in the following paragraphs.

DIRECTORY This option allows you to select the data directory for the File List. When Directory is selected, you are prompted to enter a new drive and directory path.

LIST The List option displays the File List for the default directory. When List is selected, you have the following options to choose from: SuperCalc, 1-2-3, Print, Macro, Config, and All. The following list shows each option and the filename extension it looks for to compile a list of files to be in the display list.

Option	Filename Extension
SuperCalc	.CAL
1-2-3	.WKS and .WK1
Print	.PRN
Macro	.XQT
Config	.CFG
All	any

Select the option indicated to display only those files having the desired filename extension.

PATH The Path option allows you to set data paths to be used in data searches. The paths are lists of drives and directories where data might be stored. When SuperCalc 5 searches for data, it does so in the following order:

The default directory
Spreadsheet datapath directories
Global datapath directories
System AUTOEXEC.BAT (used only if no Global datapath has been set up)

If the file cannot be found after searching all these paths, the File List is displayed.

When the Path option is selected, you are presented two options, Global and Spreadsheet. Each is briefly described here.

Global This option allows you to set a datapath for the entire SuperCalc session. You can use the path for future sessions by using the Global command to save it in your configuration file. The Global option gives you three options. *Edit* lets you edit or enter a datapath. *Clear* removes the existing global datapath for the current session. Use the Global command to remove the datapath from your configuration file. *Zap* resets the global datapath to the last global datapath saved by using the Global command.

Spreadsheet This option allows you to set a datapath for the current spreadsheet. This datapath is saved with the spreadsheet. The Spreadsheet option gives you two options. *Edit* allows you to enter or edit a spreadsheet datapath. *Zap* deletes the spreadsheet datapath.

APPLICATIONS

The File command gives you a large number of choices in the way you set up your datapaths. You can have a datapath for each individual spreadsheet, one for the default directory, and one for global searches. Use the File command to set up paths and assign them to a special key to automate your search. Set up a path to access often-used files. Set up paths for different categories of data, different subjects—the possibilities are limited, but probably by the hardware.

TYPICAL OPERATION

To use and become familiar with the File command, follow the steps listed here. Begin with the spreadsheet in the Ready mode.

1. Type **//F**. The following dialog panel appears at the bottom of the screen.

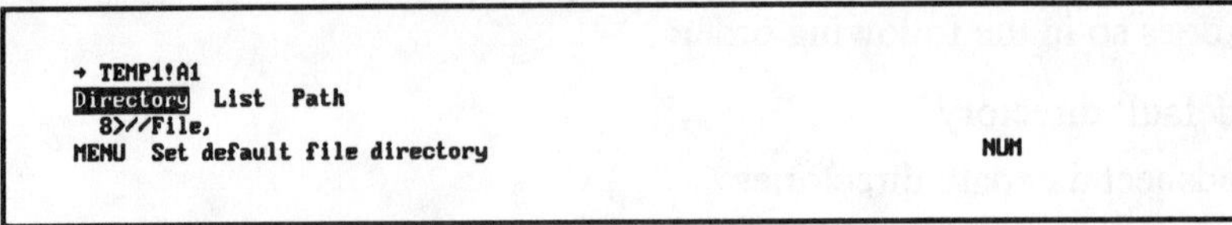

2. You are prompted to select an option. Select Directory, and press **Enter**. The following dialog panel appears.

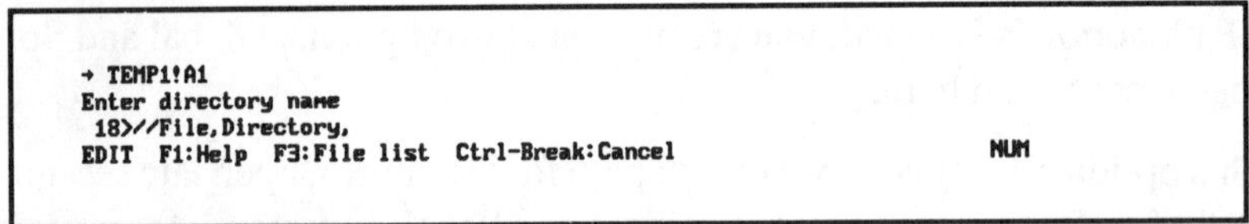

3. You are now prompted to enter a directory name that you are making the default directory. Enter the name and press **Enter**. Your entry is installed as the default directory and you are returned to the spreadsheet in the Ready mode.

4. To display the file list for the default directory, type **//F** and then select List from the options. Press **Enter** and the following dialog panel appears.

```
→ TEMP1!A1
SuperCalc  1-2-3  Print  Macro  Config  All
 13>//File,List,
MENU  List .CAL files                                      NUM
```

5. You are prompted to select from a list of options which allows you to select for display files in the default directory having certain filename extensions. You can also select to have all the filenames in the directory displayed. Select All and press **Enter**, and the files in the default directory are displayed. Press **Esc** to return to the spreadsheet.

6. To set up a path for SuperCalc 5 to take when searching for a file, select the Path option. Press **Enter**, and the following dialog panel appears.

```
→ TEMP1!A1
Global  Spreadsheet
 13>//File,Path,
MENU  Edit search paths for session (Global) or a sheet (Spreadsheet) NUM
```

7. You are now prompted to select Global or Spreadsheet. Select Global to install the path for the entire session. If you are going to make this path the one you are going to use for future work, use the Global command to save it. After selecting Global, the following dialog panel appears.

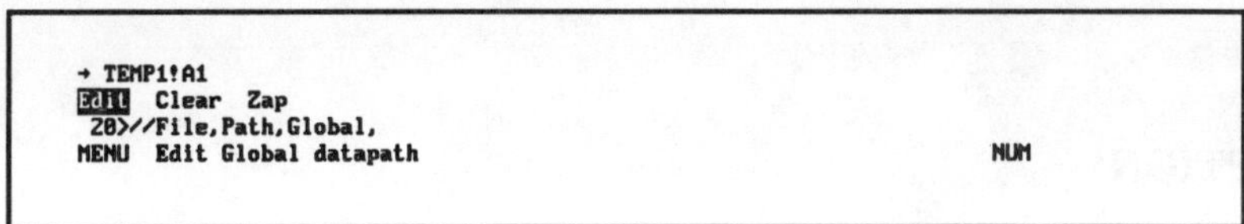

You are prompted to select Edit, Clear, or Zap. Select Edit to enter or edit a path. Clear removes the existing global path for the current session. Zap resets the global path to the one last saved with the Global command.

8. Press **Esc** until you are returned to the spreadsheet in the Ready mode.
9. Select Spreadsheet to install a path to be used only with the current spreadsheet. You can save this path with the spreadsheet. Selecting Spreadsheet brings up the following dialog panel at the bottom of the screen.

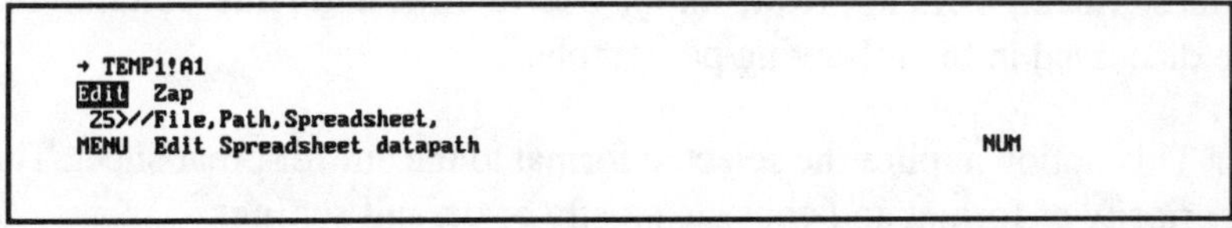

10. You are prompted to select Edit or Zap. Select Edit to enter or edit a path entry. Select Zap to remove the spreadsheet path. Subsequent file searches use the global path if one is set.
11. Press **Esc** until you are returned to the spreadsheet in the Ready mode.
12. Turn to Module 5 to continue the learning sequence.

Module 14
FORMAT

DESCRIPTION

The Format command gives you the ability to make certain choices about the way your spreadsheets are presented on your display and the way your spreadsheets are printed. This command has you make many selections if you wish, but the selections affect only the way the cells in a spreadsheet are presented. The contents of any cell are unchanged. The Format command sets up the display formats that define how numbers appear, justify text and values, and select the appearance of dates and times. You can also set column widths and hide a cell or column of cells.

The Format command offers you the option of choosing which of the four levels of formatting done in SuperCalc 5 that your format choices are applied to. The main options menu includes Global, Column, Row, Entry, User-define, and Hide-column. Each of the options are discussed in the following paragraphs.

GLOBAL This option applies the selected format to the entire spreadsheet. This level is the lowest priority of format and consists mostly of default settings.

COLUMN The Column option sets the format for a specified column range. Formats set at the Column level take precedence over settings at the Global level.

ROW The Row option sets the format for a specified row range. Row level formats override both the Global and Column level settings.

ENTRY The Entry option sets format for individual cells and cell ranges. This level is the highest format level and overrides Row, Column, and Global format settings.

USER-DEFINE This option allows you to set the formats for numeric, date, and time formats. When User-define is selected, Number and Date are the options. Number sets a numeric format, and Date covers both date and time formats.

HIDE-COLUMN This option allows you to hide from view or keep from being printed a column or column range you specify. When you select Hide-column, you enter the range, select Yes, and column and column letter are taken off the screen. The cell contents and format values are not disturbed. The column is restored by selecting Hide-column again, specifying the same range, and selecting No.

After you have selected a format level and designated the area to be formatted, the format options menu is displayed.

Three types of format options can be applied to numeric data at each level. Each cell can have one option of each type applied to it at the same time. The types of format options and the name of each option in each type are shown here.

Numeric	Integer, General, Exponential, $, *, User-defined, Number
Alignment	Right, Left, and Center
Cell-Hiding	Hide

All of the options for the format levels are listed here, and a short description of the function of each is given.

Accept	Puts selected formats in the specified range.
Integer	Displays whole numbers only.
General	Displays whole numbers, decimals, and exponents when number is greater then the column width.
Exponential	Displays numbers in exponential form.
$	Indicates currency; number is displayed with two digits after decimal point.
Right	Aligns numbers, dates, times at right edge of column.
Left	Aligns numbers, dates, times at left edge of column.
Center	Centers numbers, dates, times within columns.
Text	Positions text in cells. Options are Right, Left, or Center justification.
*	Represents a postive integer. One * = 1, five * = 5. Good for simple graphing.
User-defined	Sets custom number, time, date formats. Options are Number (1-8) and Date (1-8). Each selects 1 of 8 formats for the displayed data.
Hide	Hides cell contents.
Default	Removes format options previously set at the selected level. Returns to default settings.
Width	Column width can be set to any number 0 - 127.

The User-define option lets you set up to eight formats each for numbers and for dates and time. You set these formats up to be selected through the User-defined option for the format levels. When you select User-define, you are next prompted to select Number or Date. Select Number, and a menu for customizing number displays appears. Select Date, and a menu for customizing date and time displays appears. Use the help line on the dialog panel as you go through the customization process for either option.

APPLICATIONS

The Format command can be used to design spreadsheets for special reports or to design forms. Spreadsheets can be layed out to be printed on forms by ordinary printers. Or, displays can be set up to display only certain information for certain inputs.

TYPICAL OPERATION

To use the Format command, follow the steps listed here. Begin with the spreadsheet in the Ready mode.

1. Type **/F**. The following dialog panel appears.

```
→ TEMP1!A1
Global  Column  Row  Entry  User-define  Hide-column
 9>/Format,
MENU  Global spreadsheet format - the lowest precedence          NUM
```

2. You are prompted to select from this menu a format level, and once a level is chosen, you have other options to make use of. Select one of the four levels, and you are prompted for the range of the cells you are formatting. (In the Row option, you can select Remaining, which selects all the rows after row 255.) After your range entry, the following dialog panel appears, no matter which level you selected.

```
Accept  Integer  General  Exponential  $  Right  Left  Center  Text  *
User-defined  Hide  Default  Width
 16>/Format,Global,
MENU  Apply the selected format(s) - one from each format type      NUM
```

3. After you have made the selections for your format, return to the main options menu. Select User-define and you are prompted to select Number or Date. Choose Number, and the following screen appears.

```
USER-DEFINE NUMBER FORMAT MENU

Format        Currently Defined Format                    Zero as  Scaling
 Set                                                       Blank   Factor
  1.    $-11,111,111.11                                     No       0
  2.    $-11,111,111.11                                     Yes      0
  3.    ($11,111,111.11)                                    No       0
  4.    ($11,111,111.11)                                    Yes      0
  5.    $-11111111                                          No       0
  6.    -11,111,111                                         No       0
  7.    (11,111,111)                                        No       0
  8.    -1111111111.11%                                     No       0

→ TEMP1!A1
Quit  1  2  3  4  5  6  7  8  Zap
 28>/Format,User-define,Number,
MENU  Finished defining formats; return to /Format menu         NUM
```

4. This screen lets you set the format for eight number displays. Set any or all of them any way you like, then you return to the Number-Date menu and select Date. The following screen appears.

```
USER-DEFINE DATE FORMAT MENU

        Format                Example (using March 8, 1980  7:09:10 AM)
    1.  _BM/BD/YYYY                  3/ 8/1980
    2.  DD-MMM-YY                   08-Mar-80
    3.  DD-MMM                      08-Mar
    4.  MMM-YY                      Mar-80
    5.  MM/DD/YY                    03/08/80
    6.  MM/DD                       03/08
    7.  YY-MM-DD                    80-03-08
    8.  DD.MM.YY                    08.03.80
    T.  BH:TT:SS_AM/PM               7:09:10 AM

        Use M, BM, MM, MMM, MMMM or R   for month
        Use D, BD, DD,                  for day
        Use Y, YY, YYYY                 for year
        Use WWW, WWWW                   for weekday
        Use BH, HH                      for hour
        Use BT, TT                      for minute
        Use BS, SS                      for second
        Use A/P, a/p, AM/PM, am/pm      for clock
→ TEMP1!A1
Quit  1  2  3  4  5  6  7  8  T  Zap
 26>/Format,User-define,Date,
MENU  Finished defining formats; return to /Format menu         NUM
```

5. After you complete the customizing of the date-time groups, return to the main options menu.

6. Select Hide-column, and the screen prompts you to select a column or range of columns you are hiding. After your entry, you are prompted to verify your intent to hide the specified range by choosing No or Yes. Choose No to return to the spreadsheet, and Yes to hide the range.

7. Turn to Module 15 to continue the learning sequence.

Module 15
GLOBAL

DESCRIPTION

The Global command sets the basic spreadsheet defaults for SuperCalc 5. Settings made through this command can be effetive immediately or applied to the suceeding spreadsheets. The many defaults and settings are made through the main options menu, which includes the options in the following list. Each main option is described in the paragraphs that follow the list.

Optimum	Formula
Keep	"
Graphics	Labels
Spreadsheet	Protection
Evaluation	Border
Values	Next
1-2-3	Tab
+	Unprotected
–	Zoom

OPTIMUM This option presents you with three choices: Present, Next, and Quit. When Present or Next is selected, the menu and help line on the dialog panel guide you through changes you make to the current settings.

Present alters the settings of the current spreadsheet if any.

Next alters the settings for future spreadsheets. The defaults set by either of these options are saved in configuration files, of which there can be as many as necessary.

Quit returns you to the main options menu.

KEEP The Keep option saves the choices you made through the options in the Global command. Keep does not save spreadsheets, so be sure to save them before you use any command that would erase them. When you select Keep, you are given four options: Yes, No, To, and From.

Yes saves the current default settings to a file called SC5.CFG, which contains the settings for startup of SuperCalc 5. If the file already exists, you choose to Backup, Change or Overwrite.

No returns you to the spreadsheet and no default setting changes are saved.

To saves the current settings to a file you name. As in the Yes option, if the file exists, you have a choice to make.

From loads default settings from a file you specify. After naming the file, you select All, Spreadsheet, or Graphics. All uses both spreadsheet and graphics setting that are in the file. Spreadsheet uses all the spreadsheet settings, but graphics settings are not used. Graphics gives you several choices about which graphics settings are used.

GRAPHICS The Graphics option provides choices for hardware selection and layout of your output. The choices are contained in the four options presented when Graphics is selected: Quit, Device, Layout, and Options. Each option is described in the following paragraphs.

Quit returns you to the spreadsheet in the Ready mode.

Device displays the Device Selection menu, which installs the correct settings for the printer or plotter you are using. You are prompted to indicate whether you are using a black and white or color printer, or a plotter. A list of supported devices is displayed for each choice.

Layout allows you to alter the layout for graphs to be done on your plotter. You can select the page size, chart size, and chart/page offset from the Layout menu which is displayed when this option is selected.

Options displays a menu which lists interface settings for communication with printers, plotters and modems. The menu includes Auto, Parallel, Serial, DOS, Check, Zap, and Quit.

Auto overrides any default settings to select the settings recommended by the device manufacturer.

Parallel selects the parallel data port which sends data from your computer. Choose LPT1, LPT2, or LPT3.

Serial selects the serial data port which sends data from your computer. Com# allows you to choose one of four serial ports. Baud selects the data transmission rate for your modem. Parity selects the type of parity bit, if any, for your transmission. Data-bit selects the number of bits in the data word of your transmission. Stop-bits determines the location of the stop bit in the data word.

DOS selects output setting as specified by DOS.

Check makes sure that the printer is ready before sending data to it. Yes checks the printer and warns you if the printer is not ready; No sends data without checking the printer status.

Zap resets the defaults to their status as of the time when you last used the Keep option.

Quit returns you to the main options menu.

SPREADSHEET The Spreadsheet option selects a spreadsheet printer and interface settings for it, extended ACSII or standard character tables, and fonts to apply to cells in your spreadsheet if you are using a supported laser printer or PostScript-compatible printer. Options for the Spreadsheet menu are Quit, Cartridges, Device, Fonts, Options, and Translation-tables. Each is briefly described in the following paragraphs.

Quit returns you to the spreadsheet in the Ready mode.

Cartridges allows users of Hewlett-Packard LaserJet to select from one to three plug-in cartridges or Softfonts. You select from 1, 2, or 3 to specify a plug-in cartridge, or choose Softfont, which also prompts you to select 1, 2, or 3. Quit returns you to the Spreadsheet Options menu.

Device sets the correct defaults for a character printer you use to print spreadsheets. You are prompted to indicate the type of printer you are using by selecting B&W-printers or Color-printers. A Device Selection menu is displayed for either selection, which lists supported printers.

Fonts defines up to eight type fonts for application to cells and ranges of your spreadsheet if you are using a laser or PostScript-compatible printer. Options in the Font menu are Default, 1, 2, 3, 4, 5, 6, 7, and Quit. Default defines the font which is the default for the entire spreadsheet, and each number defines a separate font. You are guided through the definition of each of the eight fonts by the Help line of the dialog panel. Quit returns you to the Fonts options menu.

Options displays the menu which lists the output settings for interfacing with printers, plotters, and modems. The options are identical to the ones in the Graphics option, with the inclusion of a Form-feed option which allows you to select whether or not to issue a form-feed command to the printer between pages.

Translation-tables gives you the choice of selecting the 96-character ASCII set, or the PC Extended ASCII character set. PC Extended ASCII is the default.

EVALUATION This option determines the way that SuperCalc 5 evaluates and processes data. The option menu for Evalution includes Quit, Order, When, Iteration-control, and Range. Each option is briefly described in the following paragraphs.

Quit Returns you to the spreadsheet in the Ready mode.

Order controls the order in which your spreadsheet is recalculated. Options for Order are Dependent, Row, Column.

Dependent waits to calculate any formula until any forward references in the formula are completed. This is the default for spreadsheet calculation.

Row calculates the spreadsheet a row at a time, going left to right across each row before going down to the next one. Forward or circular references are automatically recalculated according to the current iteration setting.

Column calculates the spreadsheet down each column from top to bottom before going right to the next one. Forward or circular references are automatically recalculated according to the current iteration setting.

When determines the time that a spreadsheet will be recalculated and offers you the choice of Auto or Manual.

Auto recalculates the entire spreadsheet after new data has been entered, or after the spreadsheet is modified.

Manual holds all calculations until the F9 key is pressed.

Iteration-control allows you to build models containing circular formulas and goal-seeking models. In some cases, spreadsheets with forward or circular references require multiple calculations to reach the correct results. Iteration-control lets you specify the maximum number of iterations or lets SuperCalc 5 continue until the desired degree of precision is reached, or the resolution Delta. Select options from the Iteration-control menu, and you will be guided through their operation by the Help line on the dialog panel.

Range selects the range of the spreadsheet to be recalculated. Type a hyphen (-) to clear the current range selection and recalculate the entire spreadsheet.

VALUES This option displays the status of global settings for the current spreadsheet. Press Esc to return to the main options menu; press any other key to display the next screen.

1-2-3 This option puts SuperCalc 5 into the Lotus Compatibility mode. All commands from this point on will be interpreted according to 1-2-3 menus. Return to SuperCalc 5 menu with /Worksheets, Global,sc5.

The remaining options are toggles, that is, they are turned on or off. When the option is selected, it changes state from what it was. Each toggle is turned on by +, no matter what the previous state, and each is turned off by –, no matter the state. Each toggle option is listed and the on and off functions given.

Formula	On—Formula cells display cell contents. Off—Formula cells display cell values.
"	On—Formula entry mode is active. Off—Text entry mode is active.
Labels	On—Named ranges in formulas are displayed. Off—Cell references in formulas are displayed.
Protection	On—Protected cells cannot be altered. Off—Protected cells can be accessed.
Border	On—Row and column border of spreadsheet is illuminated. Off—Row and column border of spreadsheet is not illuminated.
Next	On—Spreadsheet cursor automatically advances in the current direction (last direction moved). Off—Spreadsheet cursor does not move automatically.
Tab	On—Cursor can be positioned only in non-blank, non-protected cells. Off—Cursor can be positioned in any cell.
Unprotected	On—Spreadsheet cells can be accessed and altered. Off—Spreadsheet cells cannot be accessed or altered.
Zoom	On—Systems with EGA boards display 43 lines on the screen; systems with VGA boards display 50 lines on the screen. Off—Standard display format controls the screen.

APPLICATIONS

With the Global command you can change format and display settings and defaults, and modify output and performance. You can save special defaults for use on special files only and change the type of output device that you are using. Also, you can alter the order in which your spreadsheets are calculated. Defaults and format settings can be reveiwed by issuing a single command.

TYPICAL OPERATION

To use the Global command, follow the steps listed here. Begin with the spreadsheet in the Ready mode.

1. Type **/G**. The following dialog panel appears at the bottom of the screen.

```
Optimum  Keep  Graphics  Spreadsheet  Evaluation  Values  1-2-3  +  -
Formula  "  Labels  Protection  Border  Next  Tab  Unprotected  Zoom
  9>/Global,
MENU  Optimize spreadsheet features                                NUM
```

2. You are prompted to select an option. Select Optimum by typing **O**. The following dialog panel appears.

```
→ TEMP1!A1
Present  Next  Quit
 17>/Global,Optimum,
MENU  Change settings for the present or future sessions
```

3. This panel prompts you to choose to have your settings apply to the present spreadsheet or to the next one and all after. The options are Present, Next, or Quit. If Present or Next is chosen, settings are applied as indicated and you are returned to the spreadsheet. If Quit is chosen, you are returned to the spreadsheet with no action taken.
4. Return to the main options menu by pressing **Esc**. Select Keep by typing **K**. The following dialog panel appears.

```
→ TEMP1!A1
Yes  No  To  From
 14>/Global,Keep,
MENU  Keep current settings as defaults - press F1 for details     NUM
```

5. This dialog panel prompts you to choose Yes or No to saving the current defaults, to choose To for saving the default settings in a file you designate, or to choose From to load a file containing defaults that you are using. Return to the main options menu by pressing **Esc**.

6. Select Graphics by typing **G**. The following dialog panel appears.

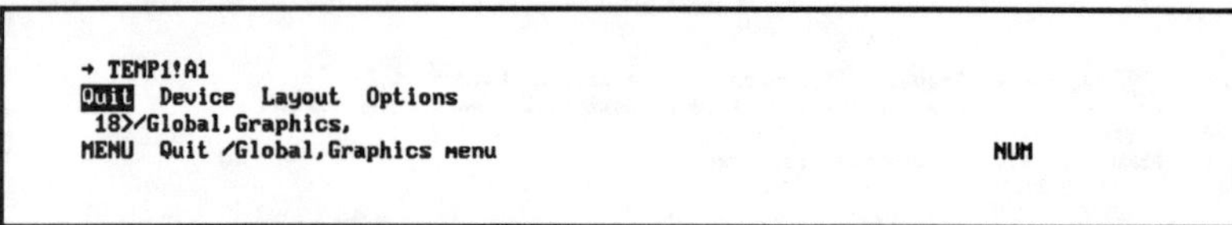

7. This panel gives you the selections to choose a black and white printer, color printer, or plotter. Select Device to make this choice. Then, if you chose the plotter, you can select Layout to design the page layout for the plotter. Options lets you choose parallel or serial output ports and configure the port for the type of peripheral you are working with. Return to the main options menu by pressing **Esc**.

8. Select Spreadsheet by typing **S**. The following dialog panel apprears.

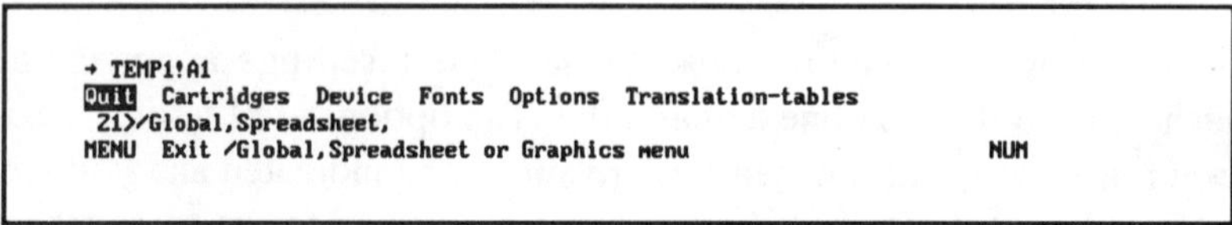

9. This panel prompts you to make choices for the printer or other peripheral to which you are sending a print file. Cartridges lets you specify a font if you are using a laser printer or PostScript-compatible printer. Device selects a black & white or color printer, and Fonts lets you define fonts used in other commands. Options sets up the communication between your computer and the peripheral you have chosen to use. Translation-tables selects the ASCII character set you are to use. Return to the main options menu by pressing **Esc**.

10. Select Evaluation by typing **E**. The following dialog panel appears.

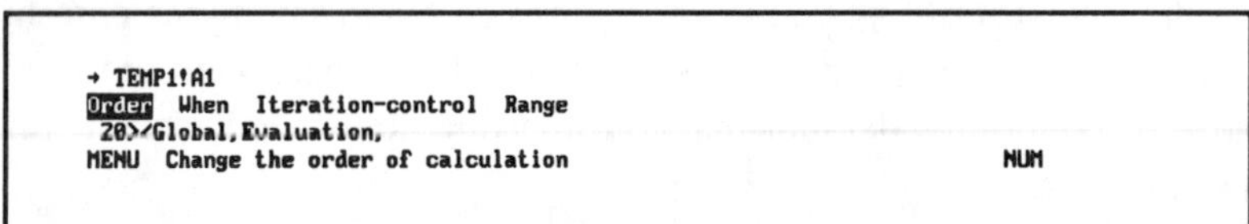

11. This panel prompts you to choose a method for evaluation and processing your spreadsheet data. Order gives you choices for evaluation by row, column, or dependency on other values. When selects manual or automatic recalculation of spreadsheets, and Iteration-control lets you exercise control over formulas that are forward-referenced, or circular. Range allows you to specify the part of the spreadsheet to be evaluated. Return to the main options menu by pressing **Esc**.

12. Select Values by typing **V**. The following screen appears.

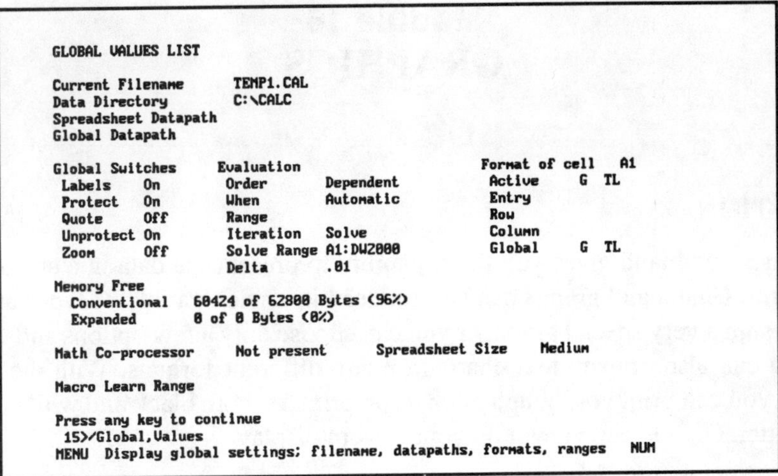

13. This screen shows you the settings of many of the default values that you have set or that have not been changed. This screen gives you a chance to review the defaults and decide on other possible choices. Return to the main options menu by pressing **Esc**.

The other options of the spreadhseet command are toggles and are turned on and off by selecting the option, or selecting the option and typing + or –.

14. Press **Esc** until you are returned to the Ready mode.

15. Turn to Module 25 to continue the learning sequence.

Module 16
GRAPHICS

DESCRIPTION

The Graphics command gives you the capability to present the data in a spreadsheet in graphic form. Charts and graphs can be produced in a wide variety of types and styles. You can design a very special graph, or you can choose only a few options and view your graph. You can also prepare text charts in many different formats. With the Graphics command, you can print your graph or chart on printers, both black and white and color, or on a plotter. Or, you can view it on your system display.

The versatility of the Graphics command is notable, yet it is not overly complicated. The options for the Graphics command are:

View	Global
Type	Name
Data	Plot
Labels	Zap
Axis	Quit
Options	

These options are contained in the main options menu, from which you select those options necessary to produce the chart or graph you desire. Each option is described in the following paragraphs.

VIEW This selection execute the drawing of a graph, using the choices that you have previously made for type of graph, data range, labels, and etc.

TYPE This option allows you to choose from among several different types of graphs. The choices are Bar, Pie, Dual, Line, Area, Hi-Lo, X-Y, Radar, and Word. After you make the choice of graph type, you are returned to the main options menu.

DATA When the Data option is chosen, the Chart Data And Options menu is displayed. This menu is a fill-in-the-blank screen, and you are prompted to enter the range of data you are graphing. There are ten columns on the menu, representing ten bars, lines, etc. that a graph can contain. Each column with a range entered will be represented on the graph. Below the series range, there are choices to be made if you want to change the characteristics of the graph. Use the help line to do some customizing of your graph.

LABELS The Labels option lets you select the labels and titles for your graph. The options available to you are Quit, Axis-labels, Legend-labels, Data-labels, and Titles. Each of these options (except Quit, of course) leads you to a fill-in-the-blank menu. Select the Axis-labels option and the Axis Label Definition And Options menu is displayed. This menu accepts your entry for the X-axis label range. Also, you can choose options for both the X-axis and Y1 and Y2 axes. The help line on the dialog panel describes each option as you move the cursor to it. Select Legend-labels, and the Legend Label Definition And Options menu is displayed. You are prompted to enter the range for the legend label. Again, you have options to choose from and can determine the location of the legends on your graph. Use the help line on the dialog panel to assist you as you make your choices. Select Data-labels, and the Data Label Definition and Options menu is displayed. This menu prompts you to enter the range for the labels you assign to the data in your graph. You can then customize those labels by using the options available. Once more, use the help line to get you through the options. Select Titles, and you are shown the Title Definition Menu. This menu allows you to manually enter text for the top title, subtitle, title footnote, and axis and legend titles. Quit returns you to the main options menu.

AXIS The Axis option prompts you to make choices about axis scaling and attributes and is available only to the charts with axes; Bar, Line, Area, X-Y, Hi-Lo, and Radar. When the Axis option is selected, the Axis Scaling Definition menu is displayed. Also contained in this option is the Axis Options menu, which is accessed by pressing the PageDown key. You return to the first menu by pressing the PageDown key. Pressing the Esc key returns you to the main options menu. The options for either of these menus are briefly described by the help line to assist you in making your choices.

OPTIONS This option allows you to make variations in your graph or chart. When you select Options, the Chart Options menu is displayed. The options for different types of graphs and charts differs, so the menu differs for each graph or chart type. The selected chart type is shown in the upper right-hand corner of the display. The options for each of the chart types are briefly explained by the help line on the dialog panel when the option is under the menu cursor. Use this assistance to make your graph the way you want it.

GLOBAL The Global option prompts you to make settings for peripherals that you use to print or display your graph. Select Global and three options are offered: Quit, Drivers, and Options. Each is briefly explained in the following paragraphs.

Quit returns you to the main options menu.

Drivers allows you to make settings for using a plotter for your output, or for sending chart files to other graphics-oriented file formats. Selection of one of these options will send all future outputs of the Plot option to the device or file selected. Three options are available to you in the Drivers menu: Normal, PIC-file, and CGI. Normal sends outputs to the default device, selected by the Global command. PIC-file puts chart files in a PIC file, which is a Lotus graphics format. You supply the filename, and the extension .PIC is added. CGI sends the chart files to the CGI (Computer Graphics Interface) device or file. CGI has several options, and you can use the help line to know what you are choosing.

Options displays the Global Options menu. This menu contains monitor and printer settings that will enable SuperCalc 5 to communicate with the devices you specify. The help line again explains the choices you have.

NAME This option saves or loads charts that you specify. The current chart and all charts that you designate with this option will be saved when you use the Save command to save your spreadsheet. A spreadsheet can have an unlimited number of named charts saved with it. Options for Name are Retrieve, Store, Delete, and Zap. Each is explained in the following paragraphs.

Retrieve loads a chart that has been saved using the Store option. You are prompted for the name of the chart you are retrieving, or press F3 for a list of existing charts. The chart that you load will overwrite the current chart, but the data in your spreadsheet is not affected.

Store lets you save the current chart. You are prompted for the name of the chart, and after you have stored it, you can modify or erase the current chart without affecting the stored chart.

Delete does just what it says. You are prompted for the name of a chart you are deleting. Enter the name, or press F3 and choose from the list of named charts. Delete does not affect the current chart. To clear the current chart, use the Zap command in the main options menu.

Zap deletes all named charts, but does not affect the current chart. The current chart is the only one left after using Zap while in the Name option.

PLOT The Plot option sends the current chart to the plotter or printer you have specified with the Global command. After the current chart has been plotted, you are returned to the spot in the program where you were before plotting.

ZAP The Zap option erases the current chart from working memory. You are prompted to verify your command by responding to the Yes or No options presented when you select Zap. Select Yes, and the current chart is erased from memory and all defaults are reinstated. Select No and the Zap is canceled, and you are returned to the chart.

QUIT The Quit option, when selected, takes you out of the Graphics command and returns you to the spreadsheet.

APPLICATIONS

With the Graphics command, you can present data in many different graphical formats. You can print, plot, or view on a screen the charts and graphs you create. Your outputs can be in color or black and white. You can preview your creation, then make changes to suit your needs. SuperCalc 5 can output 71 colors, allowing for a very bright output if your tastes run in that direction. Lines and text in your chart or graph can be varied in many ways, or you can simply enter a range to graph, and the defaults in place will produce a graph for you. You can also put your data into other graphical formats for use as a base for viewgraphs, slides, and other optical media.

TYPICAL OPERATION

To use the Graphics command, follow the steps listed here to go through the command and options structure. Begin with the spreadsheet in the Ready mode.

1. Type **//G**. The following dialog panel appears.

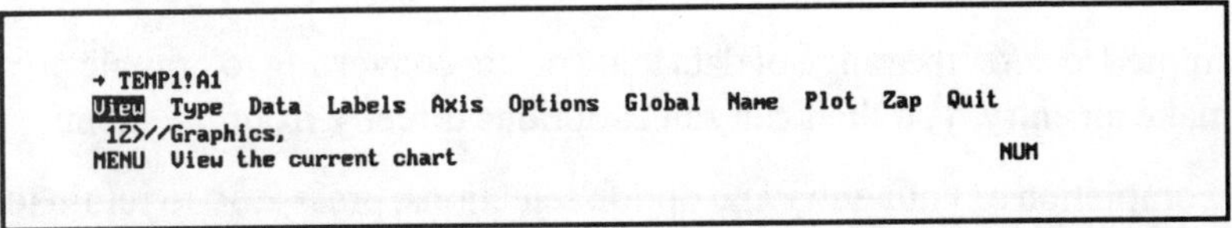

2. You are prompted to select an option from the menu presented. To build a chart, your first selection should be to select the type of graph or chart you want. Select Type by typing **T**. The following dialog panel appears.

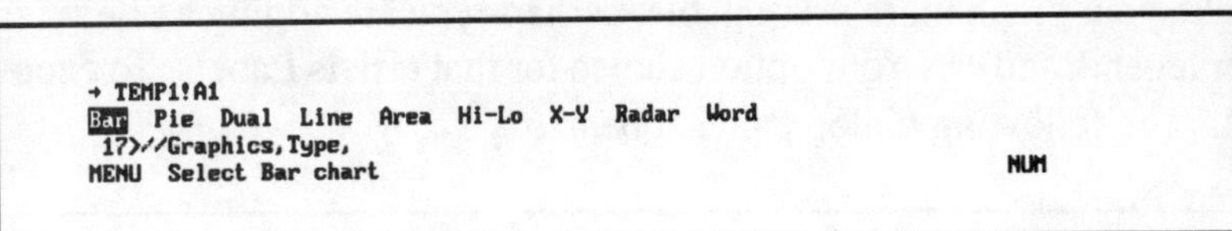

3. You now select the type of chart or graph you are building. Make your selection, then press **Enter**. You are returned to the main options menu. Now that you have chosen the type of graph you want, you need to specify a range that tells SuperCalc 5 where the data is that you are graphing. Therefore, your next selection is Data. Select Data by typing **D**. This causes the following screen to appear.

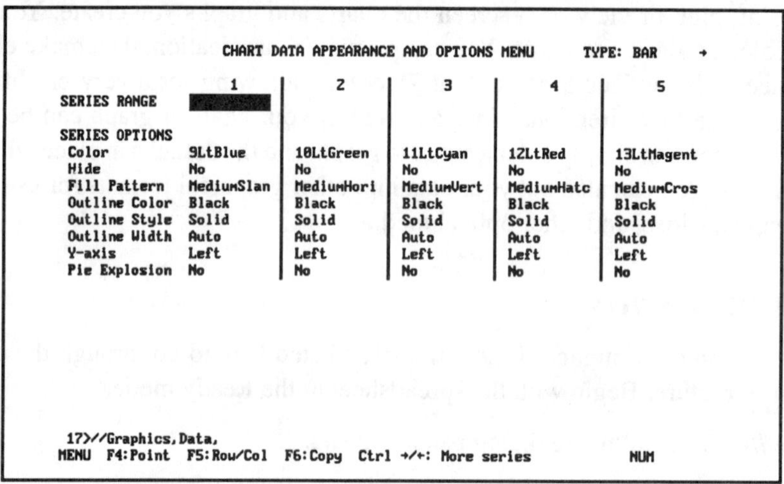

You are prompted to enter the range of data that you are converting to graphic presentation. After you make an entry, you then can select options directly from the menu.

4. After completion of your entry and option selections, press **Esc** to return to the main options menu. You now have defined the two most important parts of your graph, the type and the data to use. As a matter of fact, you can see your graph with only lines (or other symbols), but no text, by selecting the View option. Type **V** to make that selection. After a few seconds of charting, your graph or chart appears on your screen. Press **Esc** to return to the main options menu.

5. To make your graph more presentable, perhaps you are adding a title, a legend, axis title or legend, and etc. Your option choice for that task is Labels. To choose Labels, type **L**. The following dialog panel appears.

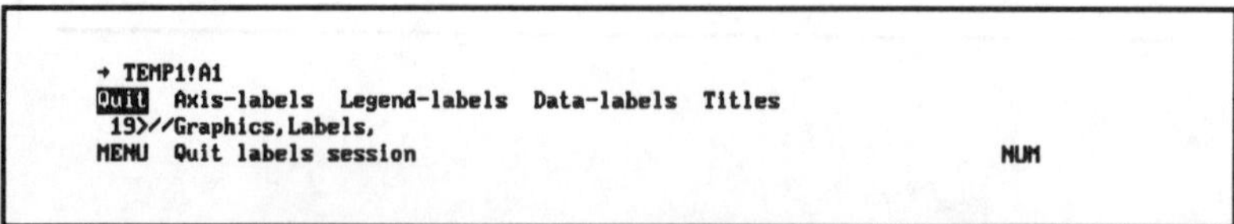

6. You are prompted to select the title or legend you are adding. You can add one of each to your graph if you like. To add an axis label, select Axis-label by typing **A**. The following screen appears.

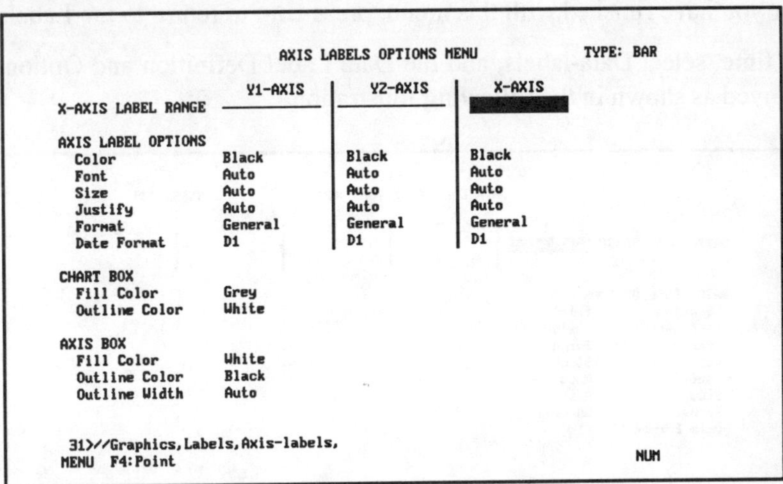
AXIS LABELS OPTIONS MENU TYPE: BAR

	Y1-AXIS	Y2-AXIS	X-AXIS
X-AXIS LABEL RANGE			
AXIS LABEL OPTIONS			
Color	Black	Black	Black
Font	Auto	Auto	Auto
Size	Auto	Auto	Auto
Justify	Auto	Auto	Auto
Format	General	General	General
Date Format	D1	D1	D1
CHART BOX			
Fill Color	Grey		
Outline Color	White		
AXIS BOX			
Fill Color	White		
Outline Color	Black		
Outline Width	Auto		

31>//Graphics,Labels,Axis-labels,
MENU F4:Point NUM

In this menu, you are prompted to enter a range for the X-axis labels, then choose options. The help line explains each option if you need any help with your choices.

7. After your entries are complete, press **Esc** to return to the Labels options menu.

8. Now select Legend-labels by pressing **L**. This displays the Legend Label Definition and Options menu, shown in the following illustration.

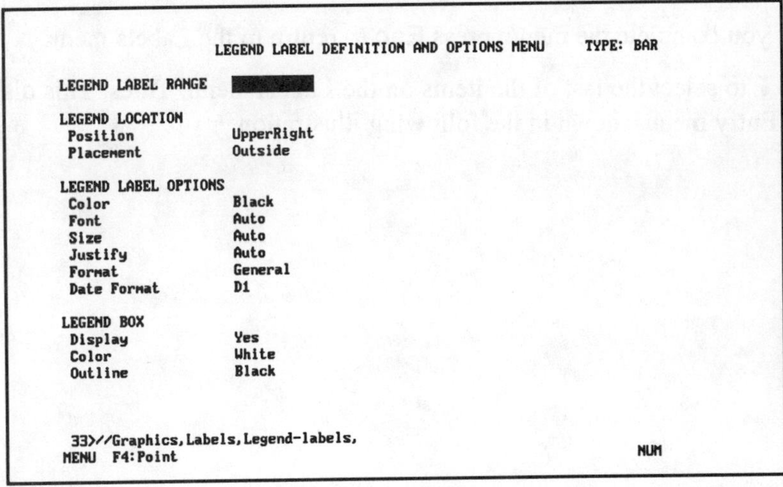
LEGEND LABEL DEFINITION AND OPTIONS MENU TYPE: BAR

LEGEND LABEL RANGE	
LEGEND LOCATION	
Position	UpperRight
Placement	Outside
LEGEND LABEL OPTIONS	
Color	Black
Font	Auto
Size	Auto
Justify	Auto
Format	General
Date Format	D1
LEGEND BOX	
Display	Yes
Color	White
Outline	Black

33>//Graphics,Labels,Legend-labels,
MENU F4:Point NUM

You are prompted to enter the range that contains the name for your legend labels. After you enter the range, you again have options to select from. Use the help line to assist you in choosing options.

9. After you have finished with this menu, press **Esc** to return to the Labels menu.
10. This time, select Data-labels, and the Data Label Definition and Options menu is displayed as shown in the following illustration.

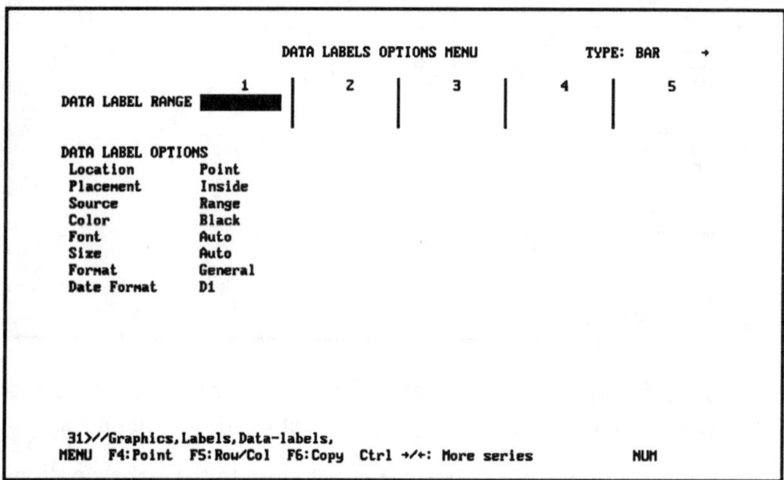

This menu allows you the choice of using something other than the data values from the Chart Data and Options menu. You are prompted to enter a range for the labels you are using. After your entry, you can select options for the data labels.

11. After you complete the menu, press **Esc** to return to the Labels menu.
12. Type **T** to select the last of the items on the Labels menu, Titles. This displays the Title Entry menu, shown in the following illustration.

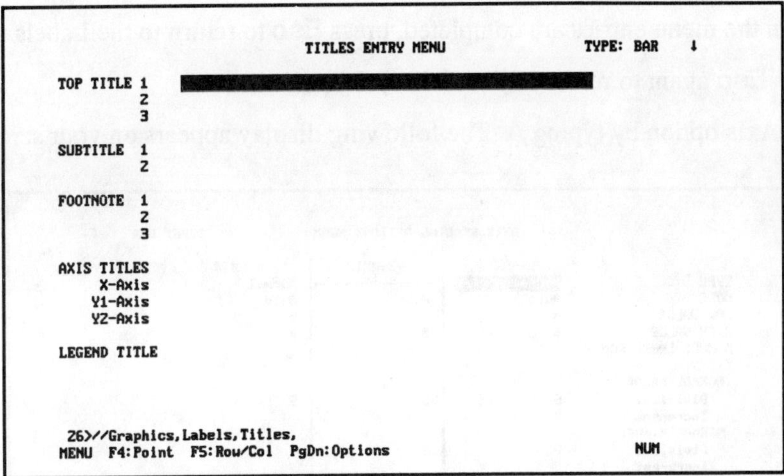

This menu prompts you to enter a range for any of the listed titles, or to type it directly on the menu. The first three titles can have up to three lines each.

13. After your titles are entered, press **Page-Down** to access the Title Options menu, shown in the following illustration.

```
                          TITLES OPTIONS MENU           TYPE: BAR   ↑

                COLOR      FONT       SIZE      JUSTIFY    POSITION

TOP TITLE       Black      Auto       Auto      Auto

SUBTITLE        Black      Auto       Auto      Auto

FOOTNOTE        Black      Auto       Auto      Auto

AXIS TITLES
  X-Axis        Black      Auto       Auto      Auto       Auto
  Y1-Axis       Black      Auto       Auto      Auto       Auto
  Y2-Axis       Black      Auto       Auto      Auto       Auto

LEGEND TITLE    Black      Auto       Auto      Auto


Black
 26>//Graphics,Labels,Titles,
MENU  F4:Point  F6:Copy  PgUp:Title Menu                 NUM
```

This menu allows you to choose options for each of the titles you just entered. Use the help line for assistance in making your choices.

14. When the menu entries are completed, press **Esc** to return to the Labels menu.
15. Press **Esc** again to return to the main options menu.

Select the Axis option by typing **A**. The following display appears on your screen.

```
                         AXIS SCALING OPTIONS MENU              TYPE: BAR   ↓

                          Y1-AXIS        Y2-AXIS        X-AXIS
TYPE                      Normal                        Normal
MODE                      Auto           Auto           Auto
LOW VALUE                 0              0              0
HIGH VALUE                0              0              0
MANUAL LABEL RANGE
TICKS:
 NORMAL MAJOR
   Divisions              5              5              5
   Increment
 NORMAL MINOR
   Divisions              0              0              0
   Increment
 LOG MAJOR
   Divisions/Decade       1              1              1
   Decades/Division
 LOG MINOR
   Divisions/Decade       9              9              9
   Decades/Division

Normal
 17>//Graphics,Axis,
MENU  F4:Point  PgDn:Options                                      NUM
```

This is the Axis Scaling Definition menu. On this menu, you define the scale of the X and Y axes. The help line lets you know what your options are so you can make a good choice. From this menu, you can access the Axis Options menu.

16. Press **Page-Down** and the following screen appears.

```
                         AXIS APPEARANCE OPTIONS MENU           TYPE: BAR   ↑

                         COLOR      WIDTH      STYLE      POSITION
X-AXIS
   Axis                  Black      Auto       Solid
   Tick                  None       Auto                  Outside
   Major grid            None       Auto       Solid
   Minor grid            None       Auto       Solid

Y1-AXIS
   Axis                  Black      Auto       Solid
   Tick                  Black      Auto                  Inside
   Major grid            Grey       Auto       Solid
   Minor grid            None       Auto       Solid

Y2-AXIS
   Axis                  Black      Auto       Solid
   Tick                  Black      Auto                  Inside
   Major grid            Grey       Auto       Solid
   Minor grid            None       Auto       Solid

Black
 17>//Graphics,Axis,
MENU  F4:Point  F6:Copy  PgUp:Axis Menu                           NUM
```

This menu allows you to select the characteristics of the axes, grids, and tick marks.

17. Use the help line to get your selections made, then press **Page-Up** to return to the Axis Scaling Definition menu. From that menu, press **Esc** to return to the main options menu.

18. Select the Options option by pressing **O**. the following display appears.

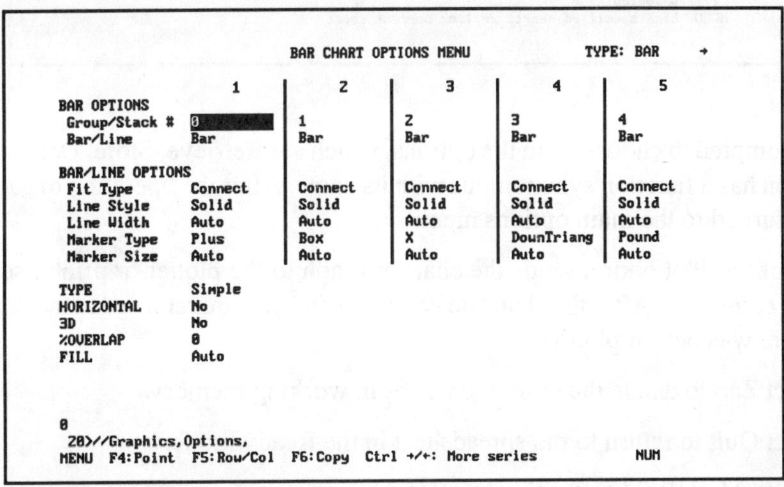

The Chart Options menu shows you the options for each of the major chart types. The menu displayed changes to reflect the differences in each chart type when the selected type is changed by the Type option. The options for each type of chart are explained on the help line, which allows you to make the choice you want.

19. When you are finished with the menu, return to the main options menu by pressing **Esc**.

20. Select Global by typing **G**. The following panel appears.

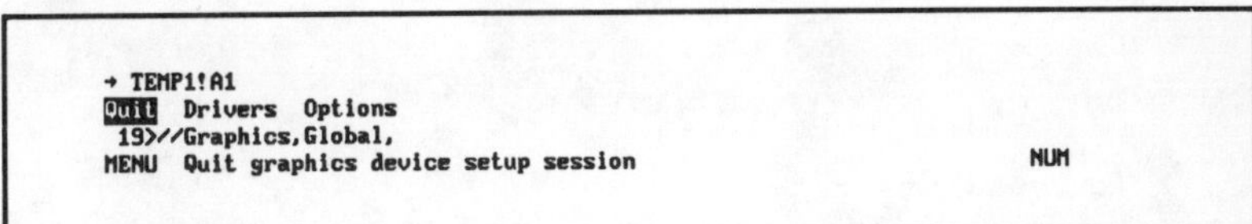

21. You are prompted to select Quit, Drivers, or Options. Select Quit and you are returned to the main options menu. Select Drivers and you can make choices about the devices or files that your chart is sent to. Select Options and you can make settings to configure your system to operate with your particular printer or monitor.

22. Once your choices have been made and you are back in the main options menu, select the Name option. The following dialog panel appears.

```
→ TEMP1!A1
Retrieve  Store  Delete  Zap
 17>//Graphics,Name,
MENU  Load specified chart; replace current chart                    NUM
```

You are prompted to choose from the options, which are Retrieve, Store, Delete, and Zap. Each option has a function synonomous with its name. After the operation of each option, you are returned to the main options menu.

Selection of the Plot option sends the chart or graph to the plotter or printer selected by the Global command. After the chart file has been sent, you are returned to the place where the program was before plotting.

23. Select Zap to delete the current chart from working memory.
24. Select Quit to return to the spreadsheet in the Ready mode.
25. Turn to Module 24 to continue the learning sequence.

Module 17
IMPORT

DESCRIPTION

The Import command reads data files created by other programs such as spreadsheets and databases, converts them into SuperCalc 5 format, then loads them into the current spreadsheet. Import converts as much data as possible from the foreign file to the SuperCalc format.

The Import command operates similarly to the Export command, but in the opposite direction. Files created by foreign programs are read and converted to SuperCalc format, then loaded into the current spreadsheet, according to your option selections. Formats that the Import command can convert to SuperCalc format are:

XDIF

DIF

CSV

NUMBERS

TEXT

VISICALC

dBASE

Selection of the format which you are importing leads you to other options, which are explained with each format in the following paragraphs.

XDIF The XDIF format is convertable to SuperCalc by the Import command. All formulas and display formats are converted. Options for the XDIF format are Replace, All, Values, Consolidate, and Part. Each option is briefly described here.

Replace clears the existing spreadsheet from memory, then loads all of the converted file into the current spreadsheet. If the current spreadsheet has been edited, SuperCalc will ask for confirmation before executing the import command, as the current spreadsheet is lost by importing a file.

All converts a foreign file, then loads it into the current spreadsheet. The current spreadsheet is not cleared, so the converted file is written directly over the spreadsheet that was in memory. If a small imported file replaces a larger spreadsheet with this option, data to the right and below the converted file will still exist. You must decide if this is a problem, then act to resolve it.

Values converts the entire imported file into SuperCalc, but only the calculated values of formulas in foreign files are converted, not the complete formulas. If it is possible to convert display formats from the foreign file, they are included.

Consolidate combines the corresponding cells of the converted file and the current spreadsheet and puts the result in the spreadsheet cell. Note that addition is the only consolidation operation allowed by this option.

Part allows you to select a part of the foreign file for importation. You select a from range in the foreign file and a to range in the current spreadsheet. The from range must be in the format of the file being imported. Note that some formats contain only row entries. To view the options for the Part selection, type a comma (,) after the from entry. The options include All, Values, +, –, *, and /. The All option imports all of the specified part of the foreign file. The Values option imports all of the foreign file except that it converts only the calculated values of formulas, not the formulas. The +, –, *, and / options perform the indicated arithmetic operation in consolidation of the corresponding cells of the converted file and the current spreadsheet.

Each of the previously described options appear in some combination as options in each of the formats. You are referred to these descriptions as these options appear later in this module.

DIF This option converts the standard DIF format into SuperCalc spreadsheet format. For this format, you must inform SuperCalc whether the file to be imported is Rowwise or Colwise. Rowwise indicates that each record in the file is a spreadsheet row, and Colwise indicates that each record in the file is a spreadsheet column. Options for the DIF format include Replace, All, Consolidate, and Part.

CSV The CSV option converts files created in the comma separated values format to the SuperCalc format. Formulas can be imported in this format by enclosing them in backslash characters (\). Including a statement such as \sum(a1:a20)\ in a CSV file results in the statement SUM(A1:A20) after conversion. Options for the CSV format are Replace, All, Consolidate, and Part.

NUMBERS This format option converts numeric files into SuperCalc format. Numbers converts only numbers and text enclosed by double quote marks. Each line in the file is put on a row in the current spreadsheet, and each number or double-quoted text is put into a cell. The entry in each cell is truncated to 240 characters. Options for this format are Replace, All, and Part.

TEXT The Text format option imports an ASCII file as text and puts one line of the ASCII file on a row in the current spreadsheet. The input line of the ASCII file is limited to 240 characters and truncated at that point.

VISICALC The VisiCalc format option converts VisiCalc data files to the SuperCalc format. The conversion includes all data including formulas and values, with the following exceptions.

1. @AND and @OR functions in VisiCalc allow unlimited arguments, while SuperCalc allows only two. To retain formula accuracy, nested AND or OR functions are generated during conversion. If the converted formula exceeds 240 characters, a message appears on your screen.
2. Formulas in Boolean expression that evaluate TRUE or FALSE in VisiCalc result in 1 or 0 in SuperCalc.
3. Any + formula prefix on VisiCalc is removed when converted to SuperCalc. A VisiCalc formula such as +A1+B1 would be converted to A1+B1 in SuperCalc format.
4. VisiCalc displays 21 rows on a screen, while SuperCalc displays 20 rows. Conversion of a VisiCalc file that had been saved with the cursor on the 21st row results in a SuperCalc screen with the cursor on row 20 and the top row forced off the screen. Any conversion that results in conflict between retaining the original screen and retaining the original cursor position is decided in favor of the original cursor position.
5. A screen split with the Window command and title locks in place for each window is treated differently by VisiCalc and SuperCalc. VisiCalc keeps the lock in each window, while SuperCalc does not keep the lock in the second window. In converting to the SuperCalc format, the lock in the second window is kept, as though it had been set by the spreadsheet originator.
6. Repetitous text in VisiCalc repeats across column width only. After conversion to SuperCalc, repetitous text will repeat across the row to a non-empty cell, the same way that SuperCalc does.

Options for the VisiCalc format are Replace, All, and Part.

dBASE The dBASE format option converts dBASE III files into SuperCalc spreadsheet format. In the conversion, TRUE and FALSE evaluations are converted to 1 and 0, and memo fields are not converted. The dBASE format has two options which are not present in any other format. They are Names and Extract. Each is described later in this module. Befor using either of them, you must refer to the Data module to define the Input, Criterion, and Output ranges. For importing a dBASE file, SuperCalc uses the ranges in the following manner:

1. Each dBASE record is read into the input range. The range must be at least two rows deep.
2. The record is evaluated against the data in the criterion range if any is there.
3. If the record is accepted, it is put in the output range. The output range must be of sufficient size to handle the incoming records.

The first row of each range is reserved for field names. They are entered manually or can be imported with the Names option.

Names This option reads field names from the dBASE file into the SuperCalc criterion range. The names then must be copied into the input and output ranges and can be repositioned. Once the names have been imported, selection criteria can be entered to determine which dBASE records are imported.

Extract This option reads dBASE records into the input range, compares them to the selection criteria, then adds the accepted records to the output range. Options for this command are Replace and All.

APPLICATIONS

The Import command allows you to take advantage of the power and features of SuperCalc 5 to manipulate data created in other programs. Formats accepted by the Import command are used by the majority of the programs that contain data which would benefit by processing in SuperCalc 5.

TYPICAL OPERATION

To use the import command, follow the steps listed here, beginning with the spreadsheet in the Ready mode.

1. Type //, then select Import and press **Enter**. The following dialog panel appears.

```
→ TEMP1!A1
XDIF  DIF  CSV  Numbers  Text  VisiCalc  dBase
 10>//Import,
MENU  SDI file format                                  NUM
```

You are prompted to select a format from the menu shown. After selecting a format, you are prompted to enter the name of the foreign file you are importing. SuperCalc 5 will add the proper extension to the filename.

Press Enter, and you are presented with a screen giving you the options for the format you selected.

If you select XDIF, the following panel appears.

```
← TEMP1!A1
Replace  All  Values  Consolidate  Part
 28>//Import,XDIF,example1.bak,
MENU  Erase current spreadsheet before importing
```

You are prompted to select an option from this menu.

Select All, Values, or Consolidate, press Enter, and the import is done. You are returned to the spreadsheet with the imported file in it, in the Ready mode.

Select Replace and you are prompted to confirm your intent to import a file, as the current spreadsheet will be lost. Select Yes or No and press Enter. The import is done, and you are returned to the spreadsheet with the imported file in it, in the Ready mode.

Select Part and you are prompted for a from range and a to range. After entering your selections and pressing Enter after each, you are prompted by the option menu that appears as shown on the following dialog panel.

```
← TEMP1!A1
All  Values  +  -  *  /
 39>//Import,XDIF,example1.bak,Part,A1,A1,
MENU  Import part of spreadsheet including formulas
```

2. Select the option for your needs and press **Enter**.

The import is done and you are in the spreadsheet in the Ready mode. If you selected DIF, the following panel appears after you have made your filename entry.

```
← TEMP1!A1
Colwise  Rowwise
 27>//Import,DIF,example1.bak,
MENU  Import records as columns
```

3. Select Colwise or Rowwise to indicate the record orientation of the file you are importing and press **Enter**. The following panel appears for either choice made on the previous screen.

```
← TEMP1!A1
Replace  All  Consolidate  Part
 35>//Import,DIF,example1.bak,Colwise,
MENU  Erase current spreadsheet before importing
```

4. The options for this screen are very similar to the ones seen in the XDIF format. The only difference is that the Values option has been made part of the Part option of this screen. Select Part and make a to and from entry, pressing **Enter** after each. The following panel appears.

```
← TEMP1!A1
Values  +  -  *  /
 46>//Import,DIF,example1.bak,Colwise,Part,A1,A1,
MENU  Import part of spreadsheet Values only
```

Did you select CSV? The following panel is on your display if that was your choice.

```
← TEMP1!A1
Replace  All  Consolidate  Part
 20>//Import,CSV,TEMP1,
MENU  Erase current spreadsheet before importing
```

The options are the same for CSV as they were for DIF after the record orientation choice was made.

5. Press **Esc** until you are returned to the Import options menu.
6. For the format selections Numbers, Text, and VisiCalc, you are prompted to enter the file to import. After your entry, press **Enter** and the following panel appears.

```
→ TEMP1!A1
Replace  All  Part
 31>//Import,Numbers,example1.bak,
MENU  Erase current spreadsheet before importing
```

7. Press **Esc** until you are returned to the Import options menu.

8. Each option on this menu is familiar to you from earlier use, so make your selection and press **Enter** to execute the command. If dBASE was your selection, the following dialog panel appeared after your filename entry.

```
→ TEMP1!A1
Replace  All  Extract  Names
 29>//Import,dBase,example1.bak,
MENU  Erase current spreadsheet before importing
```

The Extract and Names options can be used only if you have defined them in the Data command. After definition, Names must be used first. After the field names are imported, data can be imported from the dBASE files with the Extract option.

9. Press **Esc** until you are returned to the spreadsheet in the Ready mode.

10. Turn to Module 12 to continue the learning sequence.

Module 18
INSERT

DESCRIPTION

The Insert command adds rows, columns, blocks, or an entire page of empty cells to a spreadsheet. When cells are added, formulas in the spreadsheet are automatically adjusted. When rows, columns, or blocks are added, current data is moved aside, formulas are adjusted, and formats retained.

When current data is moved aside to insert cells, the data is moved according to the type of insert done. When inserting a cell or cells in a row, the data in the specified row and all rows below it are moved down to make space for the insert.

Inserting a column or columns moves to the right the specified column and all columns to the right of it. A block insertion moves data down or to the right to accomodate the insertion. Insertion of a page is done where you specify, and all pages behind the inserted page are re-numbered.

If an insert of rows or columns would push a cell past the last row or column of the spreadsheet, SuperCalc 5 does not allow the insert. Unless you change the size of your spreadsheet, an appropriate number of cells must be deleted from the insert for it to be allowed. To increase the size of your spreadsheet, refer to the module for the Global command. Any inserted cell takes on the Global or General display format.

APPLICATION

The Insert command is very useful in adding places for new data in the middle of a spreadsheet. Also, adding pages to a spreadsheet can be done with the Insert command.

TYPICAL OPERATION

To illustrate the use of the Insert command, the file created in Module 20 is used. Follow the steps listed here, and begin with the spreadsheet in the Ready mode.

1. Load the example file by typing **/L EXAMPLE1.SC5** and pressing **Enter**. Press **R** and the file is loaded.

2. Type **/I**. The following dialog panel appears on your display.

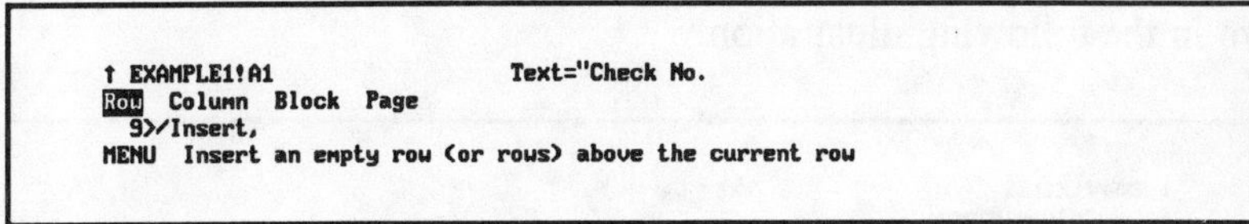

```
↑ EXAMPLE1!A1                 Text="Check No.
Row  Column  Block  Page
 9>/Insert,
MENU  Insert an empty row (or rows) above the current row
```

3. To insert a row of blank cells, select Row from the options. Press **Enter** and the dialog panel appears as shown in the following illustration.

```
↑ EXAMPLE1!A1                 Text="Check No.
Enter Row Range
 14>/Insert,Row,1
POINT F1:Help F2:Edit F3:Names Home:1st End-Arrow:last Ctrl-Break:Cancel
```

You are prompted to enter the number of the row into which you are inserting a row of blank cells.

4. Type **7**, then press **Enter**. The row is inserted, you are returned to the spreadsheet in the Ready mode, and the following screen appears.

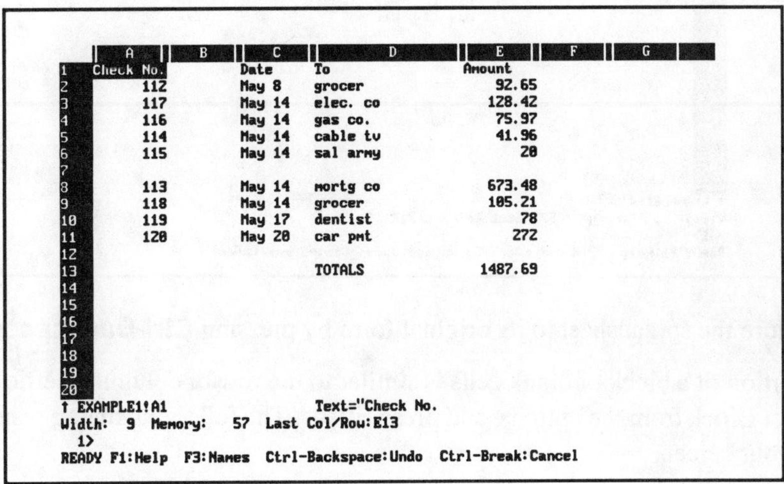

	A	B	C	D	E	F	G
1	Check No.		Date	To	Amount		
2	112		May 8	grocer	92.65		
3	117		May 14	elec. co	128.42		
4	116		May 14	gas co.	75.97		
5	114		May 14	cable tv	41.96		
6	115		May 14	sal army	20		
7							
8	113		May 14	mortg co	673.48		
9	118		May 14	grocer	105.21		
10	119		May 17	dentist	78		
11	120		May 20	car pmt	272		
12							
13				TOTALS	1487.69		
14							
15							
16							
17							
18							
19							
20							

```
↑ EXAMPLE1!A1                 Text="Check No.
Width:  9  Memory:   57  Last Col/Row:E13
 1>
READY F1:Help  F3:Names  Ctrl-Backspace:Undo  Ctrl-Break:Cancel
```

5. Return the spreadsheet to its original form by pressing **Ctrl-Backspace**.

6. To insert a column of blank cells, the sequence is similar to the row insertion. Type **/I**, select Column from the options, and press **Enter**. The dialog panel appears as shown in the following illustration.

```
↑ EXAMPLE1!A1                    Text="Check No.
Enter Column Range
 17>/Insert,Column,A
POINT F1:Help F2:Edit F3:Names Home:1st End-Arrow:last Ctrl-Break:Cancel
```

You are prompted to enter the letter of the column into which you are inserting a column of blank cells.

7. Type **A**, then press **Enter**. The column is inserted, you are returned to the spreadsheet in the Ready mode, and the following screen appears.

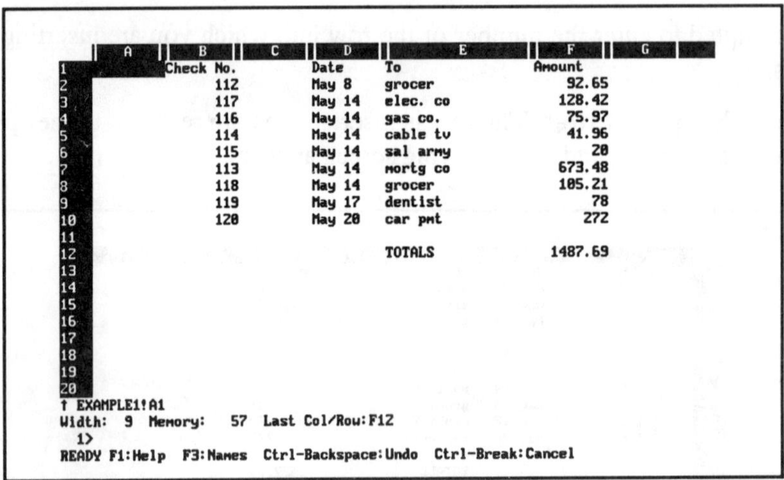

	A	B	C	D	E	F	G
1		Check No.		Date	To	Amount	
2		112		May 8	grocer	92.65	
3		117		May 14	elec. co	128.42	
4		116		May 14	gas co.	75.97	
5		114		May 14	cable tv	41.96	
6		115		May 14	sal army	20	
7		113		May 14	mortg co	673.48	
8		118		May 14	grocer	105.21	
9		119		May 17	dentist	78	
10		120		May 20	car pmt	272	
11							
12					TOTALS	1487.69	
13							
14							
15							
16							
17							
18							
19							
20							

↑ EXAMPLE1!A1
Width: 9 Memory: 57 Last Col/Row:F12
1>
READY F1:Help F3:Names Ctrl-Backspace:Undo Ctrl-Break:Cancel

8. Restore the spreadsheet to its original form by pressing **Ctrl-Backspace**.

9. Insertion of a block of blank cells is similar to the row or column insertion. Type **/I**, select Block from the options, and press **Enter**. The following dialog panel appears on your screen.

```
↑ EXAMPLE1!A1                    Text="Check No.
Enter Range
 17>/Insert,Block,A1
POINT F1:Help F2:Edit F3:Names Home:1st End-Arrow:last Ctrl-Break:Cancel
```

10. You are prompted to enter the range of a block into which you are inserting blank cells. Type **A6:C8**, press **Enter**, and the following screen appears.

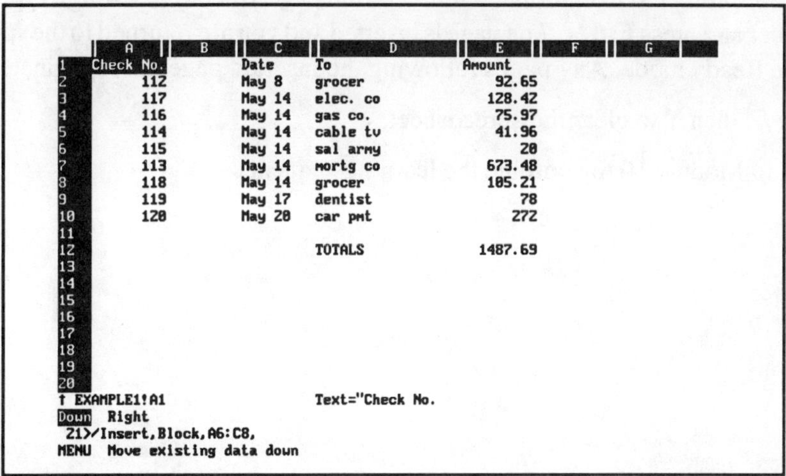

11. You are now prompted to select whether to move the current data in the cells where you are inserting blank cells Down or to the Right. Select either, press **Enter**, and the insert is done. You are returned to the spreadsheet in the Ready mode and the following screen appears.

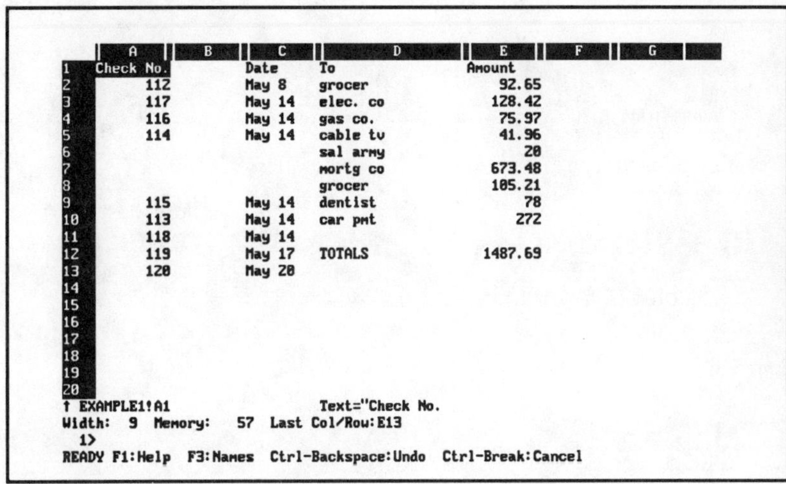

12. Inserting a page consists of the same sequence as the other insert options. Type **/I**, select Page from the options, and press **Enter**.

13. You are prompted to enter the number of the page you are inserting. Type the page number and press **Enter**. The page is inserted and you are returned to the spreadsheet in the Ready mode. Any pages following the inserted page are repaginated.

14. Type **/Z** then **Y** to clear the spreadsheet.

15. Turn to Module 10 to continue the learning sequence.

Module 19
JUSTIFY

DESCRIPTION

The Justify command allows you to justify text over a specified width which you select. The text may be justified left, right, or centered within the specified range of columns. The Justify command differs from the Format command as it operates on a block of cells, rather than operating within a single column. This command also contains a "word-wrap" option which can function similar to a word processor.

In the Justify command, three options are available: single, multiple, and word-wrap. A description of each is included in the following paragraphs.

SINGLE The Single option justifies text over a width specified as a range of columns. The text must begin in the first column of the specified range, and only the text in the first column will wrap. Justification stops at the first non-text cell encountered.

MULTIPLE The Multiple option allows you to wrap text which may be interrupted by a non-text cell. The text must begin in the first column of the specified range, and justification stops when two consecutive non-text cells are encountered.

For either the Single or Multiple option, you choose to justify your text to the left, right, or center. In left or right justification, the text is moved flush to the left or right, word-wrapping to conform to the range specified. As much text as possible is included on each line, with a single blank space between each word. Center justification centers each line in the specified range, line by line. If a text string is too long to center or right justify within the range, the string is not moved.

WORD-WRAP The Word-wrap option lets you type continously without pressing Enter. A specific width is chosen for the text, and when text is typed, the part that fits the selected width is entered automatically. The cursor then moves down one row, and the remaining data on the entry line moves to the beginning of the entry line. All text is left justified. If right or center justification is desired, you must use the Single or Multiple option after the entry is complete. Word-wrap will terminate when you press Enter with no text on the entry line, move the cursor outside the column range, try to write in a protected cell, fill up all available memory, or press Esc. If the specified range is a single cell, the preceding rules apply with an added termination caused by trying to write in a non-blank cell, protected or not.

APPLICATIONS

The Justify command permits the addition of text columns, comments, or various text strings to your spreadsheet. The Word-wrap option functions as a word processor for continuous text entry.

TYPICAL OPERATION

To illustrate the use of the Justify command, text must be entered, since the Single or Multiple options can be used only after text has been entered. Follow the listed steps, beginning with spreadsheet in the Ready mode.

1. Type in the text of the applications paragraph of this module and press **Enter**. Your text will only be displayed on the first row, but don't be concerned, as it is all there for our example.

2. Type **/J**. Your screen appears as shown in the following illustration.

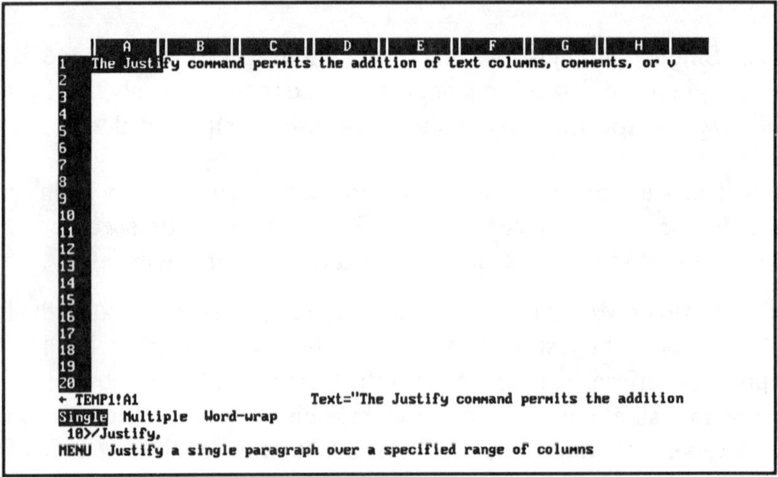

3. You are prompted to select an option. For this example, select Single and press **Enter**.

4. You are now prompted to enter the range of columns within which you are justifying the text. Type **A1:C1** and press **Enter**. The dialog panel of your spreadsheet appears as shown in the following illustration.

```
+ TEMP1!A1                              Text="The Justify command permits the addition
Left  Center  Right
 23>/Justify,Single,A1:C1,
MENU  Left-justify the text as it wraps over the specified range
```

5. Your prompt now is to select how your text is justified. Select Left, press **Enter**, and your text is justified according to your specifications. You are returned to the spreadsheet in the Ready mode, and the following screen appears.

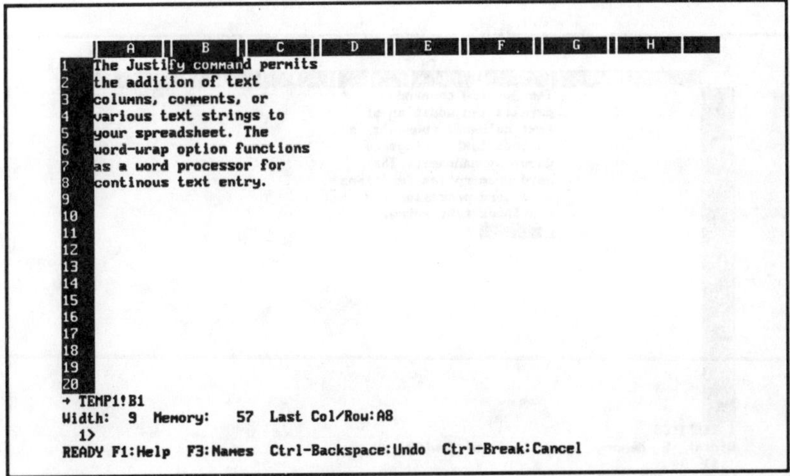

6. For the next example, clear your spreadsheet (use the blank command) and type **/J** and select Word-wrap. Press **Enter**, and the following screen appears.

```
+ TEMP1!A1
Go  Range  Width
 20>/Justify,Word-wrap,
MENU  Enter text width (maximum characters per line)                NUM
```

7. You are prompted to select from Go, Range, or Width. However, you must first enter the range of columns within which to wrap the text. Therefore, select Range, press **Enter**, type **C1:E10** and press **Enter** again.

8. You are returned to the options menu and again prompted to select an option. Select Go to begin text entry, or select Width to alter the width of the text you are about to enter. The default width is 65 characters, or you can extend the width to as much as 240 characters. For this example, select Width, press **Enter**, type **27** (3 column widths), and press **Enter** again. You are returned to the options menu.

9. Now select Go, press **Enter**, and make your text entry (use the text in the Applications paragraph again). The text wraps within the specified columns. When your entry is complete, press **Enter** to put the last of your text in the spreadsheet. Your screen should be similar to the following one.

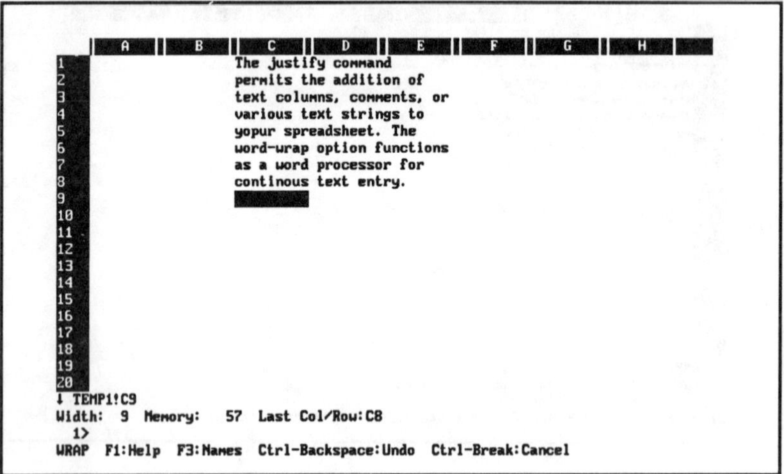

10. Press **Enter** to return to the spreadsheet in the Ready mode.

11. Use the Zap command to clear the spreadsheet.

12. Turn to Module 23 to continue the learning sequence.

Module 20
LOAD

DESCRIPTION

The Load command reads a disk file to load stored speadsheet cell contents into the current spreadsheet. All or part of the file can be loaded into a location you specify. Options include formula adjustment, values only, and consolidation arithmetic. Named ranges and chart descriptors (formats, headings, chart types) may also be loaded into the current spreadsheet.

After you have entered a filename, you have the following options: Replace, All, Values, Consolidate, Part, Names, Graphs, and Single. A description of each option is included in the following paragraphs.

REPLACE The Replace option clears the current spreadsheet and loads all of the named file. If you have edited the current spreadsheet and not saved it, a message will be displayed to remind you to do so. If you need to save the current spreadsheet, select No to cancel Replace. Select Yes to continue the Load command.

ALL The All option loads all the pages of spreadsheet in the specified file exactly as they were saved. If you have been working on a spreadsheet, it is a good idea to save the spreadsheet and use the Zap command to clear it and load to a blank spreadsheet. All writes a file over anything in your current spreadsheet, so the use of Zap eliminates any possibility of extraneous data showing up with the file you have loaded.

VALUES The Values option loads only the calculated values of any formulas in the specified file and entry level display format data. Formulas are not loaded.

CONSOLIDATE The Consolidate option combines corresponding cells of the specified file and the current spreadsheet, and the result is entered in that cell in the current spreadsheet. Cells are combined using the addition operation of consolidation arithmetic. Cells not affected are text cells, control text cells, protected cells, date and time cells, N/A cells, ERROR cells, and cells having string value results.

PART The Part option loads only a portion of the specified file, with you designating the portion to be loaded. In a partial load, SuperCalc 5 loads only cell contents and entry level formats. Any other format or default value is ignored.

When you select the Part option, you are prompted to enter the range of the source file you are loading and the location in the current spreadsheet where to load it. After you have entered the "from" range, type a comma (,) to display the Part options. An option menu appears on the dialog panel, and each option is briefly described in the following paragraphs.

No-adjust The No-adjust option, when selected, instructs SuperCalc 5 not to adjust formulas when a partial file is loaded.

Ask The Ask option prompts you to make a formula adjustment for each cell to be loaded that contains a formula. The entry line displays the formula and the prompt line displays the source cell. Select Yes if an adjustment is needed, or No if none is required.

Values The Values option loads only calculated values to the current spreadsheet where a source file cell contains a formula. Formulas are not loaded. Dates change to their DVAL function value, and times change to their TVAL function value.

+ The + option adds each file cell value to the corresponding spreadsheet cell value and places the numeric sum in the spreadsheet cell.

– The – option subtracts each file cell value from the corresponding spreadsheet cell value and places the numeric difference in the spreadsheet cell.

***** The * option multiplies each file cell value by the corresponding spreadsheet cell value and places the numeric result in the spreadsheet cell.

/ The / option divides each spreadsheet cell value by the corresponding file cell value and places the numeric quotient in the spreadsheet cell.

NAMES The Names option loads named ranges in the specified file into the current spreadsheet. Named ranges are part of the spreadsheet, are saved when the Save command is used, and are loaded with the use of the All or Replace options of the Load command. Names loaded are added to the current name list. Note that duplicate names could possibly re-define existing names.

GRAPHS The Graphs option loads chart descriptors from the specified file into the current spreadsheet. When you select the Graphs option, you are prompted to select All or Single. All loads all chart descriptors in the specified file into the current spreadsheet. Single prompts you for the name of a single chart descriptor to load.

SINGLE The Single option loads one page of the spreadsheet in the specified file into the current spreadsheet. When you select single, you are prompted for the page number to load.

APPLICATIONS

Load retrieves data files and enters the data into the current spreadsheet in several different ways, so that some of your job could possibly be taken care of by selecting the right options before loading your file. You have the option of combining spreadsheets, loading parts of spreadsheets, consolidating data, and using graphics data from other spreadsheets. Load is a very versatile command, but there are several special situations to be aware of, and they are listed here.

1. Protected cells are unaffected except by Replace. The Replace option will write over protected cells.
2. A "MEMORY FULL" message may appear if you load a large spreadsheet created with a prior version of SuperCalc. SuperCalc 5 uses more memory than previous versions.
3. When you load named ranges using the Part option, the name must be defined in both the specified cell and the current spreadsheet.
4. Loading a chart descriptor from a specified file overwrites a chart descriptor of the same name in the current spreadsheet.
5. To load Lotus 1-2-3 files, you must specify the appropriate extension (.WK1 or .WKS).
6. The last occupied row or column cannot be greater than the current spreadsheet boundary as set with the Global command.

TYPICAL OPERATION

To use the Load command, you must specify a file to load. So that a file is available for use as you go through the Recommended Learning Sequence, create the one shown in the following illustration.

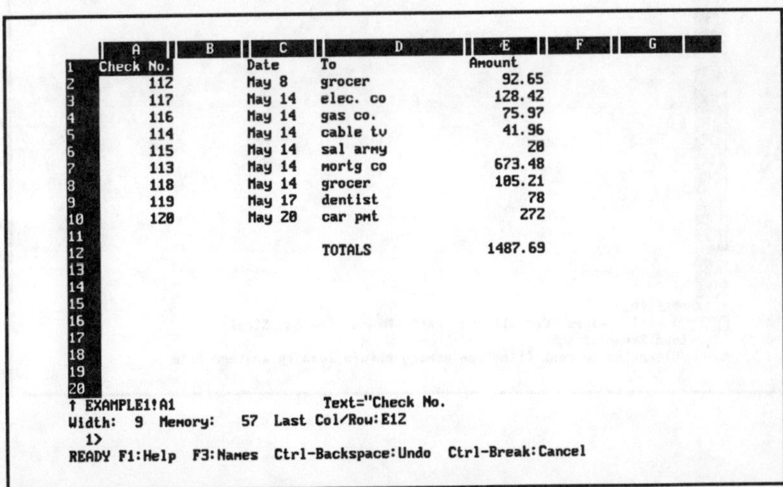

After you have completed the file, give it the name EXAMPLE1.SC5. Save the file by typing /S EXAMPLE1.SC5. Press Enter and type A to complete saving the file. With a file to use for our exercises, we can now begin our operations. Follow the steps listed here for instructions on use of the Load command. Illustrations are included showing the results of examples in the instructions. Begin with the spreadsheet in the Ready mode.

1. Type **/L**. The dialog panel appears as shown in the following illustration.

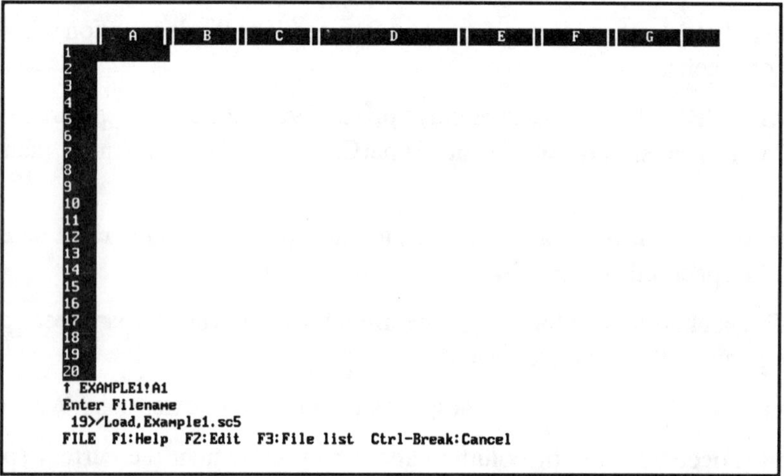

2. You are prompted to enter a filename. Type **EXAMPLE1.SC5** and press **Enter**, and the Options menu appears on the dialog panel as shown in the following illustration.

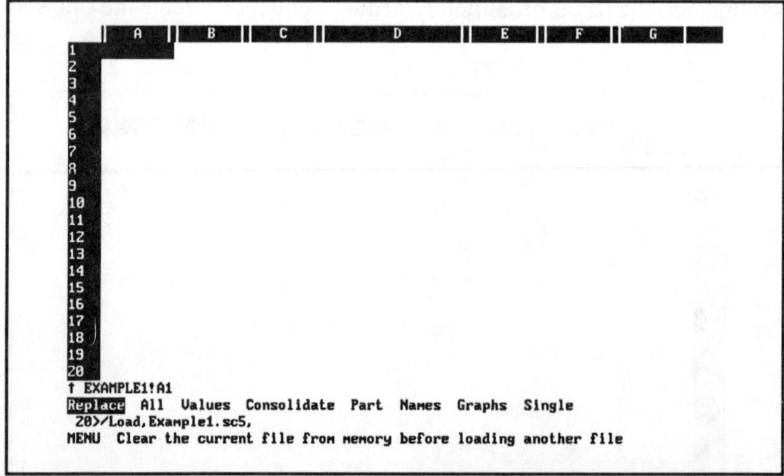

3. Select Replace by highlighting it with the menu cursor and pressing **Enter** (or by typing R). You are now asked by SuperCalc if you are sure you want to erase the spreadsheet in memory, as this is what happens with the Replace option. Select No, and you are returned to the main options menu. Select Yes, and the file is loaded. If a spreadsheet was in memory before the load operation, it is erased. The Replace option clears all data from the current spreadsheet before loading the specified file. The following screen appears.

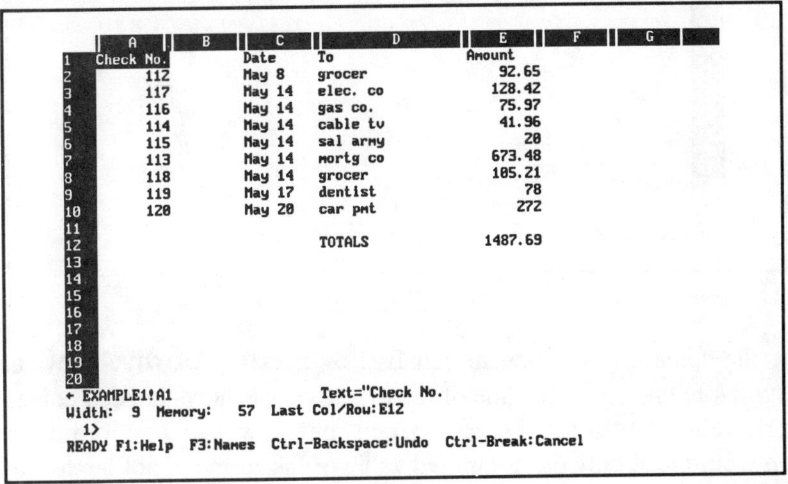

	A	B	C	D	E	F	G
1	Check No.		Date	To	Amount		
2	112		May 8	grocer	92.65		
3	117		May 14	elec. co	128.42		
4	116		May 14	gas co.	75.97		
5	114		May 14	cable tv	41.96		
6	115		May 14	sal army	20		
7	113		May 14	mortg co	673.48		
8	118		May 14	grocer	105.21		
9	119		May 17	dentist	78		
10	120		May 20	car pmt	272		
11							
12				TOTALS	1487.69		
13							
14							
15							
16							
17							
18							
19							
20							

← EXAMPLE1!A1 Text="Check No.
Width: 9 Memory: 57 Last Col/Row:E12
1>
READY F1:Help F3:Names Ctrl-Backspace:Undo Ctrl-Break:Cancel

4. To use the All option, type **/L EXAMPLE1.SC5** and press **Enter**.

5. Select All from the Options menu by highlighting it and pressing **Enter** (or by typing A), and the file is loaded.

The All option loads the file directly over the current spreadsheet without first clearing it. If the file being loaded has blank cells in it, data in those cells of the previous spreadsheet will show up in the spreadsheet just loaded. Also, if the spreadsheet being loaded is smaller than the spreadsheet being displaced, some data will be untouched and show up in your spreadsheet after loading. The screen displayed will be the same as the previous illustration.

6. To show an example of the Values option, clear the current spreadsheet by typing **/Z** and then **Y**. (This operation used the Zap command to clear the spreadsheet that was displayed on your screen.)

7. Now type **/L EXAMPLE1.SC5** and press **Enter**.

8. Select the Values option by typing **V**. The following spreadsheet appears.

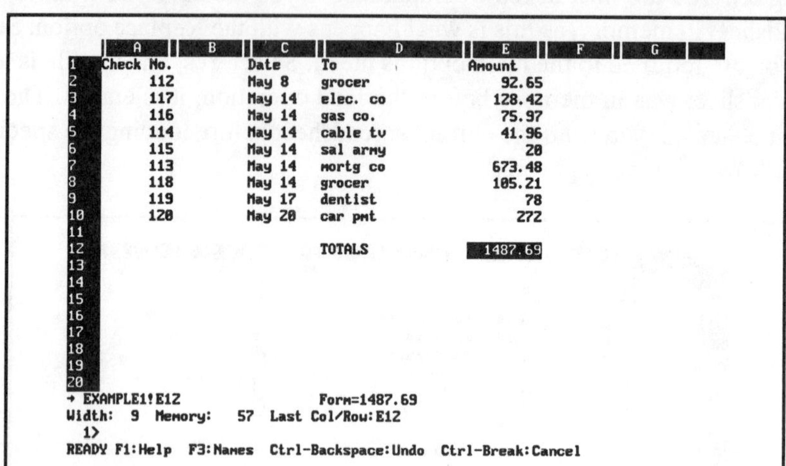

	A	B	C	D	E	F	G
1	Check No.		Date	To	Amount		
2	112		May 8	grocer	92.65		
3	117		May 14	elec. co	128.42		
4	116		May 14	gas co.	75.97		
5	114		May 14	cable tv	41.96		
6	115		May 14	sal army	20		
7	113		May 14	mortg co	673.48		
8	118		May 14	grocer	105.21		
9	119		May 17	dentist	78		
10	120		May 20	car pmt	272		
11							
12				TOTALS	1487.69		
13							
14							
15							
16							
17							
18							
19							
20							

→ EXAMPLE1!E12 Form=1487.69
Width: 9 Memory: 57 Last Col/Row:E12
1>
READY F1:Help F3:Names Ctrl-Backspace:Undo Ctrl-Break:Cancel

9. Move the spreadsheet cursor to cell E12 by pressing **Down Arrow** and **Right Arrow**. Note that the status line of the dialog panel shows the cell contents to be a numeric value of 1487.69. If the actual cell content were to be a formula, the Values option would load only the computed value of the formula, not the formula itself.

10. Clear the spreadsheet by using the Zap command as done in step 6.

11. To load a partial spreadsheet, type **/L EXAMPLE1.SC5**.

12. Press **Enter** and select Part from the Options menu. You are now prompted to enter the source range of the partial spreadsheet you are loading. Type **A1:C10**.

13. Press **Enter**, and you are prompted for the destination range in the spreadsheet where you are loading the data. However, you may choose from an options menu if you type a comma (,). The Options menu includes No-adjust, Ask, Values, +, – , *, and /. If you have chosen an option, press Enter. If you did not use an option, do not press Enter.

14. Enter the destination range by typing **A1:C10**. Press **Enter**, and the partial load is done. You are returned to the spreadsheet in the Ready mode, and your spreadsheet is as shown in the following illustration.

```
  |   A   ||   B   ||   C   ||   D   ||   E   ||   F   ||   G   ||   H   |
1  Check No.          Date
2        112          May 8
3        117          May 14
4        116          May 14
5        114          May 14
6        115          May 14
7        113          May 14
8        118          May 14
9        119          May 17
10       120          May 20
11
12
13
14
15
16
17
18
19
20
→ EXAMPLE1!A1                 Text="Check No.
Width:  9 Memory:    57  Last Col/Row:C10
   1>
READY F1:Help  F3:Names  Ctrl-Backspace:Undo  Ctrl-Break:Cancel
```

To become familiar with all the options of the Load command, you can create example spreadsheets, then load them to gain the knowledge about them that only practice can bring about. Your use of the Load command can be a time saver, where applications permit.

15. Type **/Z** then **Y** to clear the spreadsheet.
16. Turn to Module 29 to continue the learning sequence.

Module 21
MACRO

DESCRIPTION

The Macro command gives you the capability to create, save, run, and do analysis and debug on macros. You can also convert Lotus 1-2-3 macros to SuperCalc 5 macro format.

Macro operations are done in different modes, which are indicated on the right side of the help line when they are active. Function keys are used to invoke the macro modes and functions. The function keys that invoke modes and other operations are listed in the following table, with a brief desciption of what each does.

Key	Mode	Description
Alt-F2	STEP	Turns STEP mode on/off
Alt-F3		Displays the Macro Name/Range Directory.
Alt-F4	LEARN	Turns LEARN mode on/off
Alt-F5		Executes the specified macro
Alt-F6	DIRECT	Turns DIRECT mode on/off
Alt-F8	ASTEP	Turns ASTEP mode on/off after turning on STEP mode with Alt-F2.
Alt-a		Executes a macro named \a or a file named A\aqt (a can be any letter).
F8		In STEP mode, single steps the character position within a cell. Resumes macro execution in MACRO mode.
	MACRO	Indicates a macro is currently active.

The Macro command options work in conjunction with the macro modes to allow you to create your macros. Options for the macro command include Learn, Read, Write, eXecute, Analyze, Breakpoint, Convert, and Trace. Each of the options is briefly explained in the following paragraphs.

LEARN This option must be used before going into the Learn mode. You must specify a range where the macro is to be stored, then you can use Alt-F4 to go into the Learn mode. The range must be large enough to contain the entire macro, as you are taken out of the Learn mode when the end of the range is reached. Enter keystrokes manually by invoking the Direct mode while in the Learn mode. Pressing Enter puts the keystrokes in the macro.

READ The Read option allows you to enter a file macro into your spreadsheet in the spot you specify. A file macro is simply a macro created on a spreadsheet, then saved using the Write option of the Macro command. Read gives you a choice of options about how you read in your file macro. They are All, Macros-only, Labels-macros, or Comment-macros. A brief description of each follows.

All reads all three columns, Labels (left column), Macros (center column), and Comments (right column). The columns must be continous.

Macros-only reads only the macros column.

Labels-macros reads only the labels and macros columns.

Comment-macros reads only the comments and macros columns.

WRITE This option saves a spreadsheet macro to a file macro. As mentioned, the file macro is a macro created on a spreadsheet and saved using this option. The name for your file macro must conform to DOS conventions, and an extension (.XQT) is added by SuperCalc 5 unless you specify otherwise. To save the entire macro, you need only specify the cell containing the top statement of the macro if the macro is continous and has no blank cells. The save stops at the first blank cell or at the end of the range specified. Write options are the same as the Read options, with the exception that they write the various columns to a file macro in place of reading them from a file macro. If the file macro you are writing is already in existence, you will first be prompted to Backup, Change, or Overwrite when you save the current macro.

EXECUTE The eXecute option invokes a file macro from any spreadsheet. After you invoke this option, you are prompted to enter the filename for the file macro. The filename extension is assumed to be .XQT, unless you enter the extension that was used when the macro was saved. You can also execute a macro by using the Alt key with a one-letter file macro name. An example is that if you pressed Alt-C, the file macro named C.XQT would be executed.

TRACE This option allows you to control the execution of a macro so that you can review the effect of each step in the macro. The trace can be output to the screen, the screen and a printer, or the screen and a file. These outputs are selected by the options of the Trace menu, Console, Printer, and File. Console is the default. The function of each option is explained in the following paragraphs.

Console displays the trace output on the system display only.

Printer sends the trace output to the display and to the printer. Printing continues until the end of the macro, or until Ctrl-Break or Alt-F2 is pressed. Resume printing by pressing Alt-F2.

File sends the trace output to the display and creates an ASCII text file. Options for File are Open and Close. Selection of Open creates a .PRN file or reopens the existing one. The file is open until closed or another option is chosen. Select Close to close an opened file.

BREAKPOINT This options lets you insert up to eight breakpoints in a macro to assist you in isolating problems. When an executing macro reaches a breakpoint, it is automatically sent into the STEP mode. You then can view each step execution. Execution of the macro is resumed when the STEP mode is turned off by a command in the macro. Breakpoint options include 1-8 and Zap. An explanation of each follows.

1-8 selects the number for a breakpoint in a macro. Each macro can contain eight breakpoints. When the breakpoint number is selected, you have three options: Location, Condition, and Zap. Each are briefly explained here.

Location sets an unconditional breakpoint at a specifed location. You have further options when Location is selected. You select Spreadsheet or File to indicate where the macro is that gets the breakpoint. Spreadsheet indicates a macro in the current spreadsheet or in working memory, and File indicates a file macro. Either of these options will prompt you for the location of where the breakpoint is to be installed.

Condition sets a breakpoint that is triggered when the output of a conditional formula equals a preset value. Triggering the breakpoint causes the macro execution to go into the STEP mode.

Zap clears a specified breakpoint. Zap clears all breakpoints.

ANALYZE This option allows you to analyze a macro structure and create a report of the analysis. The report can be viewed on the display, sent to a printer, or to a file. The report can list a number of different items, and you can select what you want in the report. Options for Analyze are Go, Range Type, Output, and Quit. Each is breiefly described in the following paragraphs.

Go executes the Analyze command with the selected options.

Range prompts you to specify the range of the macro to be analyzed.

Type allows you to select the parts of the macro to be analyzed and listed in the report. Options for this selection are Contents, Transfers, and Modifies. The help line can assist you in making these and other option selections.

Output lets you choose where to send the report. The options are Console, Printer, or File. Console sends the report to the display. Printer sends the report to your printer. File sends the report to a file with a .PRN extension. If the file exists, you are prompted to choose whether to Backup, Change, or Overwrite the existing file.

CONVERT This option converts Lotus 1-2-3 macros into SuperCalc 5 syntax, and converts those macros converted from Lotus to SuperCalc back to Lotus. Options for Convert include 1-2-3 and SC. Each is described here.

1-2-3 converts Lotus 1-2-3 macros to SuperCalc 5 syntax. Most Lotus macro commands are converted to equivalent items in SuperCalc. Slash commands remain in Lotus slash command syntax, since SuperCalc has a full Lotus menu tree and interprets most of the Lotus slash commands as SuperCalc equivalents. Before conversion of a Lotus macro, you must select the Unprotect command and the All option, as the Lotus macro cells are all protected. The Unprotect, All removes their protection. The only slash commands not converted are Graph and some of the Format options. These commands have no effect, but will not stop execution of the macro.

SC returns a converted Lotus macro to its original state.

For either of the options, you are prompted to select All or Range to indicate whether you are converting all the macro or the range of the partial macro to convert.

Some special cases for conversions are listed here:

1. A 1 is placed after a slash (/) that is followed by a first letter of a command from the Lotus menu. This signals SuperCalc to read following characters as Lotus commands.
2. The /X option used by earlier versions of Lotus is contained in the commands recognized by SuperCalc and is available as an option for macro conversions.
3. In Lotus, pressing Enter after cell entry does not advance the cursor. For a conversion, set the Global command Next option to off so the cursor does not advance when the macro is run.
4. You cannot split function names or bracketed commands. You may split the parameters.
5. Ranges cannot be split.
6. Logic functions cannot be split.
7. The @(DATE(year,month,day) function cannot be split.

APPLICATIONS

The Macro command is useful for automating entries or functions that occur regularly in a spreadsheet. Numeric entries that can be determined by earlier results in a spreadsheet, conditional formulas, or just about anything that can be reduced to a formula is made easier to work with by using the Macro command. Formulas can be linked to other parts of a spreadsheet, or to other spreadsheets.

TYPICAL OPERATION

To use the Macro command to build, edit, or run a macro, follow the steps listed here. Begin with the spreadsheet in the Ready mode.

1. Type **//M**. The following dialog panel appears.

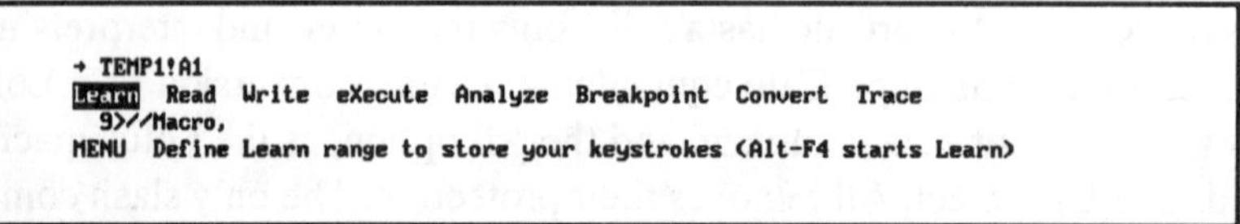

2. Building a macro is done through the Learn option. To select that option, type **L**. You are prompted by this option to enter the range where your macro is stored. If you do not make an entry for the range and press Enter, the file macro directory is displayed (.XQT extensions). Press Enter on this display and the subdirectories are displayed. Press Esc twice to return to the options menu. Press **Alt-F4** to go into the Learn mode. You can enter data in one of two ways. Use the Read option to load a file macro or a macro in memory, or enter the Direct mode by pressing Alt-F6 to enter from the keyboard. Each keystroke in the Learn mode is entered in the Learn range. After your entry is complete, Press **Alt-F4** to exit the Learn mode.

3. Select the Read, Write, or eXecute option and you are prompted for a filename to locate the data that is to be processed. After your entry, the Read and Write options further prompt you for instructions about what part of the file to use or what to do if the file exists. The help line assists you by explaining the options.

4. Select the Analyze option from the main options menu by typing **A**. The following dialog panel appears.

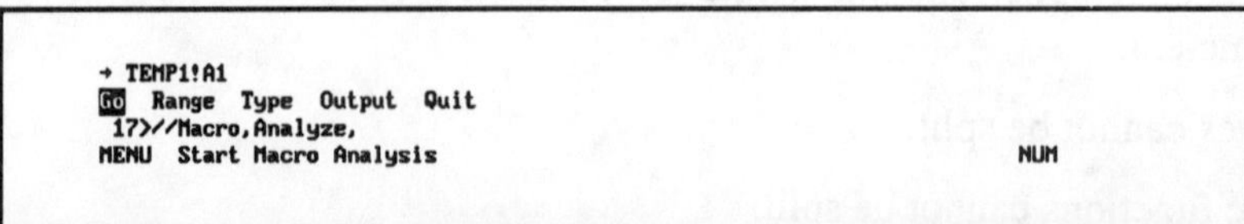

5. The options menu prompts you to make a selection. Your first choice must be Range, so type **R**. Enter the range of the macro you are analyzing. After your entry, press **Enter**, and you are returned to the options menu. Next, select Type by typing **T**. You see another menu that allows you to select the type of report for your analysis. Let the help line assist you in choosing the makeup of the report. After the report format is complete and you are back in the Analyze options menu, you can select Ouptut to choose where the report is sent. Then select Go to execute the analysis. Use Quit to return to the main options menu.

6. Select Breakpoint from the main options menu by typing **B**. The following dialog panel appears.

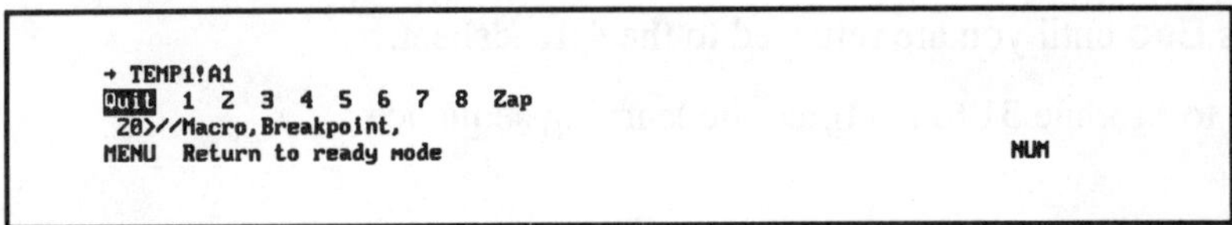

7. This options menu gives you a selection of breakpoints to put into your macro. Select one of the numerical options, and you are further prompted for type and location of the breakpoint data. The help line gives you necessary information to make your selections. Use Zap to clear all the breakpoints from the current macro. After the breakpoints information is complete, you are returned to the main options menu.

8. Select Convert from the main options menu by pressing **C**. The following dialog panel appears.

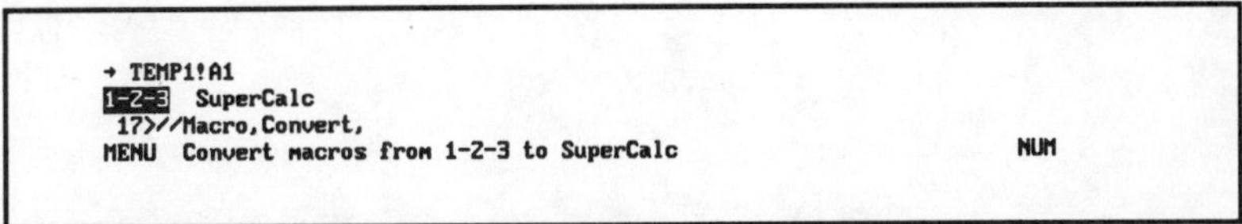

You are prompted to instruct SuperCalc 5 to convert Lotus 1-2-3 macros to SuperCalc format, or to convert macros back to Lotus that had been converted to SuperCalc. Either selection prompts you to select whether you are converting all of the macro, or the range you are converting. After conversion, you are returned to the main options menu.

9. Select the Trace option from the main options menu by typing **T**. The following dialog panel appears.

```
→ TEMP1!A1
Console  Printer  File
 15>//Macro,Trace,
MENU  Trace a macro, show results on-screen                          NUM
```

You are prompted to select whether the trace data is to be sent to the screen, printer, or to a file. If the File option is selected, the help line explains the options you have.

10. Press **Esc** until you are returned to the spreadsheet.
11. Turn to Module 31 to continue the learning sequence.

Module 22
MOVE

DESCRIPTION

The Move command moves the contents of the cells in a row range, column range, or block to a new location. Formulas are adjusted for their new location, and rows and columns can be transposed. Options for the Move command are Block, Row, Column, and Page. A description of each option is contained in the following paragraphs.

BLOCK The Block option moves a specified block of cells from its present location to a specified destination. Any data in the destination cells is overwritten. Two options are available when the Block option is selected, Normal and Transpose. A brief description of each is contained in the following paragraphs.

Normal The Normal option moves the contents of the source cells to the new location with no change except for the automatic adjustment of any formula.

Transpose The Transpose option moves the contents of the source cells to the new location,and puts the row data into columns, and column data into rows. References to the transposed cells are adjusted to reflect the new location. Only blocks can be transposed.

ROW The Row option moves a row range up or down on a spreadsheet. Rows between the new and old locations are automatically moved to fill in the spreadsheet, and formulas are adjusted for the new location.

COLUMN The Column option moves a column range right or left on a spreadsheet. Columns between the new and old locations are automatically moved to fill in the spreadsheet, and formulas are adjusted for the new location.

PAGE The Page option moves a page within a file to a new location in the pagination of the file. Pages in the file are renumbered to reflect the changed page order.

APPLICATIONS

The Move command allows movement of existing data to other locations in a spreadsheet without having to re-enter it. Major changes to an existing spreadsheet can be done easily with the Transpose and Block options, drastically cutting the time required to create an almost completely new spreadsheet.

TYPICAL OPERATION

To illustrate the use of the Move command, the example spreadsheet is subjected to Move operations. Follow the listed steps, and begin with the spreadsheet in the Ready mode.

1. Type **/L EXAMPLE1.SC5** and press **Enter**. Type **R** to load EXAMPLE1.SC5 into your spreadsheet.
2. Type **/M**. The Move Options menu is displayed on the dialog panel as shown in the following illustration.

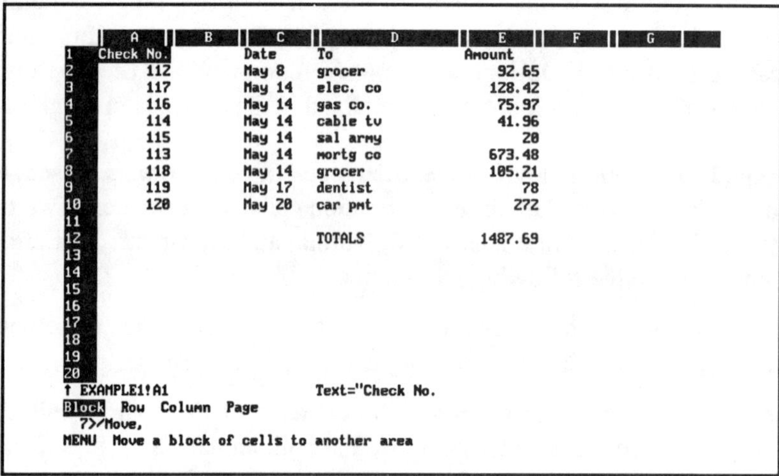

You are prompted to select Block, Row, Column, or Page from the Options menu. Start the example by moving a row.

3. Select Row and press **Enter**. You are prompted to enter a row or range of rows to move.
4. Type **12**, press **Enter**, and you are prompted to enter the row in which you want the specified row to be placed.
5. Type **14**, press **Enter**, and the row is moved. You are returned to the spreadsheet in the Ready mode, and the following screen appears.

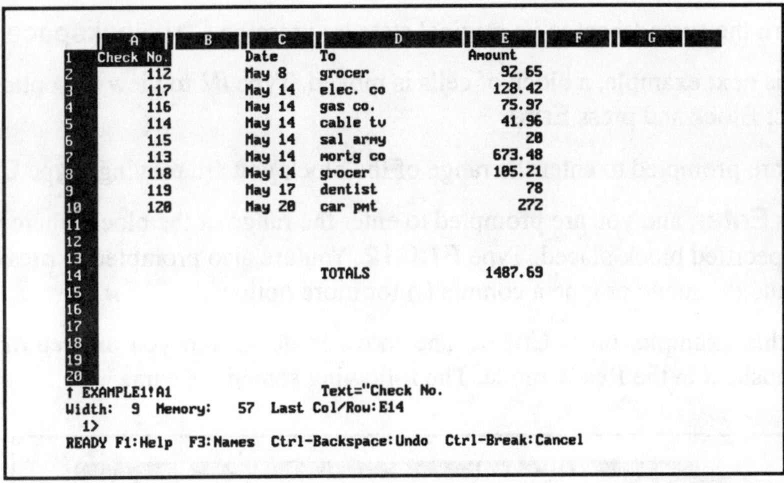

6. Return the spreadsheet to its original state by pressing **Ctrl-Backspace**.
7. For another example, move a column using the Move command. Type **/M** and select the Column option.
8. Press **Enter**, and you are prompted to enter the letter of a column that you are moving. Type **E**.
9. Press **Enter**, and you are prompted to enter the letter of the column in which you want the specified column to be placed. Type **F**.
10. Press **Enter**, and the move is done. You are returned to the spreadsheet in the Ready mode, and the following screen appears.

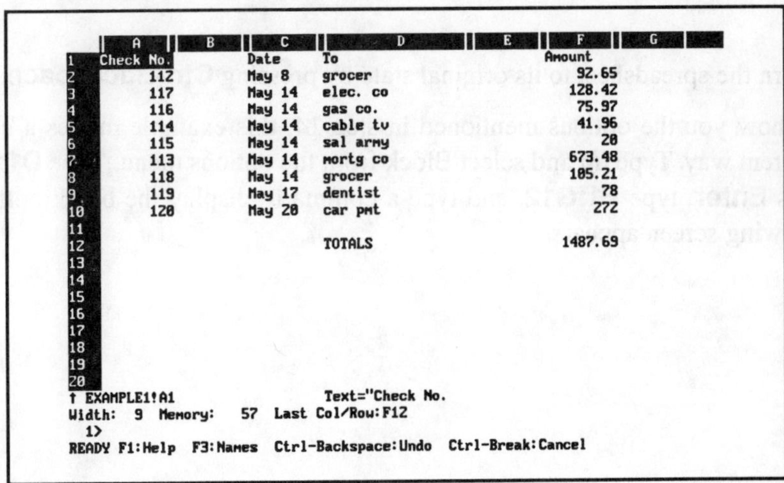

11. Return the spreadsheet to its original state by pressing **Ctrl-Backspace**.
12. In this next example, a block of cells is moved. Type **/M** to view the options menu. Select Block and press **Enter**.
13. You are prompted to enter the range of the block you are moving. Type **D1:E12**.
14. Press **Enter**, and you are prompted to enter the range of the block where you want the specified block placed. Type **F1:G12**. You are also prompted to press Enter to execute the move or type a comma (,) for more options.
15. For this example, press **Enter**. The move is done, and you are returned to the spreadsheet in the Ready mode. The following screen appears.

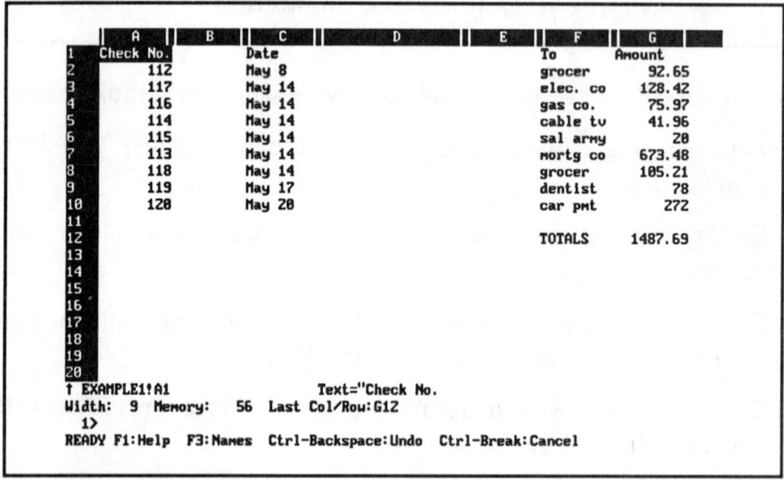

16. Return the spreadsheet to its original state by pressing **Ctrl-Backspace**.
17. To show you the options mentioned in step 14, this example moves a block in a different way. Type **/M** and select Block from the options menu. Type **D1:E12** and press **Enter**, type **F1:G12**, and type a comma to display the block options. The following screen appears.

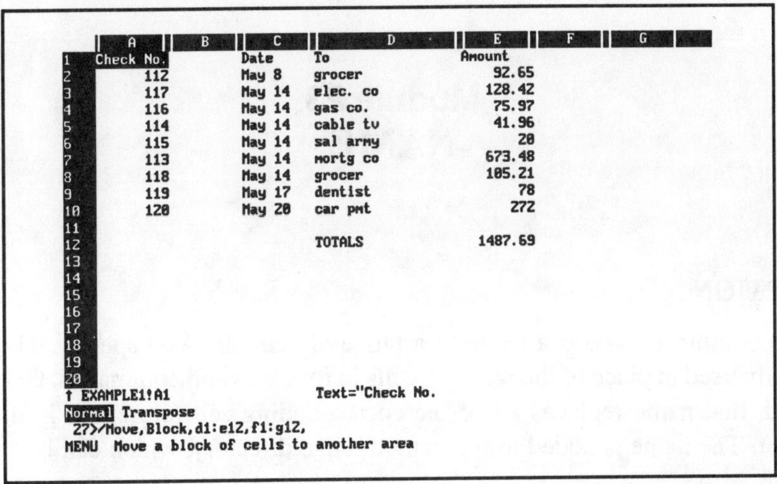

You are prompted to choose between Normal and Transpose. Typically, if you are doing an ordinary move, you do not get to this screen as you have executed the move from the last prompt. To get here, you must have wanted to use the Transpose option.

18. Select the Transpose option.
19. Press **Enter**, and the move is done, but the rows are in columns, and the columns are in rows. You are returned to the spreadsheet in the Ready mode. Use the Right Arrow to move the spreadsheet row until column E is at the left edge of the screen, and the following screen appears.

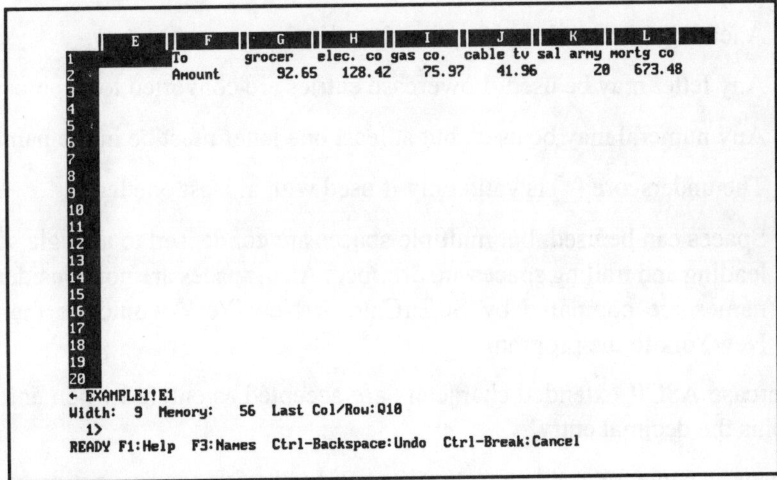

20. Type **/Z** then **Y** to clear the spreadsheet.
21. Turn to Module 18 to continue the learning sequence.

Module 23
NAME

DESCRIPTION

The Name command assigns a name to a range of cells that you specify. The name is subsequently used in place of the range of cells in formulas and commands. Once a name is assigned, that name replaces all of the corresponding cell references in the current spreadsheet. The name is added to the named range directory, which can be viewed by pressing F3.

Options for the Name command are Create, Delete, Labels, Table, and Zap. Each of the options is described in the following paragraphs.

CREATE The Create option assigns a name to a range. You must name a range before you can reference it by anything other than the row-column designation. To create a named range, you specify the name and then the corresponding range. In creating a named range, you must adhere to the following restrictions on name selection:

1. A name can be up to 32 characters long.
2. Valid characters for a range name:
   a. A leading backslash (\) is optional as the first character only.
   b. Any letter may be used. Lowercase entries are converted to uppercase.
   c. Any numeral may be used, but at least one letter must be in the name.
   d. The underscore (_) is valid only if used with at least one letter.
   e. Spaces can be used, but multiple spaces are condensed to a single space, and leading and trailing spaces are dropped. Also, spaces are not considered when names are compared by SuperCalc 5. New York would be the same as NewYork to the program.
3. Uppercase ASCII extended characters are accepted as entered when entered with Alt plus the decimal entry.
4. If you use a name for a cell range that is a valid cell reference or function, you cannot reference that cell or function until the name is deleted. SuperCalc 5 displays an advisory message informing you that you are re-defining a cell reference or function. For example, if you name the range A1:C5 as G2, you cannot reference G2.

DELETE The Delete option removes a name from its corresponding range. The cell range designation in the row-column format replaces the name in all corresponding references.

LABELS The Labels option gives you the capability to name several ranges at once from labels in your spreadsheet.

Options available when Label is selected are Right, Down, Left, and Up. The option names indicate where the labels are located in relation to the ranges they are naming.

Right	The ranges are directly to the right of their labels.
Down	The ranges are directly below their labels.
Left	The ranges are directly to the left of their labels.
Up	The ranges are directly above their labels.

The defined range must have its names in the perimeter row or column adjacent to the range in the direction specified by the option selected. For example, selecting right means that the names would be in the left column, and the range would be to the right of the names. If the range consists of a single column or row, each name is assigned only to the adjacent single cell.

Any cell not conforming to naming conventions is ignored by the Labels option. However, if a cell contains characters in the text that are not legal for a name, the characters are converted to a space and the operation continued.

TABLE The Table option puts the names and associated ranges in the named range directory in a spreadsheet so that you can print them out for future reference. Format of the spreadsheet is two columns, one containing the name, the other containing the range associated with the name on the same row.

ZAP The Zap option deletes all the named ranges in a spreadsheet. You are prompted for confirmation if you select this option, as its effect could be traumatic if used in error.

The named range directory contains all of the named ranges in the current spreadsheet. You view the named range directory by pressing F3 and can access it from the Ready, Entry, Audit, or Point modes. The help line at the bottom of the dialog panel displays the full name and its associated range. With the named range directory on the screen, pressing Enter puts the name of the current selection on the entry line of the dialog panel. Press F4 to put the range of the current selection on the entry line. Press Esc to exit the named range directory and return to the spreadsheet.

APPLICATIONS

You can use names anywhere that you expect ranges. Once you have assigned a name to a range, all formulas and functions referencing that range start using the name for the reference.

TYPICAL OPERATION

To illustrate the use of the Name command, make use of the sample spreadsheet created in Module 20. Follow the listed steps, beginning with the spreadsheet in the Ready mode.

1. Load the sample spreadsheet by typing **/L EXAMPLE1.SC5**. Press **Enter** and type **R**. The example spreadsheet is loaded.
2. Type **/N**. The following screen appears.

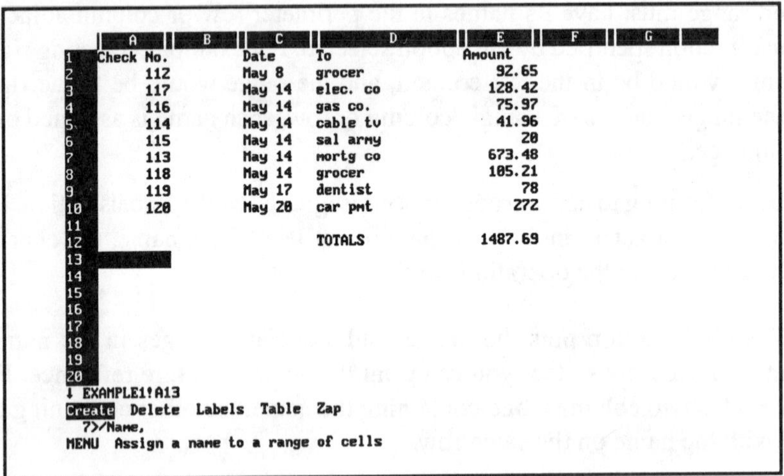

3. You are prompted to select an option. For the first of several examples, select Create. Press **Enter**, and you are prompted to enter a name for the range you are defining.
4. Type **Dollar** and press **Enter**.
5. You are now prompted to enter the range you are defining. Type **E2:E10**. Press **Enter**, and the range E2:E10 of your spreadsheet is represented by the name "Dollar."
6. Check the Named Range Directory by pressing **F3**. The following screen appears.

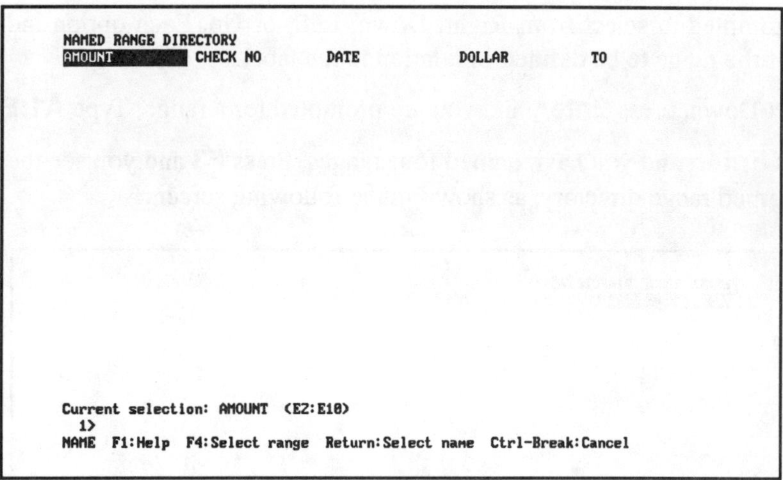

7. Return to the spreadsheet by pressing **Esc**.
8. The next example deletes a single name from the named range directory. Type **/N** and select Delete.
9. Press **Enter**, and you are prompted to enter the name you are deleting. Type **Dollar** and press **Enter**.
10. The name is deleted. To verify the deletion, press **F3** and look at the named range directory. It is blank.
11. This example uses the Labels option to name several ranges at once. Type **/N** and select Labels.
12. Press **Enter**, and the following screen is displayed.

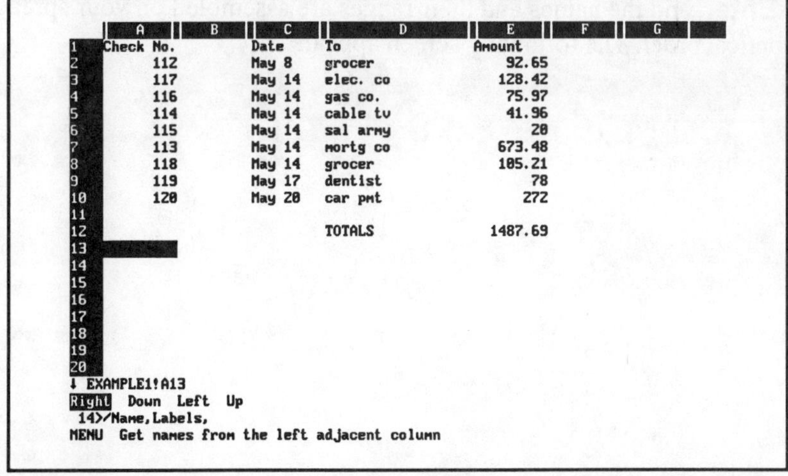

You are prompted to select from Right, Down, Left, or Up. Each option indicates the direction of the range to be defined in relation to the label.

13. Select Down, press **Enter**, and you are prompted for a range. Type **A1:E10**.
14. Press **Enter**, and you have named four ranges. Press **F3** and you see the names in the named range directory, as shown in the following screen.

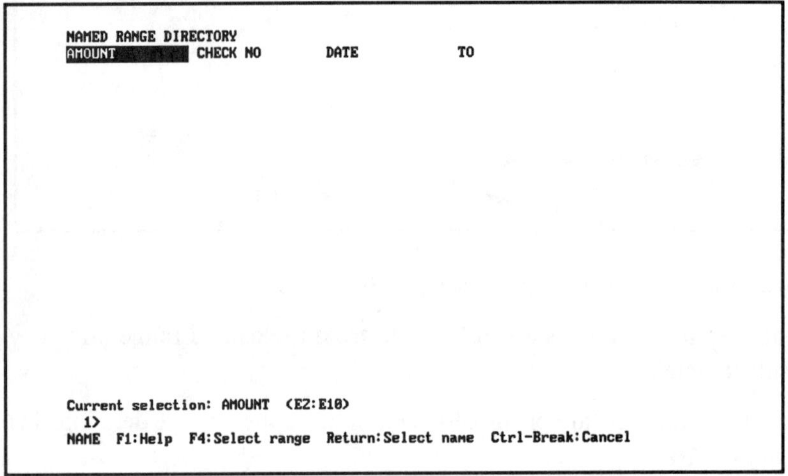

15. Return to the spreadsheet by pressing **Esc**.
16. For an example of the Table option, type **/N**, select Table, and press **Enter**.
17. You are prompted to enter the range of the spreadsheet in which the named ranges are located. Type **A1:E10**.
18. Press **Enter**, and the names and their ranges are assembled on your spreadsheet in alphabetical order. The following screen appears.

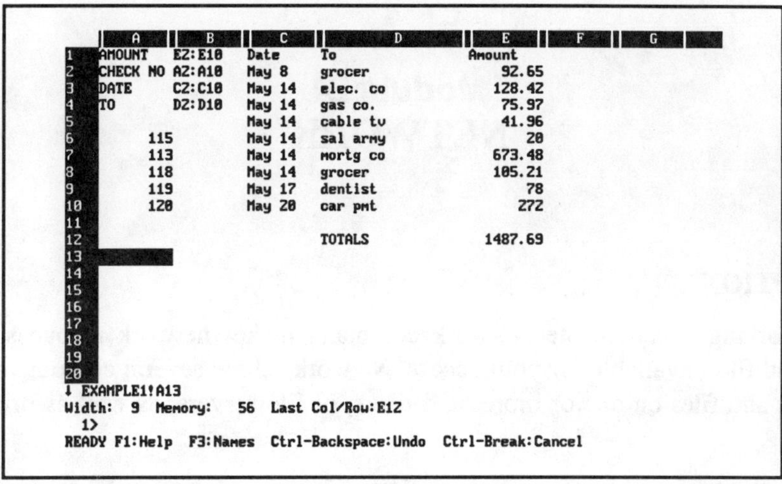

19. To show the use of the Zap option, the named range directory can be cleared as an example. Type **/N** and select Zap.

20. You are prompted to select Yes or No. Select No, press **Enter**, and you are returned to the spreadsheet in the Ready mode.

21. Select Yes, press **Enter**, and all names are deleted from the named range directory of the current spreadsheet. Press **F3** to view the empty named range directory.

22. Use the Zap command to clear the spreadsheet.

23. Turn to Module 32 to continue the learning sequence.

Module 24
NETWORK

DESCRIPTION

In a networking situation, the Network command makes network resouces, such as printers and files, available for your access. Networks allow several computers to share disk space and files on one or more hard disks, or file servers, as well as printers and plotters.

The Network command has four main options. They are Directory, Lock, Unlock, and Output. Each of the options is described in the following paragraphs.

DIRECTORY This option allows you to link to, or unlink from, a file server directory. The Linked Network Directories screen is displayed by selecting this option. Options under Directory are Quit, Link, and Unlink.

Quit returns you to the main options menu.

Link links you with a directory on the network using this syntax:

//Network,Directory,Link(drive)\\(server name)\ (directory name)

or

//Network,Directory,Link,(drive),(item)@(group)@(org)

Unlink disconnects you from the network.

LOCK The Lock option protects your files from being accessed by any unauthorized user. It gives you the exclusive right to save a file under its current filename. Locking is automatic when you load a file from a file server. If a file is locked, you can still read and revise it in browse mode, but you must save it under another filename. You can lock as many files as you wish, to prevent others from altering them during a work session, but the number of files you can lock at one time depends on the limits of DOS or your network system.

UNLOCK The Unlock option unlocks files that were locked by the Lock option. Selection of this option displays the Locked Files Directory, so that you can unlock files. You simply enter the filename you want unlocked, press Enter, and the file is unlocked.

OUTPUT The Output option allows you to send print files or other data to one of three network ports. Choose the Output option and you are offered LPT1, LPT2, LPT3, or Quit. Quit returns you to the main options menu. Select a port, and you can choose Redirect or End-redirection.

Redirect sends data to a printer through the file server using the following form:

//Network,Outout, LPT1,Redirect,\\SRV1\LAS

where SRV1 is the file server and LAS is the printer.

End-redirection sends print files to your local printer, instead of to the network printer.

APPLICATIONS

The Network command can link and unlink you from any file server. You can access and share files with the other members of the network. You can direct files to network printers or switch them back and forth between your printer and the network printer.

TYPICAL OPERATION

To go through the Network command, follow the steps listed here. Begin with the spreadsheet in the Ready mode.

1. Type **//N**. The following screen appears.

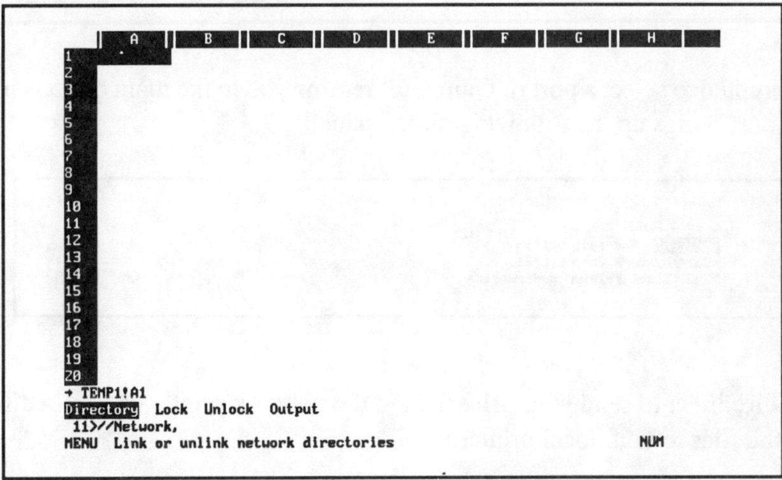

2. You are prompted to select Directory, Lock, Unlock, or Output. Select Directory and you are prompted to Link, Unlink, or Quit. If you are connected to a network, select Link and enter the correct syntax, and you are in. Select Unlink, and you are

prompted to enter the name of the file server. Make your entry and press **Enter**, and you are out. Select Quit, and you are returned to the main options menu.

3. Select Lock, and you are prompted to enter the name of the file to lock. Enter the name, press **Enter**, and your file is locked.
4. Select Unlock, and you are prompted to enter the name of the file to unlock. Enter the name of the one previously locked, press **Enter**, and the file is unlocked.
5. Select Output and the following screen appears.

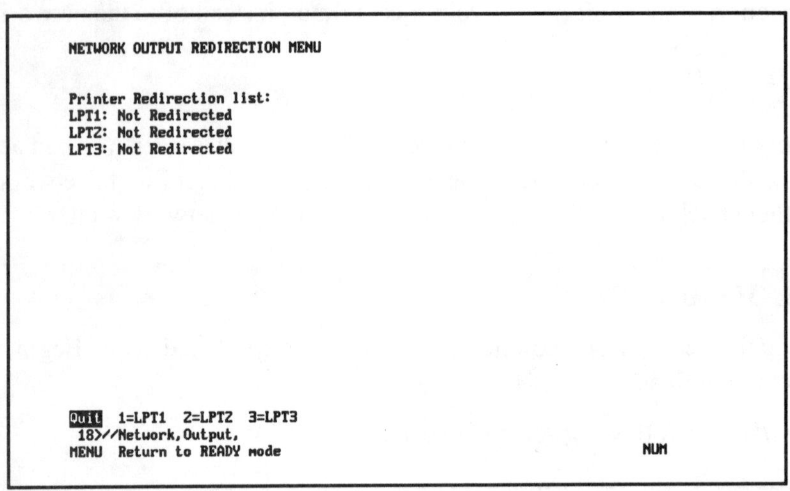

You are prompted to select a port or Quit. Quit returns you to the main options menu, but selecting a port brings up the following dialog panel.

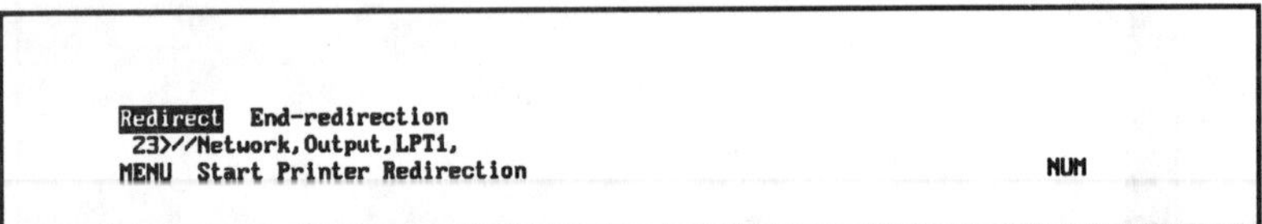

6. Select Redirect to send your print files to the network printer or End-redirection to send the files to your local printer.
7. Press **Esc** until you are returned to the spreadsheet.
8. Turn to Module 21 to continue the learning sequence.

Module 25
OUTPUT

DESCRIPTION

The Output command can write all or part of a spreadsheet to a printer or disk file, including titles, headers, footers, and margins. You can also preview the output on your display. Certain laser printers and PostScript-compatibles can add fonts, lines boxes, shading, and grids to cells and cell ranges. If you send your output to a disk, you can edit the data with any word processor that can edit an ASCII file. For word processors that cannot read ASCII, check the Import command for a possible conversion.

Options for the Output command are Printer, File, Attributes, Grid, Lines, and New-page. Printer and File are general format options, New-page is a printer command option, and the other options are part of SuperCalc's feature, Advanced Function Printing. Both groups of options are discussed in this section.

PRINTER sends your output to the printer with a default page width of 80 columns and a default page length of 66 lines. For spreadsheets exceeding the default page width, excess columns are printed on the next page.

FILE writes your output to a disk file on the default disk and directory, or where you instructed. The output is written to disk the same way as shown on your screen or as printed.

The menu selections are the same for either Printer or File. Those selections are listed here and described in the following paragraphs.

Range	Options
Go	Zap
Console	Align
Line-advance	Width
Page-advance	Quit

Range selects the spreadsheet range to output. You must select a range, as there is no default. To output an entire spreadsheet, type ALL. You can also output multiple ranges. To print multiple ranges on one page, you print one range at a time and set the printer so that it does not form feed after each range.

Go executes the output command, formatting the output according to your options and sending it to the printer or disk drive.

Console displays the output on your screen.

Line-advance sends a line feed to the printer.

Page-advance sends a form feed to the printer.

Options provides choices for all aspects of printed page format. You can design a page format to suit a special need, or allow the defaults to determine the format. As you go through the menus, the Help line on the dialog panel explains each selection.

Zap displays the output options menu, and any choice is reset to its default value.

Align resets the line and page counters in your printer. Set the printer paper to the top of the form, then select this option when beginning a new output.

Width tells you the width of a range in characters. This information is useful in setting your page size for an output.

The following options to the Output command are for use with PostScript-compatible printers and certain laser printers. The settings of these options do not show on your screen, but you can view them by using the Test command.

ATTRIBUTES This option enables you to put fonts, borders, and shading in your output. Options include Fonts, Border, and Shade (What Else!). Each of the options is briefly discussed in the following paragraphs.

Fonts adds type fonts to individual cells or ranges. You can use up to eight fonts in an output. You select from the options menu to add the default font or font 1 through 7. Each font is defined by the Global command.

Border puts border lines in specified range or ranges. This option prompts you to select where the border is to be placed, or to quit or clear any border from the specified range. Selections include Top, Bottom, Left, Right, and Outline for placement of border, and Clear to remove border. Quit gets you out of the Border option. Each of the five placement choices prompt you to select Set or Clear. Set puts the selected border in the range, or Clear removes any border from the range.

Shade puts a light shading over the specified range. You are prompted to Clear or Set the shading, and their operation is the same as for the Border option.

GRID The Grid option puts lines on all four sides of every cell in the output. Lines around the outside of the output are heavier than those in the interior. You are prompted to select Yes or No, Yes causing the grid to be placed, and No removing a grid from the output.

LINES The Lines option puts text for line drawing into cells in the specified range. You can choose horizontal or vertical and select line shading and thickness. The menu options are Horizontal and Vertical. Each option draws a line as indicated by its name, and each prompts you to define the line thickness and shading. The thickness and shading prompts are defined on the help line of the dialog panel as they are selected.

NEW-PAGE This option adds a line in your spreadsheet to put a page break in the body of your output. The break occurs above the line with the break symbol on it. Any data entered on the same row after the break symbol is not printed.

APPLICATIONS

With the Output command you can customize your printer outputs or files to be saved. You select type fonts, add lines or boxes, control the printer, and do many things associated with the output of your files.

TYPICAL OPERATION

To go through the Output command operation, follow the steps listed here. Begin with the spreadsheet in the Ready mode.

1. Type / and select Output. The options menu is displayed on the dialog panel and is shown in the following illustration.

```
→ TEMP1!A1
Printer  File  Attributes  Grid  Lines  New-page
 9>/Output,
MENU  Print or preview report
```

2. You are prompted to select whether your output is going to the printer, to a file, you are selecting attributes, a grid, lines, or adding a page break to a file. Select Printer or File, and the dialog panel below appears.

```
→ TEMP1!A1
Range  Go  Console  Line-advance  Page-advance  Options  Zap  Align  Width  Quit
 17>/Output,Printer,
MENU  Assign report range
```

Your first choice must be Range, so you can enter the output range. Then you can select other options. Select Options and you can customize your output as to titles, page layout, see drafts of the output, and control the paper feed of the printer if you are using one.

3. Return to the main options menu by pressing **Esc**. Select Attributes, and the following menu appears on the dialog panel.

```
→ TEMP1!A1
Quit  Fonts  Border  Shade
 20>/Output,Attributes,
MENU  Leave the /Output,Attributes menu
```

You are prompted to select Fonts, Border, Shade, or Quit. With these options you select a type face for your printed output, add border at selected points or all around, or add shading for effect. Each one of these options prompts you for additional selections.

4. Press **Esc** to return to the main options menu and select Grid. You are prompted to select Yes or No. Yes puts a grid in your output, and No does not.
5. Return to the main options menu and select Lines.

You choose to use Horizontal or Vertical lines. After your selection, you choose line thickness and line shading.

6. Return to the main options menu and select New-page. Your only prompt here is to enter where you want the page break.
7. Press **Esc** until you are returned to the spreadsheet in the Ready mode.
8. Turn to Module 30 to continue the learning sequence.

Module 26
PROTECT/UNPROTECT

DESCRIPTION

The Protect command prevents any modification of cell contents in a specifed range, and prevents any data from being entered in an empty cell formatted at the Entry level. Unprotect removes the protection supplied by the Protect command.

Protected cells cannot be copied, nor can they be re-written, as happens in a load operation. The Delete command does not delete a row, column, or block containing protected cells, and the Blank command does not affect any protected cell in the specified range. Only the Zap command will delete protected cells to delete an entire spreadsheet.

APPLICATIONS

The Protect and Unprotect commands provide a method for insuring that critical parts of your spreadsheets are not erased erroneously. Use the Protect command to avoid typographical errors deleting data that you could not replace except at great expense of time and sweat. As data becomes less important, use the Unprotect command to remove the protection.

TYPICAL OPERATION

Use of the Protect and Unprotect commands is very simple, and the example file is used to demonstrate its ease of use. Follow the listed steps; begin with the spreadsheet in the Ready mode.

1. Type **/L EXAMPLE1.SC5**. Press **Enter** and type **R**. The example spreadsheet is loaded.
2. Type **/P**. The display appears as shown in the following illustration.

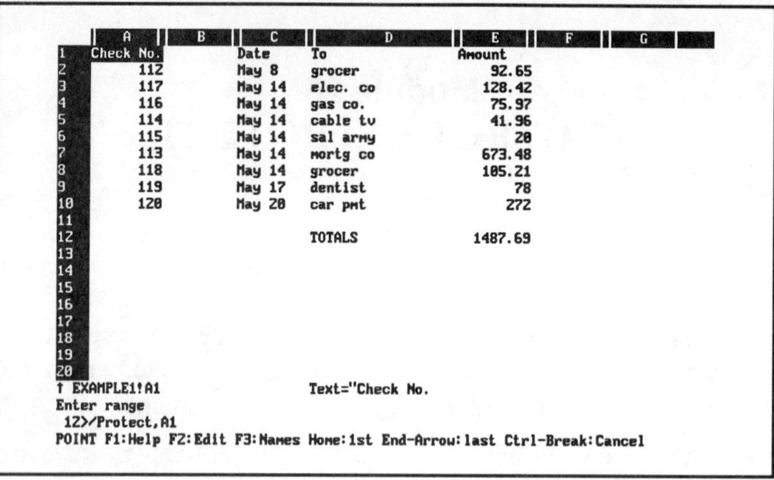

If you wish to protect only the current cell, press Enter. To protect a row, column, or block, type in the range and press Enter.

3. Type **A** and press **Enter**. You have protected Column A and are returned to the spreadsheet in the Ready mode.
4. To check the protection you just gave to the specified range, type **/D**, select Column, and press **Enter**. Then type **A** and press **Enter**. Column A is not deleted, and the following screen appears.

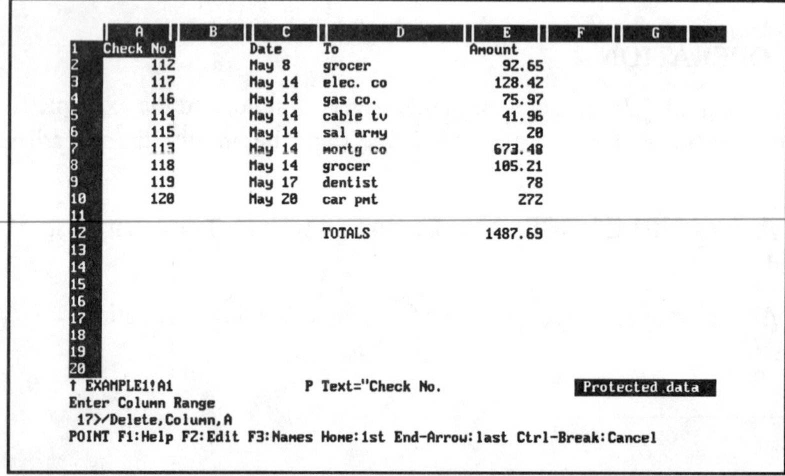

5. Press **Esc** three times to get back to the spreadsheet in the Ready mode. Then, to remove the protection from column A, type **/UA**. Press **Enter**, and the protection is gone. You are returned to the spreadsheet in the Ready mode.
6. Check the specified area's protection by using the Delete command. Type **/D**, select Column, and press **Enter**. Then type **A** and press **Enter** to display the following screen.

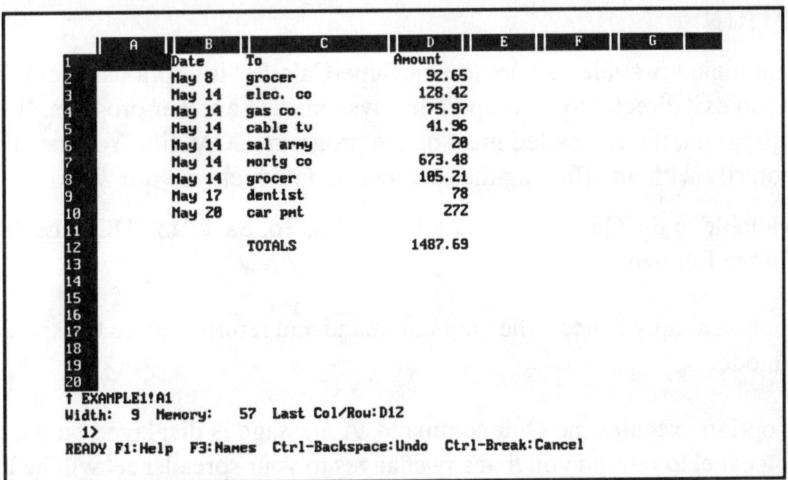

7. Use the Zap command to clear the spreadsheet.
8. Turn to Module 28 to continue the learning sequence.

Module 27
QUIT

DESCRIPTION

The Quit command provides a way to exit SuperCalc 5 with options. From the Ready mode, you can exit directly to your operating system or to another program. If the exit is to another program, the file called must be the program .COM file. You can also exit to DOS temporarily without affecting the spreadsheet in which you are working.

Options available in the Quit command are No, Yes, To, Save, and DOS. Each option is described in the following paragraphs.

NO This option simply cancels the Quit command and returns you to the spreadsheet in the Ready mode.

YES This option executes the Quit command. A message is displayed on the Help line of the dialog panel to remind you that any changes to your spreadsheet will be lost if you execute the Quit command.

TO This option allows you to exit SuperCalc 5 directly to another program. However, the file that you enter as the file you are exiting to must be the program .COM file. This must be the case, as the program you are going to must be loaded, and this file is the only one available to do so.

SAVE The Save option saves the current spreadsheet for you before exiting to the operating system. When this option is chosen, you are prompted to select either Backup or Overwrite if the file is currently on your disk. Select Backup, and the extension of the filename on disk is changed to .bak and the current file with changes is saved with the original filename and extension. Select Overwrite, and the current file is written directly over the previous version.

DOS This option allows you to exit temporarily to DOS. This gives you an opportunity to create files, look at directories, make adjustments to files, or do other jobs requiring being in DOS. After taking care of your needs in DOS, type "exit" to return directly to your spreadsheet.

If you have multiple spreadsheets in memory, the Quit command closes the current one and displays the next one. Quit will return you to your operating system if you have only one spreadsheet in memory, but you must use the //Spreadsheets command if you have multiple spreadsheets in memory.

APPLICATIONS

The Quit command is the exit from SuperCalc 5 when you are finished with a spreadsheet, temporarily or for the end of a session. Confirmation of your exit ensures data is not lost inadvertently, and you can save data directly from the Quit command. Your exit can be directly to another program, avoiding having to go through the operating system.

TYPICAL OPERATION

The Quit command is easy to use and has some options that make it quite helpful as you go through creation and editing of spreadsheets. Follow the steps listed here to see and do examples of the use of Quit. Begin with the spreadsheet in the Ready mode.

1. Load the sample file EXAMPLE1.SC5 by typing **/L EXAMPLE1.SC5**. Then press **Enter** and type **R**. Now select the Quit command from the Command menu by typing **/Q**. The following screen appears.

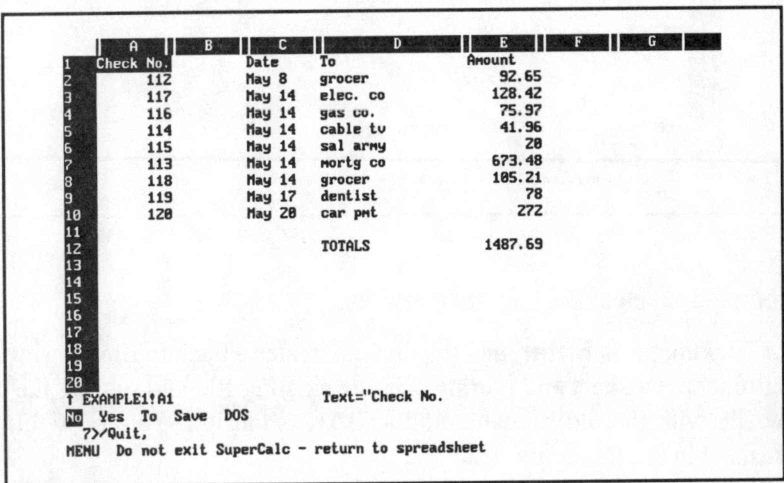

You are prompted to select from the options. If you look over the options and do not wish to continue with the Quit command, type N. You are returned to the spreadsheet in the Ready mode.

2. Select the Yes option by typing **Y**. A message is displayed inquiring to see if you have saved any changes made to your spreadsheet. If you do not wish to save the changes, type Y, and you exit the spreadsheet and SuperCalc 5 to your operating system. Type **N** to return to the spreadsheet Ready mode.

The To option provides you with a direct path to another program. You are prompted to enter the filename of the program. When the file is in another directory or on another disk drive, you must precede the filename with the appropriate drive or directory. After you have typed your entry, press Enter to execute the command. The specifed program is loaded for you.

3. The Save option can be used if you see a message that reminds you to save changes to your spreadsheet. Select Save by typing **S** while the Options menu is displayed. If you have not made changes to your spreadsheet, you are returned to the spreadsheet in the Ready mode. If you have made changes, the following screen appears when you select the Save option.

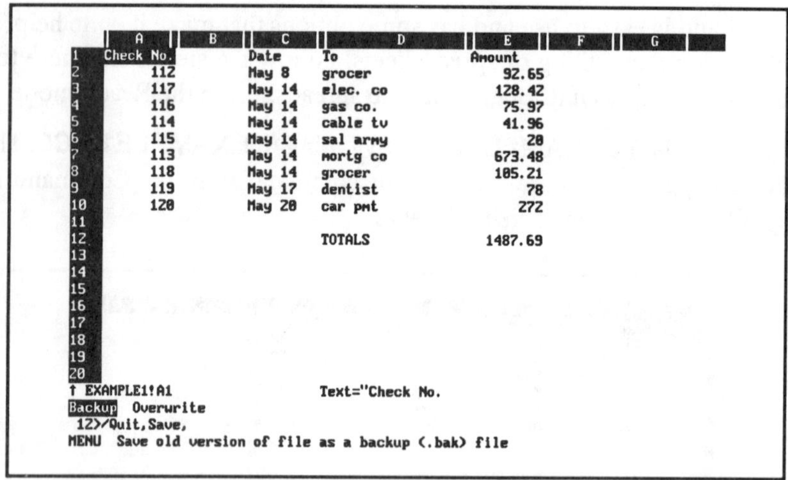

You are prompted to select Backup or Overwrite.

4. Select Backup, press **Enter**, and this option creates a backup file for you by saving the current spreadsheet and putting it in the existing file and putting the old file in a new file with the old filename and a .BAK extension. You arc rcturncd to the spreadsheet in the Ready mode.

5. Select Overwrite, press **Enter**, and the file in memory is overwritten by the current file. You are returned to the spreadsheet in the Ready mode.

The DOS option allows you to temporarily exit your spreadsheet to the DOS prompt. You can execute DOS commands without affecting the spreadsheet, but you cannot go into another program without first going back to your spreadsheet and exiting through SuperCalc 5.

6. Use the Quit command to temporarily exit SuperCalc 5 to DOS by selecting **DOS** and pressing **Enter**.
7. Return to SuperCalc 5 by typing **exit** and pressing **Enter**. You are automatically returned to the exact spot in the current spreadsheet where you were before selecting Quit.
8. Type **/Z** then **Y** to clear the spreadsheet.
9. Turn to Module 11 to continue the learning sequence.

Module 28
RESTRICT

DESCRIPTION

The Restrict command limits data input to a specified range of cells, or to occupied non-protected cells only when the Tab mode of the Global command is on. When the Restrict command is active, you are in the Input mode. To leave the Input mode, press Enter or Esc when the entry line is empty. To move the cursor around within the non-restricted area, use the Arrow, Home, and End keys. The Tab, Backspace, PgUp, PgDn, and F5 (GoTo) keys are inactivated in the Input mode. The Restrict command prompts you only for the range of cells within which you are to operate. Any other part of the spreadsheet will be restricted, and the cursor cannot be moved out of the non-restricted area.

APPLICATIONS

The Restrict command is another way to protect the data in your spreadsheet, especially when other people must enter data. Data cannot be entered in the restricted areas, and the cursor cannot be moved into the restricted areas. Restrict is useful to macro users, as it prompts for data, and response can be limited to the correct area.

TYPICAL OPERATION

To use the Restrict command, follow the steps listed here. Begin with the spreadsheet in the Ready mode.

1. Type //, and select Restrict.
2. Press **Enter**, and the following screen appears.

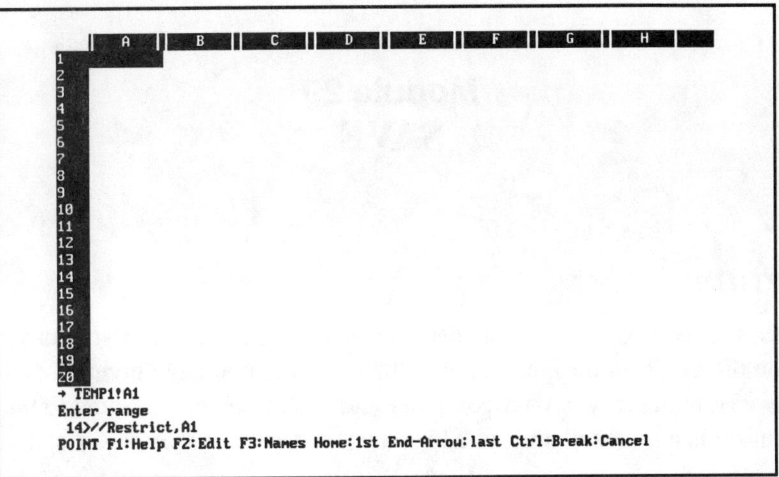

3. You are prompted to enter a range of cells which you are specifying to receive data inputs. Type **A1:C10**, press **Enter**, and you are returned to the spreadsheet in the Ready mode.
4. Use the arrow keys to move the cursor around the spreadsheet. Note that you cannot move the cursor out of the designated input area.
5. To remove the restriction and return to the Ready mode, press **Enter** (or Esc) with the entry line empty. You are returned to the Ready mode, and the cursor can be moved around the entire screen.
6. Turn to Module 14 to continue the learning sequence.

Module 29
SAVE

DESCRIPTION

The Save command takes care of the details of storing the data that you have created or modified on the disk you designate, under the filename you have given it. Save actually reads the working memory in your computer and writes the data it found to the disk. The data in memory is not erased until you load another file or exit SuperCalc 5.

When you save a file using this command, you are prompted to enter the filename. After you make the entry, the extension .CAL is added to the filename, unless you choose another. For all extensions except .WK1 or .WKS, the file is saved in SuperCalc 5 format.

Options for the Save command allow you to save all or part of the spreadsheet, cell values only, or protected or unprotected cells only. When you select Save from the command menu, you are prompted to select a filename. The default filename, or the name of the file you last loaded, is displayed on the entry line. You can use that name by pressing Enter, or you can enter a new one by simply typing it in. Pressing F3 displays the File List. After you have entered a filename, you are presented an options menu containing Backup, Change, and Overwrite if the file is found. If you want to back up the file (have an extra copy in case of problems), select Backup. This accomplishes two things. First, the file in memory automatically has the filename extension changed to .BAK. Secondly, the current file is stored in memory under the filename and extension you had originally given it. To modify the filename, select Change. If you change the name, the data will be saved under the new name. If the file on disk is no longer needed and you want to remove it, select Overwrite. This selection will completely erase the file on disk, then write the current file to disk. Be careful when using the Overwrite option, as it permanently removes a file.

After you have chosen the desired option, another set of options is offered to you. This options menu contains All, Values, Part, Duplicate, Level, Mode, and Single. A brief description of each is contained in the following paragraphs.

ALL This selection saves the entire spreadsheet, as well as some of the changed default settings. All cell contents, including display format data, are saved. Each page of the current spreadsheet is saved. A caution about the All option: If you rename a file and save it using this option, the file will be renamed in memory. If you do not wish to rename the file in memory, use the Duplicate option.

VALUES The Values option saves only the calculated value of cells containing formulas. The actual contents of the cell are not saved, only the numerical value. Cell display formats are saved, and all pages of the current spreadsheet are saved.

PART This option allows you to choose parts of a spreadsheet to be saved. When you select this option, you are prompted to enter the range of the data you are storing. After designating the range, you are prompted to select All or Values, indicating that you wish to save all the range or if you are saving only the values in the range.

DUPLICATE Use this option to save a spreadsheet under another name, without having to rename the spreadsheet in memory. Duplicate saves the current spreadsheet under the name you designate but does not rename the spreadsheet.

LEVEL The Level option allows you to save files in different SuperCalc formats. The formats available are SC5, SC4, or SC3. If the file you are working with came from an earlier version of SuperCalc, you can choose the appropriate option if you are saving it back to that version. SC3 saves files in a format compatible with SuperCalc 3 or earlier versions. SC4 saves files in a format compatible with SuperCalc 4. SC5, which is the default, saves files in a format compatible with the current version, SuperCalc 5.

MODE The Mode option lets you decide which cells are to be saved. You can choose All, Protected, or Unprotected. All saves all cells. Protected saves only the protected cells. Unprotected saves only the unprotected cells. All is the default and after each save, the default is restored.

SINGLE The Single option saves a single page of a multi-page spreadsheet. When you choose this option, you are given the same options path as if you were saving a current spreadsheet.

APPLICATIONS

The Save command is more versatile than the basic function it performs. You can rename, erase, or back up files. You can save partial files, files with only numerical values, or files with only certain types of cells. Duplicate files can be made, and files can be saved in formats of earlier versions of SuperCalc. A good use of the capabilities of this command is to save a large spreadsheet. Use the Save command to save it in two parts, by using the Part option. Another use is to protect cells you do not wish used in another spreadsheet, then select the Mode option to get only the unprotected cells.

TYPICAL OPERATION

To show the use of the Save command, we use the file created in Module 20, EXAMPLE1.SC5. Follow the steps listed here, beginning with the spreadsheet in the Ready mode.

1. Load the file by typing **/L**. Type **EXAMPLE1.SC5** and press **Enter**; type **A** and your screen should appear as in the following illustration.

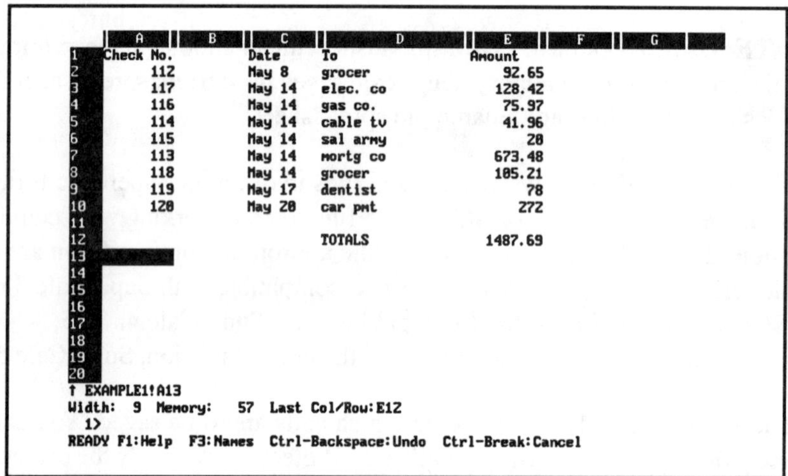

2. In this example, we create a backup file for the current spreadsheet. To use the Save comand to do this, begin by typing **/S** (note that the filename is displayed on the entry line) and pressing **Enter**. Select Backup from the options menu by using the arrow keys to move the cursor over it, then pressing **Enter**. You are then prompted to choose from the next menu, which contains several options. The menu appears on the screen as shown in the following illustration.

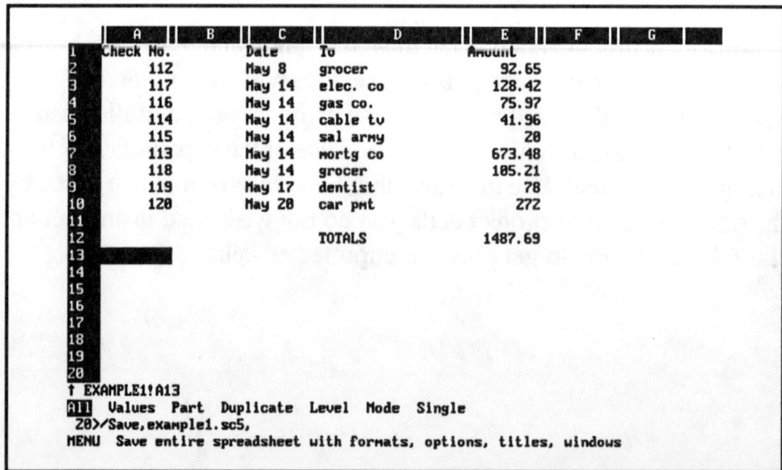

3. For this example, choose All by typing **A**, and the backup file is created. To check to see that the backup file was created, look in the directory in which it was stored.

4. To save part of a file, you can use the Part option. Start by typing **/S** and entering a new filename, AMOUNTS.CHK, as the amounts column might be helpful in a separate file for checking your checkbook. Press **Enter**, and you are prompted to choose from the options menu. Select Part by typing **P**. You are now prompted to choose All or Values, indicating if you want all the data in the range (All) or only the calculated values (Values). Select All by typing **A**. You are next prompted for the range of the data you are saving. Type **E1:E12**, press **Enter**, and you have stored the amounts column of the spreadsheet in a file called AMOUNTS.CHK. Check your default directory to make sure it is there.

5. To use the Level option, choose the format you want, press **Enter**, and you start at the main option menu. You have all the options open to you as if you are saving a file in the SuperCalc 5 format (which is the default).

The Mode option is operated by selecting the Mode option, then choosing which cells you are saving by selecting All, Protected, or Unprotected.

The Single option operates almost as if you are about to save an entire file, with all the options of the main option menu available after you select Single.

You can practice using the Save command to get used to it. Be careful when using the Overwrite option, as it erases a file then writes another in its place. You can lose data in a flash and cannot get it back.

6. Type **/Z** then **Y** to clear the spreadsheet.

7. Turn to Module 27 to continue the learning sequence.

Module 30
SPREADSHEETS

DESCRIPTION

The Spreadsheets command allows you to perform file-handling and display operations with multiple and multi-page spreadsheets. To perform these operations, spreadsheets must be open, meaning that they are in the working memory (RAM) of your computer. SuperCalc 5 allows you to open up to 255 spreadsheets at the same time, provided there is enough working memory available. To open additional spreadsheets, press Ctrl-Enter. Multi-page spreadsheets can be created with the Insert command.

To scroll among open spreadsheets and the pages within them, use Ctrl-Plus or Ctrl-Minus. Ctrl-Plus advances you to the next spreadsheet or page, and Ctrl-Minus takes you back to the previous spreadsheet or page. Spreadsheets and pages are displayed according to their order on the Open Spreadsheet Directory. Press F4 to display the Open Spreadsheet Directory.

The current spreadsheet is the one displayed on your screen, or if you are displaying more than one spreadsheet, it is the one where the cursor is currently located. The name of the current spreadsheet is shown in the dialog panel at the beginning of the status line. To include names and pages of a spreadsheet in cell and range references, use the following syntax:

name!page!cell — references one cell on one page.

name!startpage.endpage!range — references a range on a range of pages.

You can load, save, or quit individual spreadsheets or pages with the SuperCalc file handling commands, or you can save all spreadsheets in memory using the options of this command. The options are described later in this module.

The Open Spreadsheet Directory, displayed by pressing F4, shows the list of open spreadsheets. It lists the names of each open spreadsheet and the path of each file loaded from other than the current directory. Each page is listed on a separate line. Hidden spreadsheets are designated by an asterisk (*) in the H column. Move the bar cursor to select spreadsheets or pages for display.

The Referenced Spreadsheet Directory lists the names of spreadsheets that are linked to the current spreadsheet page by formula reference. This directory indicates whether the referenced spreadsheet is in memory or on disk and displays the path for each linked spreadsheet. You can change any part of the name in the FILE column, and the changed portion will be intensified to remind you what you have changed.

Some of the file handling features of SuperCalc 5 are present in more than one command. Some things to remember when working with multiple spreadsheets or multipage spreadsheets are listed here.

1. Any command that works on a single-page spreadsheet works on a spreadsheet page.
2. You can enter a range of pages within a spreadsheet when you are moving, inserting, or deleting pages.
3. You can edit the File column of the Referenced Spreadsheet Directory to associate a different filename with a name in the Name column. When you enter a different name, all link formulas using the new name will reference the new name.
4. You can load more than one single-page spreadsheet, a multipage spreadsheet, more than one multipage spreadsheet, or any combination of single-page and multipage spreadsheets if enough working memory is available.
5. Single-page spreadsheets are saved and loaded separately; multipage spreadsheets are saved and loaded as one.
6. Single-page spreadsheets are not ordered; multipage spreadsheets are ordered so that you can specify page ranges. This allows you to work in three dimensions.
7. Single-page spreadsheets can be linked to files on your disk to save working memory, multipage spreadsheets usually have all their pages in working memory to make convenient reviewing and updating the spreadsheet.

Options available for the spreadsheets command are Display, GoTo, Hide, New, Rename, Save, Unhide, Zap, and Quit. A brief description of each is contained in the following paragraphs.

DISPLAY Use the display option to display up to three spreadsheets on your screen. Select from options 1, 2, 3, Synchronize, Unsynchronize, and Zoom to set up the display. Choose 1, 2, or 3 to select the number of spreadsheets to be displayed. Synchronize scrolls the displays simultaneously, and Unsynchronize returns independent scrolling to the displays. Zoom prompts you to select Yes or No. Yes displays only the current spreadsheet in normal full-screen size. No displays all open spreadsheets.

GOTO This option displays the next, previous, or a selected spreadsheet or page according to the Open Spreadsheet Directory. Select Next to display the next spreadsheet, Previous to display the previous spreadsheet, and Specify to select a spreadsheet of your choice.

HIDE Select this option to prevent the selected spreadsheet, page, or page range from being displayed. You are prompted to select the spreadsheet, page, or page range.

NEW This option opens a new blank spreadsheet in memory.

RENAME You can change the name of the current spreadsheet with this option. The new name becomes the default filename when you save the file. You are prompted to enter the new name.

SAVE All open spreadsheets that have been modified are saved to disk by this option. You select Backup or Overwrite before saving the file. Backup creates a backup file, and Overwrite writes over the old file with the same name.

UNHIDE allows the spreadsheet, page, or page range to be displayed.

ZAP clears all open spreadsheets and returns you to a blank spreadsheet in the Ready mode. You must select from No, Yes, and Save before the clearing takes place. Select No, and you are returned to the current spreadsheet in the Ready mode without clearing the open spreadsheets. Yes clears all open spreadsheets without saving them. Save clears all open spreadsheets, first saving those with modifications since the last save. You select to Backup or Overwrite files with the same names.

QUIT closes all open spreadsheets and exits SuperCalc 5 to the operating system. You are prompted to select Yes, No, or Save. Select Yes, and you close all open spreadsheets without saving them. Select No, and you are returned to the current spreadsheet in the Ready mode. Select Save, and you close all open spreadsheets, first saving those with modifications since the last save. You select Backup or Overwrite for the files with the same names.

APPLICATIONS

Spreadsheets is very useful when the need is for several spreadsheets to be loaded at one time, and when several displays on the screen at one time is desirable. Also, creation of links between spreadsheets, whether in memory or not, can be accomplished.

TYPICAL OPERATION

To use the Spreadsheets command, follow the steps listed here. Begin with the spreadsheet in the Ready mode.

1. Type // and select Spreadsheets. Press **Enter** and the dialog panel appears as shown in the following screen.

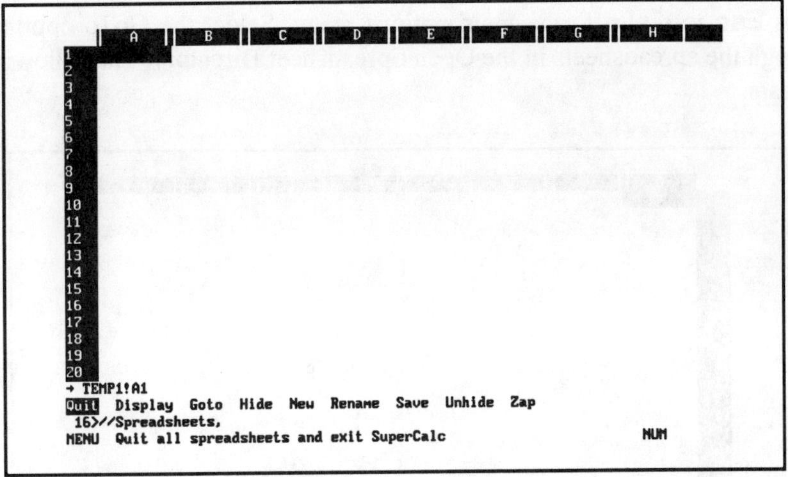

2. You are prompted to select one of the options displayed. Select Display and press **Enter**. The following screen appears.

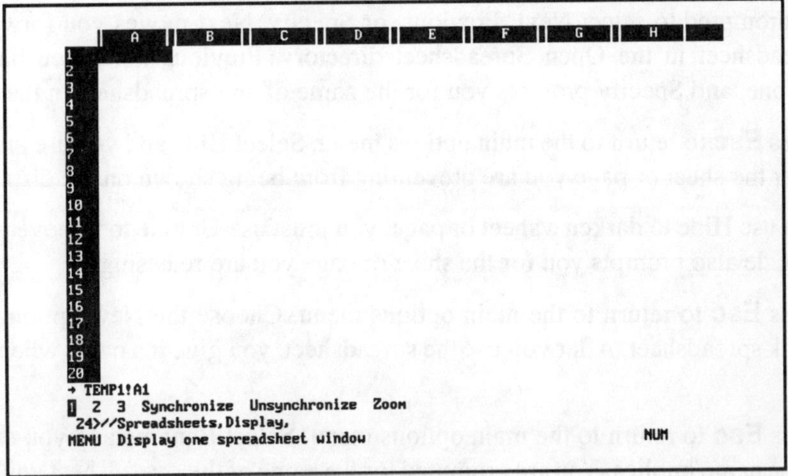

The Display option gives you the choice of displaying 1, 2, or 3 spreadsheets at one time. You can have multiple spreadsheets scrolled simultaneously by using the Synchronize option, then remove the synchronized scrolling by using Unsynchronize. Select Zoom and you can toggle between the current spreadsheet display (Yes) and displaying all the open spreadsheet windows (No).

3. Press **Esc** to return to the main options menu. Select the GoTo option to move through the spreadsheets in the Open Spreadsheet Directory. The following screen appears.

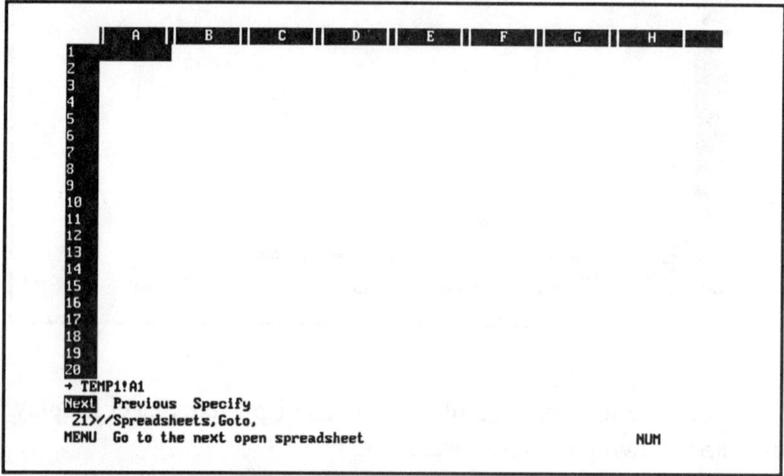

You are prompted to select Next, Previous, or Specify. Next moves you forward to the next spreadsheet in the Open Spreadsheet directory. Previous takes you back to the previous one, and Specify prompts you for the name of any spreadsheet in the directory.

4. Press **Esc** to return to the main options menu. Select Hide and you are prompted to enter the sheet or page you are preventing from being shown on the display.

After you use Hide to darken a sheet or page, you must use Unhide to remove it from the dark. Unhide also prompts you for the sheet or page you are releasing.

5. Press **Esc** to return to the main options menu. Choose the New option to open a blank spreadsheet. After you use the spreadsheet, you give it a name when you save it.

6. Press **Esc** to return to the main options menu. Select Rename and you can do just as the name implies. You are prompted for the name of the spreadsheet you are going to change, then for the new name.

7. Press **Esc** to return to the main options menu. Select Save when you have completed your multiple spreadsheet operations and have made modifications to your spreadsheets. Save closes all open spreadsheets, first saving those with modifications. You are prompted to choose Backup or Overwrite for those files already existing.

8. Press **Esc** to return to the main options menu. Select Zap to clear all open spreadsheets and return you to a blank spreadsheet in the Ready mode. You are prompted by the following screen.

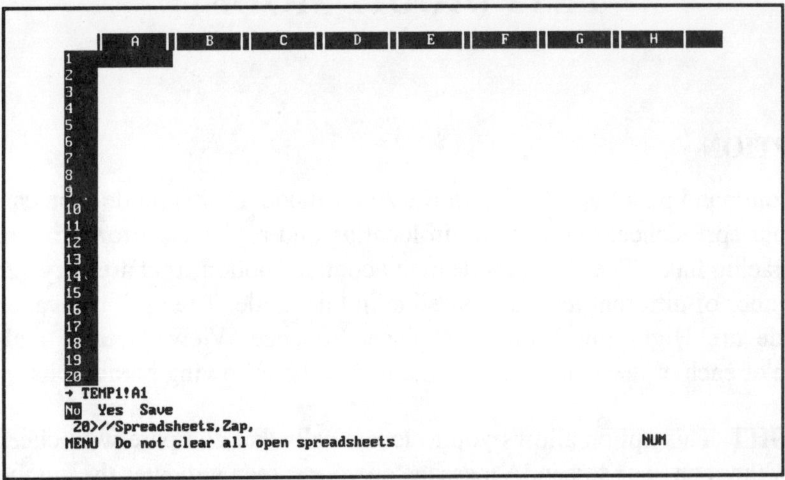

If you change your mind, select No and you are returned to the current spreadsheet in the Ready mode. Select Yes to proceed to clear all the spreadsheets. Select Save and you save any spreadsheet that has been modified before clearing it. You can again select to Backup or Overwrite if the file exists.

9. Press **Esc** to return to the main options menu. Select Quit and the following dialog panel appears in the following illustration.

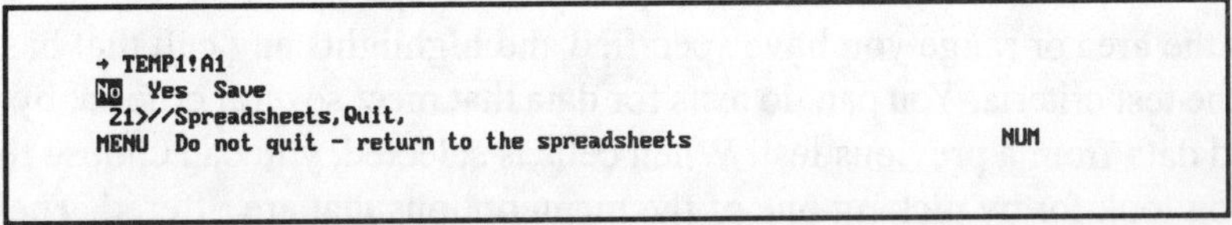

You are prompted by the same options as in the Zap operation. The only difference is that you will be returned to your operating system when the Yes or Save options are completed. No returns you to the current spreadsheet.

10. Select No and press **Enter** to return to the spreadsheet in the Ready mode.
11. Turn to Module 13 to continue the learning sequence.

Module 31
TEST (AUDIT MODE)

DESCRIPTION

The Test command puts SuperCalc 5 in the Audit mode. In this mode, you can perform tests on your spreadsheet that aid you in locating and replacing errors, finding unused data, and tracing links. The Audit mode menu contains options that are very versatile, so a large number of different tests are possible in this mode. The options available in the Audit mode are Highlight, Names, Replace, Squeeze, View, Details, and Quit. A description of each of these options is contained in the following paragraphs.

HIGHLIGHT This option allows you to locate cells that compare with citeria you set and display them on your screen. A message on your screen indicates the number of cells found. Options for this function are Area, Block, Cells, Find, Links, Modified, Output-attr, Pre-zap, Relationships, and Zap. A brief description of each is given here.

Area offers you the opportunity to select the part of the spreadsheet which is tested and to select cells on which the test is based. When Area is selected, you are prompted to make choices through the Filter or Range options. Let the help line assist you in these choices and any further option choices you make.

Block highlights the range that you select. The highlighted block can be used in further testing, but the range is not kept by SuperCalc 5 when the Audit mode is exited.

Cells tests the area or range you have specified and highlights any cell that has contents that meet the test criteria. You can do tests for data that meet several criteria, by using the highlighted data from a previous test. When cells is selected, you can choose the type of contents you look for by picking one of the menu options that are offered. The help line assists you by giving a short explanation of each choice.

Find locates cells that match the value or content criteria you set, then highlights them. When Find is selected, you choose to look for contents or value, then proceed to select the detailed options that enable you to be very selective in the cells you locate. Use the help line to guide you through the options selection.

Links locates and highlights for you all the references to another spreadsheet, then highlights them for you.

Modified determines whether or not cells affected by recalculation are highlighted or not. A Yes response to the prompt highlights all recalculated cells, regardless of whether you are in the Audit mode. No cuts off the highlighting feature.

Output-attr allows you to check for cells that have output attributes as part of their contents. Results of this test can give you a look at the expected output.

Pre-zap allows you to choose between clearing all highlights before another test is done, or adding new highlights to those in place from previous tests. Select Yes at the prompt to clear highlights from earlier tests, and No to combine test results.

Relationships looks for cells containing only formulas, and relationships between them and referenced cells. You can select the type of relationship you are looking for and whether or not to include the referenced cells as part of the output.

Zap clears all highlights from the current spreadsheet.

NAMES This option displays a list of the ranges that meet the test conditons you have set. This allows you the opportunity to check any ranges meeting your test conditions for errors. Options include Bounds, Duplicate, Overlap, Reversed, and Unreferenced. The following paragraphs contain a brief description of each.

Bounds shows you the named ranges that spread beyond the current spreadsheet's active range. The active area is that area where your data and formulas reside. The display is the Named Range Directory - Bounds.

Duplicate looks for identical cells or groups of cells that have different names. The Named Range Directory - Duplicate is displayed.

Overlap tests for any range which contains cells that are within the area of other ranges. The display of the Named Range Directory - Overlap includes any overlapping ranges.

Reversed checks for and displays on the Named Range Directory - Reversed any named range whose definition has the lower right coordinate placed before the upper left one.

Unreferenced displays the Named Range Directory - Unreferenced, which includes any named ranges not referenced by any formula in the spreadhseet.

REPLACE The Replace option searches your spreadsheet for data that you are replacing with other data. Options included in the menu give you choices about what and where you want to find and replace. The menu includes Go, Case, Labels, Match, New String, Old String, Prompt, Range, and Quit. Descriptions of each are included in the following paragraphs.

Go begins the replacement operation. This option is selected after you have chosen what to replace, the replacement data, and where to look for data to replace.

Case allows you to make your search find data that exactly matches the upper and lower case of your entry or if it need be the exact case. Select Case and the options menu prompts you to select Exact if an exact match is required, or Any if either case is permissible.

Labels prompts you to tell SuperCalc 5 if the new data you are putting into your spreadsheet contains cell references or named ranges. Select Yes to indicate that you are using named ranges, and No to indicate cell references.

Match allows you to search for string occurrences. You are prompted to choose what type of occurrence you are looking for. The help line explains each option so you can select the option to accomplish what you want to do.

New-string is for entry of the data you are entering after the old data is removed.

Old-string is for entry of the data you are replacing.

Prompt gives you the option of deciding whether or not to replace each occurrence of the old data. A Yes response lets you decide on each occurrence, and No replaces each occurrence automatically. Selection of Yes offers further choices, which are explained on the help line.

Range allows you to select the area of the spreadsheet you are searching.

Quit returns you to the main options menu of the Audit mode.

SQUEEZE This option recognizes the second and all suceeding occurences of a formula and stores them as references to the first occurrence. This can save significant memory in a spreadsheet where identical formuls are used often. Squeeze should be used before beginning the use of the Audit options.

VIEW The View option displays the spreadsheet in several different ways. You can see the spreadsheet in the normal display, see an expanded version with complete formulas displayed, or a condensed version with symbols representing the data in your spreadsheet. The options menu for View includes Formula, Map, and Normal. Each is briefly explained here.

Formula lets you see the formulas that produced the values in cells containing them. The display automatically shows columns of up to 20 characters; a formula larger than that wraps within the column. Text also wraps, unless the next cell is blank, in which case it overflows into the next cell. The Labels option of the Global command determines whether cell references or range names are displayed in the View option.

Map produces a condensed version of your spreadsheet by substituting symbols for data. The characters and what they represent are listed here.

"	Text and empty cell
f	Formula
#	Number
m	Macro

Select Standard to use the preceding symbols, or Pattern to use special characters to show patterns of formulas in your spreadsheet.

Normal returns the spreadsheet display to the normal one.

DETAILS the Details option shows all cells highlighted as a result of your most recent test. The upper part of the box on your screen shows the cell addresses of highlighted cells, and as each cell address is brought under the cursor, the contents of the cell are shown in the lower part of the box. The top row of the display gives the number of highlighted cells, and each cell is listed on the next row.

As the cursor is moved across each cell, its contents are shown on the next line. Use the Right Arrow to view cells that spill off the right edge of the screen. Press Enter with the cursor on a cell address to put the spreadsheet cursor on that cell and put that cell in the center of the display.

QUIT The Quit option returns you to the spreadsheet in the Ready mode.

APPLICATIONS

The Test command puts you in the Audit mode to locate unused data, view the spreadhseet on your screen in different ways, and spot disruptions in data patterns. You can locate formulas that have errors in them, that reference empty cells, and you can check links between formulas. Each test can be run independently or combined with the results of previous tests. Test results are displayed on your screen immediately, so that you can determine if more tests are needed. You can combine testing procedures to come up with an almost unlimited number of unique tests.

TYPICAL OPERATION

To use the Audit mode to troubleshoot and debug your spreadsheet, follow the steps listed here. Begin with the spreadsheet in the Ready mode.

1. To get into the Audit mode through the Test command, type **//T**. The help line then prompts you for another entry to show the Audit mode options. Type **/8** and the following screen appears.

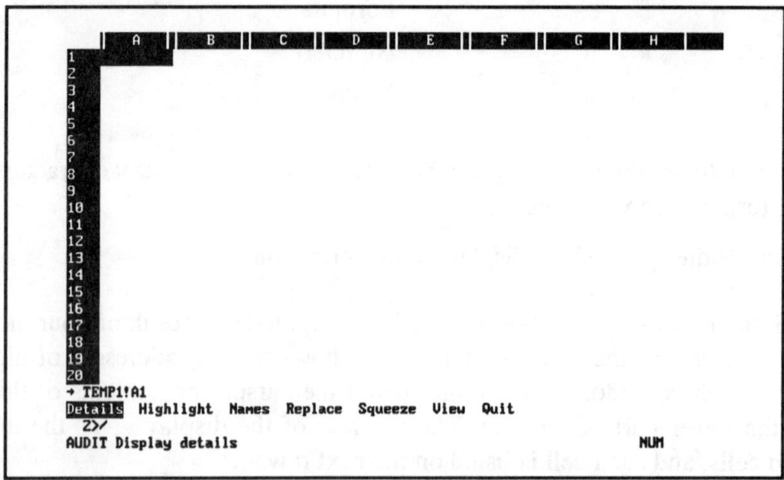

2. To set up your test, select Highlight from the options menu. Type **H**, and the following screen appears.

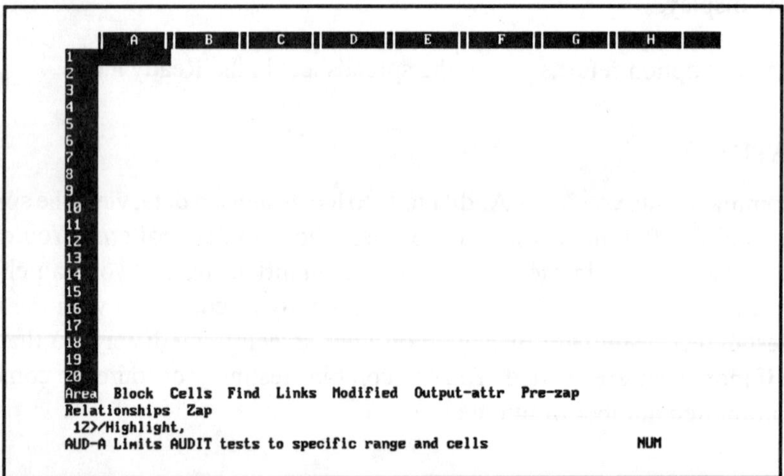

Select one of the options now displayed to define the area of your spreadsheet you are testing, then select other options to give SuperCalc 5 other details of the test you are doing. Use the information provided by the help line to get the option appropriate to your test. After your test is done, you are returned to the Audit mode options menu.

3. Select the Names option to view the Named Range Directories. Each option will display the directory containing a named range that met a test you conducted. Return to the Audit mode main options menu by pressing **Esc**.

4. To find and replace data, select the Replace option from the Audit mode main options menu by typing **R**. The following screen appears.

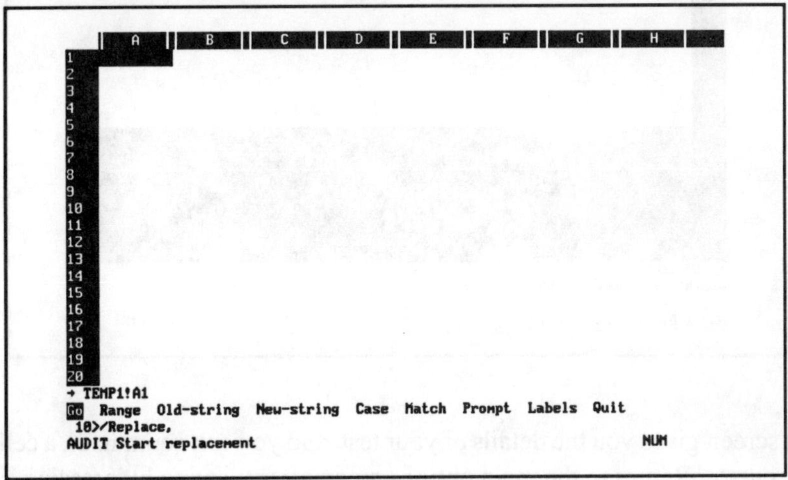

You are prompted to select options from the menu, your choice dependent on the particular operation you are doing. The help line gives you specifics about each option to ensure you get the option needed to do your test.

5. To squeeze the data in your spreadsheet so that the test size does not become unmanageable, select the Squeeze option from the Audit mode main options menu. Type **S** and the squeeze is done. You are returned to the Audit mode main options menu.

6. To view your spreadsheet in different formats, the View option is selected. Type **V** and the following dialog panel appears.

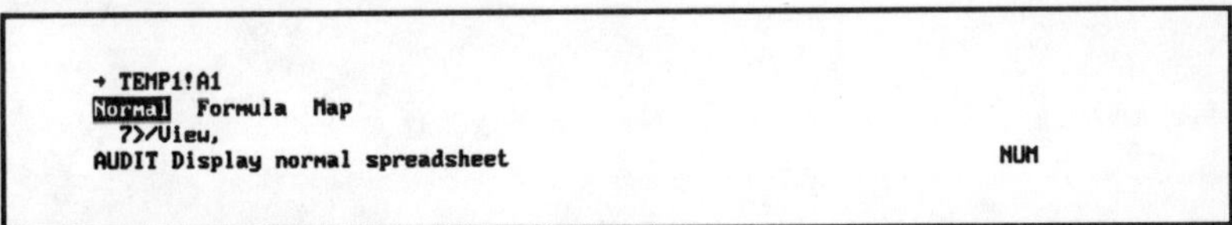

You are prompted to choose an option indicating the type of display in which you wish to see your spreadsheet. The selected display format remains the same until changed, even if you exit the Audit mode and return again.

7. To look at the results of a test, select the Details option by typing **D**. The following screen appears.

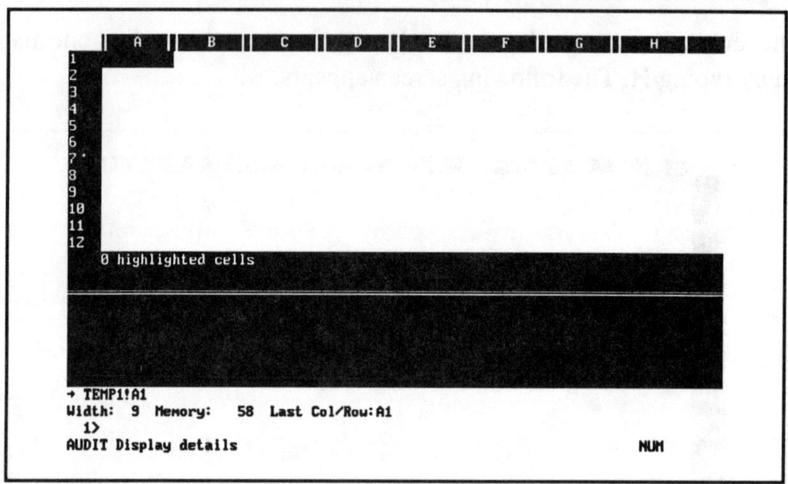

8. This screen gives you the details of your test, and you can zoom in on a cell by using your cursor. Return to the main options menu after viewing by pressing **Esc**.

You have completed the recommended learning sequence. To further advance your skills in using SuperCalc 5, work with it often and be aggressive and curious in the use of all its functions. The power and capabilities of SuperCalc 5 can be amazing when a skilled operator can put them to use.

Module 32
TITLE

DESCRIPTION

The Title command allows you to lock columns or rows in place on the display while scrolling the other columns or rows. This permits you to keep titles, reference material, or other important data on the screen while you view other data in the spreadsheet.

The Title command has several options. They are Horizontal, Vertical, Both, and Clear. These options are described in the following paragraphs.

HORIZONTAL This option locks the current row and all rows above it. The horizontal lock allows you to scroll vertically and keep the locked rows in place on the display.

VERTICAL This option locks the current column and all columns to the left of it. The vertical lock allows you to scroll horizontally and keep the locked columns in place on the display.

BOTH This option locks the current row and column and all rows above and columns to the left. With the horizontal and vertical lock, you can scroll in any direction and keep all the locked area in place on the display.

CLEAR This option removes all locks in the current spreadsheet.

A new lock can be specified, but the new lock replaces the old one. Also, cursor movement keys cannot move the cursor into a locked area. To do this, Home or F5 must be pressed. Title locks are automatically cleared when you press F5 and go to a locked cell that is off the screen above a locked row or to the left of a locked column. A title lock is also cleared if you use the Window command and the locked row or column is pushed off the screen.

APPLICATIONS

The Title command allows you to keep titles, reference data, and other important data on the screen while you scroll the rest of the screen. This can make a much easier task of reviewing a large spreadsheet that has nothing but numbers on it. You can keep track of what each row or column means as you scroll through it. Other uses are retrieving selected data from spreadsheets and row or column comparison of spreadsheet data.

TYPICAL OPERATION

The Title command is simple and easy to use. Follow the listed steps, beginning with the spreadsheet in the Ready mode.

1. Load the example spreadsheet.
2. Select the row and/or column you are locking, and move the spreadsheet cursor to the row and/or column. For this example, the cursor is left in cell A1.
3. Type **/T**. The following screen appears on your display.

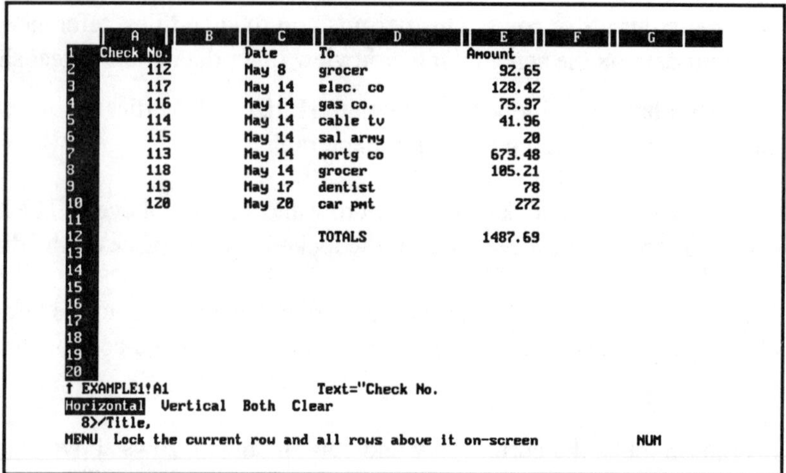

4. You are prompted to select from the four options. Select Horizontal and press **Enter**. Column A is now locked, and you are returned to the spreadsheet in the Ready mode. Move the spreadsheet cursor down the spreadsheet to verify that row 1 is locked. Position row 10 just below the locked row, and your display is as shown in the following illustration.

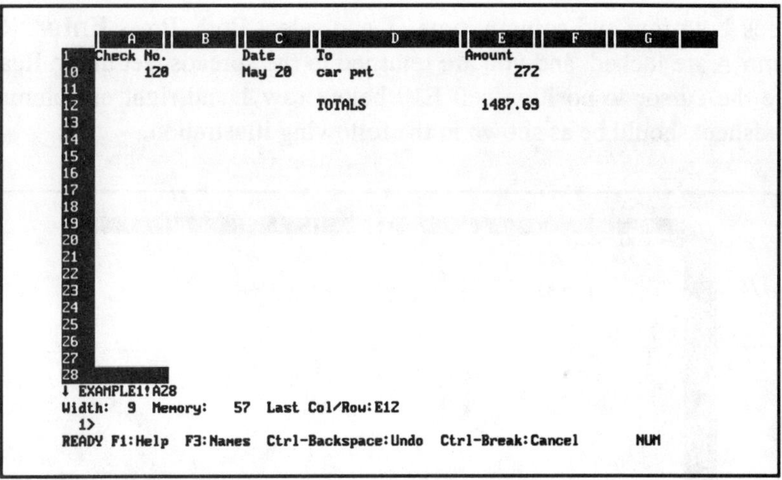

5. Move the cursor up the page until the spreadsheet is back in its original place. Notice that the cursor will not go into row 1, as it is still locked.

6. To clear the lock on row 1, type **/T**. Select Clear and press **Enter**. All locks in the current spreadsheet are now cleared, and you are back in the spreadsheet in the Ready mode.

7. To lock a column, type **/T**. Select Vertical and press **Enter**. Move the cursor to the right to scroll the columns to the left. Position column E next to column A (the locked column) and your spreadsheet should resemble the following one.

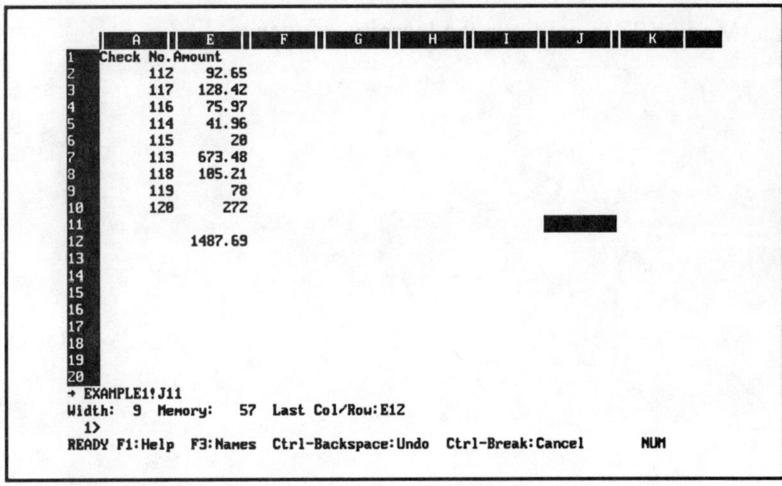

8. Move the cursor to the left to put the spreadsheet back in its original position. Clear the lock by typing **/T** and selecting Clear and pressing **Enter**.

9. To lock both row and column, type **/T** and select Both. Press **Enter**. Row 1 and column A are locked, and you are returned to the spreadsheet in the Ready mode. Move the cursor to position cell E10 below row 1 and right of column A. Your spreadsheet should be as shown in the following illustration.

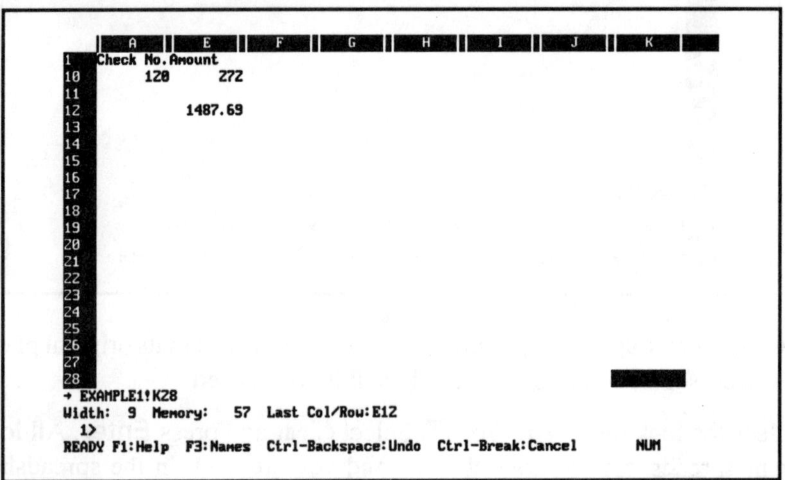

You can return the spreadsheet to its original condition and then clear the locks, or you can clear the locks and then return it.

10. Use the Zap command to clear the spreadsheet.
11. Turn to Module 33 to continue the learning sequence.

Module 33
WINDOW

DESCRIPTION

The Window command allows you to split the display into two separate parts. Each part of the screen can display distant parts of the current spreadsheet, and each window can have different options and format settings at the global level, but not at the column, row, or entry level.

The spreadsheet cursor is used to specify where the screen is to be split. The current row or column is moved down or right and the border inserted in its place. The cursor can be moved between windows by pressing F6. Each window can be scrolled independently, or they can be scrolled in unison when the cursor is moved parallel to the window split. In other words, spreadsheet columns can be scrolled synchronously when the windows are split horizontally, and rows can be scrolled synchronously when the windows are split vertically.

If a lock has been installed by the Title command, it is retained by both windows, or you may set a lock in either or both windows. You can save your spreadsheet with separate windows, but you cannot print out or otherwise get an output that will show both windows. The format of the window containing the current cell is the format used in any output.

The options of the Window command are Horizontal, Vertical, Clear, Synchronize, and Unsynchronize. These options are described in the following paragraphs.

HORIZONTAL This option splits the screen into top and bottom sections. The current row moves down, and the same border as at the top of the screen replaces it. This gives each screen a top and left border to allow the Title command to be used.

VERTICAL This option splits the screen into left and right sections. The current column moves to the right and is replaced by the border on the left of the display.

CLEAR This option removes the split screen, and the window that is above or to the left is displayed in full, and the format and settings of that window are retained.

SYNCHRONIZE This option causes both windows to scroll simultaneously as the cursor is moved in either window.

UNSYNCHRONIZE This option removes the synchronized scrolling from the windows. Unsynchronized scrolling is the default for scrolling of the windows.

APPLICATIONS

The Window command can be used for comparison of text or data in parts of the spreadsheet not displayed on the same screen, and to locate related data. Corrections and editing of data can be done in two areas of your spreadsheet without having to move back and forth.

TYPICAL OPERATION

To illustrate the use of the Window command, the example file is loaded and used to show how the Window command operates. Follow the steps listed here, beginning with the spreadsheet in the Ready mode.

1. Load the EXAMPLE1.SC5 file into the current spreadsheet. Set the spreadsheet cursor on row 11 in column A.

2. Type **/W**. The following screen appears.

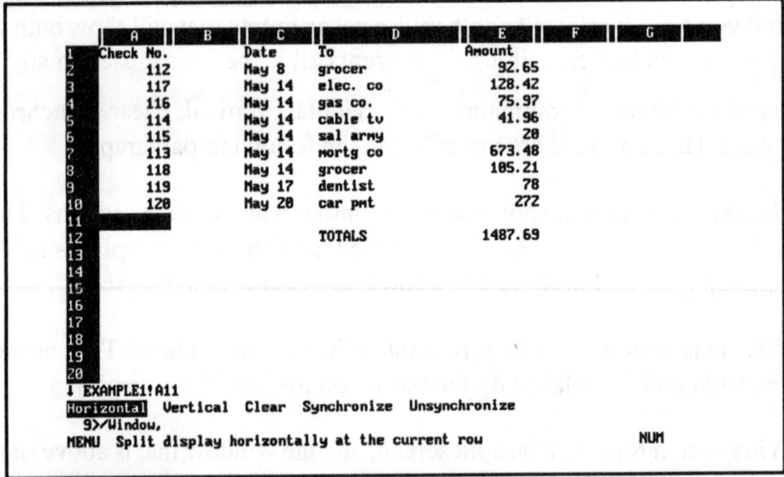

3. You are prompted to select an option. Select Horizontal and press **Enter**. The following screen appears.

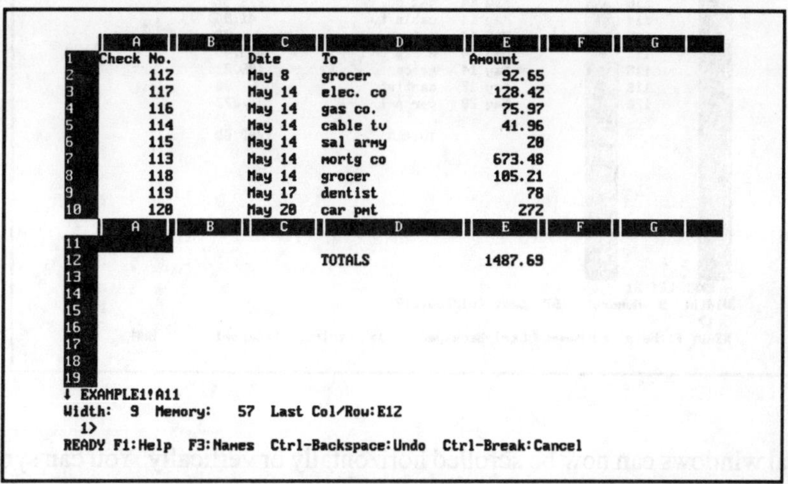

4. The spreadsheet cursor is in the bottom window. Move the cursor to scroll the spreadsheet horizontally or vertically, or both, through the window. Notice that the upper window does not scroll. Press **F6** to move the cursor to the upper window. Move the cursor to scroll the spreadsheet.

5. To scroll both windows, type **/W**. Select Synchronize and press **Enter**. Press **Right Arrow** to scroll both windows horizontally. Restore independent scrolling of the windows by typing **/W**. Select Unsynchronize and press **Enter**. The windows can now be scrolled individually.

6. Clear the windows by typing **/W** and selecting Clear. Press **Enter** and you are returned to the spreadsheet in the Ready mode.

7. Move the cursor to column B. To split the screen vertically, type **/W**. Select Vertical and press **Enter**. The following screen appears.

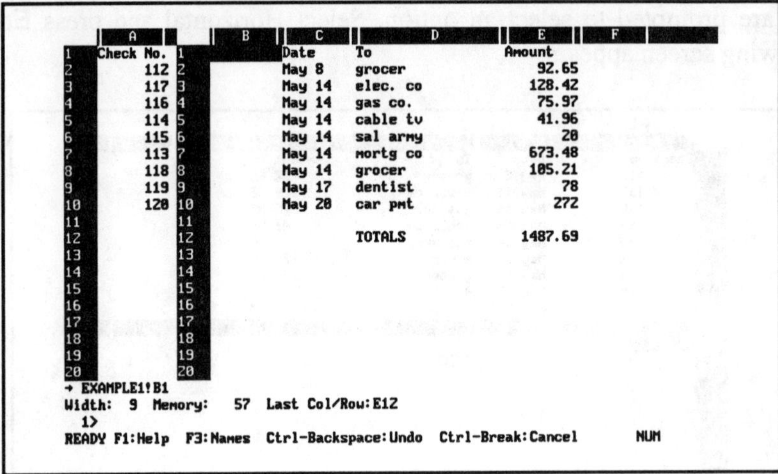

The vertical windows can now be scrolled horizontally or vertically. You can synchronize the vertical scrolling, or independently scroll each window.

8. Use the Zap command to clear the spreadsheet.
9. Turn to Module 26 to continue the learning sequence.

Module 34
ZAP

DESCRIPTION

The Zap command erases an entire spreadsheet from the working memory of your computer. After "zapping" the spreadsheet, the program returns a blank spreadsheet in the Ready mode. The file is not erased from disk storage. You are prompted for confirmation of your action through an options menu.

The options for the Zap command are No, Yes, Save, and Page. These options are described in the following paragraphs.

NO This option allows you to change your mind after selecting the Zap command. When no is selcted, you are returned to the spreadsheet.

YES This option executes the Zap command. The contents of all cells in the spreadsheet are erased. Display formats are reset to the default settings, and user-defined and output settings are reset to the settings made by the global command. Protected cells, current charts, and named ranges are all deleted. Locks put in place by the window or title commands are cleared. Zap does not clear the default data directory or any global settings.

SAVE This option saves the current spreadsheet for you before erasing it from memory. Save prompts you to select from an options menu which contains Backup and Overwrite. These options are briefly described in the following paragraphs.

Backup saves the current spreadsheet and stores it under the original filename and extension, then takes the old file and stores it under the original filename with a .BAK extension.

Overwrite saves the current spreadsheet and stores it under the original filename and extension, writing over the old version of the file.

PAGE This option erases a specified page of the spreadsheet in memory. The erasures are the same as in the Yes option.

APPLICATIONS

The Zap command is useful in clearing a spreadsheet from memory, or pages of a multipage spreadsheet in memory. It clears all data and format from a spreadsheet so that no extraneous data is left to corrupt data that is entered later.

TYPICAL OPERATION

The Zap command is illustrated by examples using the sample file created in Module 20. Follow the steps listed here, beginning with the spreadsheet in the Ready mode.

1. Load the EXAMPLE1.SC5 file.
2. Type **/Z**. The following screen appears.

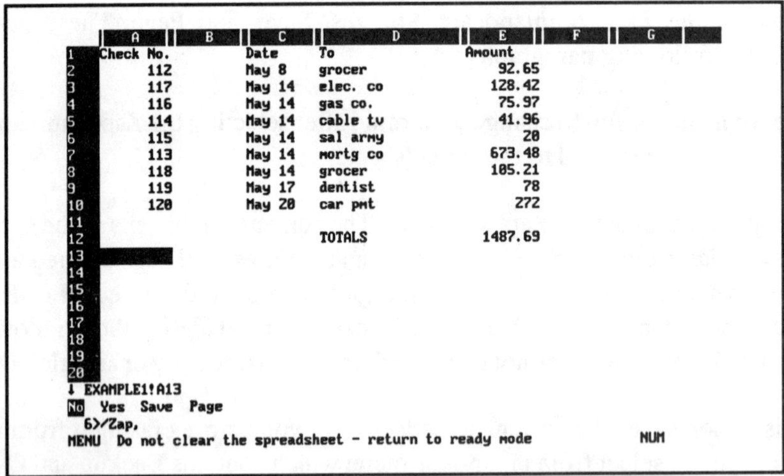

3. You are prompted to select from the options menu. Select No, press **Enter**, and you are returned to the spreadsheet in the Ready mode.
4. Type **/Z**. Select Yes, press **Enter**, and the spreadsheet is erased. You are returned to a blank spreadsheet in the Ready mode.
5. Press **Ctrl-Backspace** to restore the spreadsheet, and select Save from the options menu. Press **Enter**, and the following screen appears if you have made changes to your spreadsheet. If no changes have been made, you are returned to the spreadsheet.

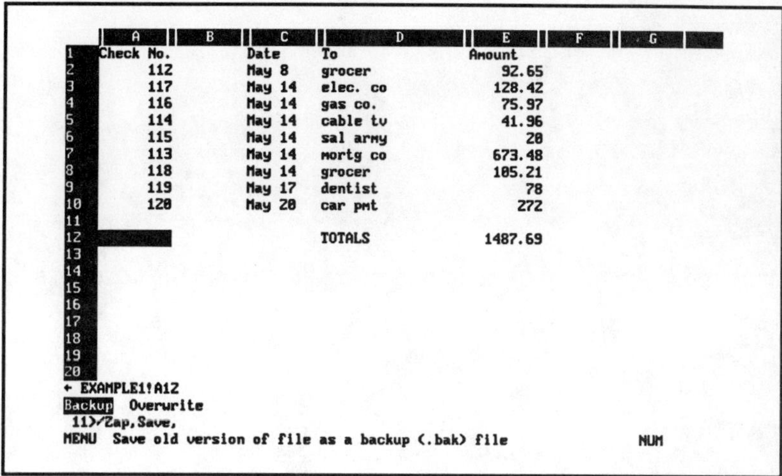

	A	B	C	D	E	F	G
1	Check No.		Date	To	Amount		
2	112		May 8	grocer	92.65		
3	117		May 14	elec. co	128.42		
4	116		May 14	gas co.	75.97		
5	114		May 14	cable tv	41.96		
6	115		May 14	sal army	20		
7	113		May 14	mortg co	673.48		
8	118		May 14	grocer	105.21		
9	119		May 17	dentist	78		
10	120		May 20	car pmt	272		
11							
12				TOTALS	1487.69		
13							
14							
15							
16							
17							
18							
19							
20							

← EXAMPLE1!A12
Backup Overwrite
11>/Zap,Save,
MENU Save old version of file as a backup (.bak) file NUM

6. You are prompted to select Backup or Overwrite. Select Backup to create a backup file which contains the old file stored under the filename with a .BAK extension, and store the current spreadsheet under the original filename and extension.
7. Select Overwrite to store the current spreadsheet under the original filename and extension, overwriting the old version of the file. No backup file is created.
8. Use the Zap command to clear the spreadsheet.
9. Turn to Module 19 to continue the learning sequence.

Appendix A
GLOSSARY OF TERMS

This appendix contains a listing of terms frequently used in computer documentation and operation. Each term is listed in boldface type, and a brief description is given for each term.

Absolute cell reference — A cell reference indicating that one or both coordinates are not to be adjusted. In SuperCalc 5, the notation F2 is an absolute cell reference to F2. To allow adjustment of the column, the notation would be F$2.

Active spreadsheet — That part of a spreadsheet whose boundary is defined by the last column and last row in which data has been entered.

AnswerScreen — The help screen provided by SuperCalc 5 that contains information about the current command, mode, or option. The help screen is called by pressing F1.

ASCII — Acronym for the American Standard Code for Information Interchange. This is the code used by SuperCalc 5 to represent the characters it displays, reads, and writes.

AUTOEXEC.BAT — A DOS batch file containing commands that execute automatically when DOS is booted.

Backup — A copy of a file, directory, or other data, made for the purpose of having the data available in the event of the loss of the working data.

Byte — A group of eight bits, storing the code to represent one character.

Cell — A location on the spreadsheet for data entry, identified by the intersection of a column and a row. The column and row intersection is the cell address, or location.

Consolidation Combining data from separate spreadsheets or from different parts of the same spreadsheet.

Column Spreadsheet cells in a vertical line. Letters are used to represent the individual columns. SuperCalc 5 allows up to 254 columns in a single spreadsheet.

Cursor diamond keys Letter key equivalents to the arrow keys. Ctrl-S moves the cursor to the left, Ctrl-E moves it up, Ctrl-X moves it down, and Ctrl-D moves it to the right.

Date value Value entered with a date function, in a format representing a date.

Device A graphics printer or plotter.

Display window The area of the spreadsheet currently shown on your screen. The window can be split to display several spreadsheets at once.

Entry level format Format settings entered for a specific cell or range of cells. This level of format settings takes precedence over any other format level.

Foreign data file Any data file created by a program other than SuperCalc 5.

Forward Reference A reference from a formula or function to a higher cell address. An example is a cell A7 that references cell H28.

Hold-down key One of three keys that are held down while pressing another key. These three keys are Ctrl, Alt, and Shift. As an example, to enter Ctrl-Backspace, the Ctrl key is held down while pressing Backspace.

Invoke Another term for execution of a macro or command.

Kilobyte The memory required to store 1024 characters. Usually referred to by its abbreviation, K. For example, my computer contains 256K of RAM.

LICS characters The Lotus International Character Set, or LICS, is translated to and from ASCII when loading and saving Lotus 1-2-3 release 2 files.

Log on To make a selected drive the current drive. For example, in DOS, make drive B the current drive by typing B: at the DOS prompt and pressing Enter.

Macro — A group of commands that can automatically perform certain functions when invoked.

Menu — The listing of options for selection of functions performed by a command, or the list of commands.

Mode Indicator — An indicator on the help line of the dialog panel that shows the current operating mode of SuperCalc 5.

Named Range — A range of cells that has been assigned a name. After assigning a name to a range, you can refer to the range by the name.

Numeric Value — Any value that can be expressed as a decimal. The value may be expressed as a numeric constant or a formula evaluation.

Peripheral — Special equipment connected to a computer to perform a designed operation. Usually a printer, monitor, or memory storage device.

Redirection — A change in the output device that receives your output.

Row — Spreadsheet cells in a horizontal line. Rows are identified by number, up to 9999 in SuperCalc 5.

Scroll — To move around the area of the spreadsheet shown on your display. The arrow keys move the cursor to areas off screen to move them onto the display.

Slash commands — The commands available to you on the command menu after typing a slash (/) or two slashes (//).

String — Textual data contained in a cell.

Time value — A date value less than 1 that is displayed as a time.

Word-wrap — A feature of SuperCalc 5 that operates similar to a word processor. Text is automatically fit into the margins and column area selected.

Appendix B
FUNCTIONS AND OPERATORS

This appendix contains a list of the operators and functions resident in SuperCalc 5. The operators are of three types: Arithmetic, Relational, and String. The functions are grouped into ten categories shown in the following list.

Logical	Calendar
Financial	Index
Statistical	Data Management Statistical
Arithmetic	Trigonometric
String	Special Purpose

The listing of an operator or function in this appendix includes a brief description of the operator or function and shows the format for it.

OPERATORS

Arithmetic These operators perform the arithmetic operations that make up the calculations done by SuperCalc 5. The operators are listed and described in table B-1.

Table B-1. ARITHMETIC OPERATORS

Operator	Operation Performed
+	Adds two numeric values.
–	Subtracts one numeric value from another.
*	Multiplies one numeric value by another.
/	Divides one numeric value by another.
%	Converts a numeric value to a percentage.
^ or **	Performs exponential multiplication of the value to which it is attached.

These operators, when used in conjunction with other operators and functions, can build a formula or function.

These formulas and functions are evaluated in algebraic procedure. This order for evaluation is ^ or **, *, %, /, +, and –.

Relational The relational operators compare values and indicate the result of the comparison with a display of the word TRUE or the word FALSE. The list of operators is contained and explained in table B-2.

Table B-2. RELATIONAL OPERATORS

Operator	Type Of Comparison	Result
=	Equals	TRUE if operands are equal, FALSE if not equal
< >	Not Equal	TRUE if operands are not equal, FALSE if they are equal
<	Less than	TRUE if value to the left of the operator is less than the one to the right, FALSE if equal to or greater than
>	Greater than	TRUE if value to the left of the operator is greater than the one to the right, FALSE if less than
<=	Less than or equal to	TRUE if the value to the left of the operator is less than or equal to the value to the right, FALSE if not
=>	Greater than or equal to	TRUE if value to the left of the operator is greater than or equal to the value to the right, FALSE if not

String SuperCalc 5 has one string operator, &. This operator combines strings by concatenation.

FUNCTIONS

The SuperCalc 5 functions are listed here and show the format and results for each.

Table B-3. FUNCTIONS

Function	Result
Arithmetic Functions	
ABS(value)	Absolute value of *value*
EXP(value)	e to the power *value*
INT(value)	Integer of *value*
LN(value)	Natural log, log base e, of *value*
LOG10(value)/LOG(value)	Log base 10 (common log) of *value*
MOD(value1, value2)	Remainder from the division of *value1* by *value2*
ROUND(value, places)	*Value* rounds to the number of *places*
ROUNDUP(value, places)	*Value* rounded up to the number of *places*
SQRT(value)	Square root of *value*
TRUN(value, places)	*Value* truncated to number of *places*
Calendar Functions	
DATE(mm,dd,yy)	Date value of specified date
EDAT(dd,mm,yy)	Same as above; European parameter order
DATEVALUE(date value or string, fstring)	Converts *string*, *date value*, or integral portion of Julian date/time into a date-formatted value
DVAL(value)	Date value of specified *value*
NOW	System date and time
TODAY	System date
TIME(hh,mm,ss)	Time value of specified time
TIMEVALUE(time value or string) or TVAL(time value or string)	Converts *string*, *time value*, or fractional portion of Julian date/time into a time-formatted value
Date/Time Reference Functions	
DAY(value)	Number of the day of the month of *date value* or integral portion of Julian date/time
HOUR(value)	Hour corresponding to hour portion of *time value* or fractional portion of Julian date/time
JDATE(date value)	Julian date of *date value*

Table B-3. FUNCTIONS (Cont.)

Function	Result
JTIME(time value)	Julian time of *time value*
MINUTE(value)	Minute corresponding to the minute portion of *time value* or fractional portion of Julian date/time
MONTH(value) /MON(value)	Number of the month of *date value* or integral portion of Julian date/time
SECOND(value)	Second corresponding to the minute portion of time value or fractional portion of Julian date/time
YEAR(value)	Number of the year of *date value* or integral portion of Julian date/time
WDAY(value)	Julian number of day of week of *date value*
Data Management Statistical Functions	
DAVG(input, offset field, criterion)	Mean (average) of value in *offset field* of *input* range that meets *criteria*
DCOUNT(input, offset field, criterion)	Number of non-blank, non-zero cells in *offset field* of *input* range that meets *criteria*
DMAX(input, offset field, criterion)	Largest value in *offset field* of input range that meets *criteria*
DMIN(input, offset field, criterion)	Smallest value in *offset field* of *input* range that meets *criteria*
DSTD(input, offset field, criterion)	Standard deviation of population for values in *offset field* of *input* range that meets *criteria*
DSUM(input, offset field, criterion)	Sum of values in *offset field* of *input* range that meets *criteria*
DVAR(input, offset field, criterion)	Population variance for values in *offset field* of *input* range that meets *criteria*
Financial Functions	
Annuities (Lifetime)	
ANRATE(payment, present value, term)	Periodic interest date
ANTERM(payment, rate, present value)	Number of payment periods
PMT(present value, rate, term)	Equal periodic payment
PV(payment, rate, term)	Present value of a series of payments

Table B-3. FUNCTIONS (Cont.)

Function	Result
Annuities (Periodic)	
BALANCE(present value, rate, term, period)	Remaining principal balance after *period* payments
KINT(present value, rate, term, period)	Amount of interest paid in *period*
KPRIN(present value, rate, term, period)	Amount of principal paid in *period*
PAIDINT(present value, rate, term, period)	Total interest paid to *period*
Onetime Investments	
CTERM(rate, future value, present value)	Number of periods (term)
COMPBAL(present value, rate, term)	Final balance in an account
RATE(future value, present value, term)	Periodic interest rate
Investing Each Period	
FV(payment, rate, term)	Future Value
IRR(guess, row/col range)	Internal Rate of Return
NPV(rate, row/col range)	Net Present Value of a group of cash returns
TERM(payment, rate, future value)	Number of periods
Depreciation	
DDB(cost, salvage, life, period)	Depreciation allowance using the double-declining balance method
SLN(cost, salvage, life)	Straight-line depreciation for one period
SYD(cost, salvage, life, period)	Sum-of-the-years digits depreciation for specified period
Index Functions	
ADDRESS(range)	Cell address of upper left cell in *range*
BEGCOL(range)	Column number of upper left cell in *range*
BEGROW(range)	Row number of upper left cell in *range*

Table B-3. FUNCTIONS (Cont.)

Function	Result
CHOOSE(x,v0,v1,...,xn)	The *x*th value from the list of values
COLCHARS(value)	Takes a number from 1 to 255 and returns the equivalent column string, A through IU
COLS(range)	Number of columns in *range*
CURADDRESS	Current cell address
CURCOL	Column number of the current cell
CURPAGE	Number of the current spreadsheet page
CURROW or CROW	Current row number
CURSHEET	Name of current spreadsheet
ENDCOL(range) /ECOL(range)	Column number of the lower right cell in *range*
ENDROW(range) /EROW(range)	Row number of the lower right cell in *range*
HLU(x, range, row offset)	Content of the cell in the horizontal table specified by *range*, beneath column *x*, in the row defined by *row offset*
INDEX(range, column offset, row offset)	The value of the cell in *range* at *column offset* and *row offset*
ITER	The current iteration count
LASTCOL or LCOL	Rightmost column number containing data
LASTROW or LROW	Bottom row number containing data
LU(value, row/col range)	Last value in *range* that is less than or equal to *value*
N(cell)	Numeric value of *cell*
ROWS(range)	Number of rows in *range*
S(cell)	String value of *cell*
THISCOL or TCOL	Column number of the cell
THISROW or TROW	Row number of the cell
VLU(x, range, column offset)	Content of the cell in the vertical table specified by *range*, across row *x*, in the column defined by *column offset*

Table B-3. FUNCTIONS (Cont.)

Function	Result
Logic Functions	
Cell Type Test	
ISBLANK(expression)	True if *expression* is a blank cell
ISDATE(expression)	True if *expression* is a date value type cell
ISERROR(expression)	True if *expression* returns ERROR value
ISNA(expression)	True if *expression* returns Not Available (N/A)
ISNUM(expression)	True if *expression* returns numeric value type
ISPROT(cell)	True if *cell* is protected
ISSTR(expression)	True if *expression* returns text or string
ISTIME(expression)	True if *expression* is a date value type cell with value <1
ISVAL(expression)	True if *expression* returns numeric value
Cell Type Assignment	
ERROR or ERR	Displays ERROR
FALSE	Displays 0 for logical value False
NA	Displays N/A for Not Available
TRUE	Displays 1 for logical value True
Conditional Logic	
AND(value1, value2)	True if *value1* and *value2* are true; otherwise False
EXACT(string1, string2)	True if *string1* and *string2* match; otherwise False
IF(cond, x, y)	X if *cond* is True; Y if *cond* is false
NOT(value)	True if *value* is False; False if *value* is True
OR(valuc1, value2)	True if any value is true; otherwise False
Statistical Functions	
AVG(list)	The average of the *list*
COUNT(list)	The number of numeric value cells in *list*
MAX(list)	Maximum value in *list*
MIN(list)	Minimum value in *list*
RANDOM	Random number between 0 and 1
STD(list)	Standard deviation of a population in *list*
SUM(list)	Sum of the values in *list*

Table B-3. FUNCTIONS (Cont.)

Function	Result
VAR(list)	Population variance of the values in *list*
Special-Purpose Functions	
@(cell)	Converts string representation of *cell* into cell address
FORMAT(cell)	Format value of *cell*
TYPE(cell)	Character that represents cell type
VALUE(string)	Numeric value of *string*
WIDTH(range)	Width of column(s) where *range* is located
String Functions	
&	Concatenation of strings
CHAR(n)	ASCII value of *n*
CODE(string)	ASCII value of first character in *string*
CONTENT(cell)	The contents of *cell* as a string
DISPLAY(value, format value or string, width)	String equal to *value* formatted according to *format string* and displayed at *width*
FIND(searchstring, string, startnumber)	Character position of *searchstring* in *string* beginning at *startnumber*
LEFT(string, n)	The first *n* characters of the string
LENGTH(string)	Length of *string*
LOWER(string)	*String* converted to lower case
MID(string, startnumber, n)	Substring of length *n* beginning with the *startnumber* character position
PROPER(string)	*String* converted to proper capitalization
REPEAT(string, n)	*String* repeated *n* times
REPLACE(originalstring, startnumber, n, newstring)	Removes *n* characters of *originalstring* at *startnumber* and inserts *newstring*
RIGHT(string, n)	Last *n* characters of *string*
STRING(x,n)	Converts *x* to string with *n* decimal places
TRIM(string)	Removes excess spaces in front and end of *string*
UPPER(string)	*String* converted to upper case

Table B-3. FUNCTIONS (Cont.)

Function	Result
Trigonometric Functions	
ACOS(value)	Arccosine of *value*
ASIN(value)	Arcsine of *value*
ATAN(value)	Arctangent of *value*
ATAN2(x,y)	Arctangent of point x,y
COS(value)	Cosine of *value*
PI	Value of pi
SIN(value)	Sine of *value*
TAN(value)	Tangent of *value*

Appendix C
SUPERCALC 5 COMPATIBILITY AND FEATURE CHANGES

This appendix contains information about the compatibility between SuperCalc 5 and previous versions of SuperCalc. Other information contained is a quick summary of the changes made to SuperCalc that resulted in SuperCalc 5.

COMPATIBILITY

In SuperCalc 5, the file format has been restructured so that chart descriptions, spreadsheet links, and string functions can be saved. With these changes, compatibility between current and earlier versions of SuperCalc has been reduced to the following two statements:

1. Existing .CAL files from any previous version of SuperCalc can be used with the current version.
2. To save a file to a previous version of SuperCalc, you must use the Level option in the Save command. SuperCalc takes care of any conversion needed or any detail. You need only to know your filenames and the way to save back to other versions to be rid of any compatibility problems.

CHANGES IN FEATURES

New and better features in the current version of SuperCalc provide you with a powerful spreadsheet that can accomplish a wide variety of tasks. New or changed features are contained in the following list. Each listed feature is briefly described.

- Recalculation - Faster, more selective.
- Graphics - Includes several two- and three-dimensional charts
- Compatibility - Use Lotus 1-2-3 commands and directly load and save Lotus files, import and export dBASE III files.
- Undo - negates the effect of the last command or entry.
- Formulas & Functions - 20 new string functions, a new time function, computed cell references, now allowed in formulas and commands.
- // Spreadsheets - new command to give you global control of open spreadsheets.

- Entry and Edit-
    1) Transpose rows and columns.
    2) Edit and copy across spreadsheets.
    3) Enter destination cell for Edit.
    4) Cursor skips a column when the Hidecolumn option of Format command set column width to zero.
    5) Blank a cell's contents with no effect on its entry levels.
    6) The Arrange command has a third sort key.
    7) You are prompted for confirmation when deleting a file.
- Twelve or twenty-four hour clock, user-defined time formats, and time functions now available.
- Word-wrap option in Justify command functions like a word processor.
- // Add-in - New command adds to current spreadsheet.
- Expanded macro capabilities- new commands, and new options for debug and foreign file conversion.
- New DOS option in /Quit command exits to the operating system temporarily.
- New options in /Output command support laser and dot matrix printers.
- Change defaults for any spreadsheet quickly by using more than one configuration file.
- New //Data command options

    Delete option takes out selected records.
    Analysis option does frequency distributions and regression analysis.
    Block option puts numbers on date labels in a range to fill it.
    Matrix option performs multiplication, inversion, and solution of up to 90 variable simultaneous equations.
    Parse system separates combined data.
    Table option makes 1- and 2-variable "what-if" tables.

- New option for /Format command lets parentheses adjust to the size of negative numbers.
- Values - new option for /Global command can show global settings on the display.
- Zoom option of Global command can expand screen if hardware is in place.
- Network can now lock more than 16 files at one time.
- Table, new option for the /Name command, lists the named ranges.

- Path and Directory, new options for //File command, allow you to determine where file searches are conducted.
- Incomplete or ambiguous filename brings up File List.
- Up to 32 megabytes of expanded memory is supported using the LIM 4 specification.
- New options for //Test command help find errors, search for a cell value, content, format or type, and do search and replace operations.

Appendix D
INSTALLING SUPERCALC 5

PC INSTALLATION

The installation of SuperCalc 5 on the hard disk drive in your system is a fairly easy task. However, before you begin the installation, please take note of two items. First, you will need to verify that there is space on your hard disk for SuperCalc 5. Approximately 5 megabytes of storage is required for the program and utilities. Second, it is a good idea to put write protect tabs on the original diskettes if they are 5 1/4" diskettes. For 3 1/2" diskettes, open the write protect slide.

The actual installation of SuperCalc 5 is best taken in steps. Perform the following steps, and you are ready to use SuperCalc 5.

1. Type **C**: and press **Enter** to bring up the C drive, then type **CD** to get to the root directory of the drive.
2. To make a directory called CALC, type **MKDIR CALC** and press **Enter**. You now have a directory called CALC.
3. Use the DOS COPY command to copy each diskette from drive A to the CALC directory on drive C. Type **COPY A:*.* C:\CALC/V** and press **Enter** to copy a diskette and verify that the copy is correct.

You are now ready to begin using SuperCalc 5.

NETWORK INSTALLATION

SuperCalc 5 can be used on networks running IBM DOS 3.1 or later. Follow the steps listed here to install SuperCalc 5 on a network.

1. Open keyfile and program directories on the network server hard disk.
2. Invoke the ACTIVATE program that is part of SuperCalc 5.
3. Use ACTIVATE to copy SuperCalc 5 to the network.
4. Pledge SuperCalc 5 diskettes to the network so users can access the program.

The ACTIVATE program is provided for the network administrator only. Network users should not use the program.

SETUP

After installation is complete, consider setting up some of the parameters for your spreadsheets and peripherals. Refer to Modules 14 (Format) and 15 (Global) to find out more about these settings.

Appendix E
SUPERCALC EXERCISES

1. About This Book
   a. Where can electronic worksheets be used?
   b. How might you use the examples in this book?
   c. Where can SuperCalc commands be found in this book?
   d. What are the hardware requirements for SuperCalc 5?
   e. What should you know before learning SuperCalc 5?
2. SuperCalc 5 Overview
   a. Describe the organization of the typical worksheet.
   b. What is a cell?
   c. Describe the meaning of R3C8.
   d. How large is the SuperCalc 5 worksheet?
   e. What kind of information may be entered into a cell?
   f. What is an absolute cell reference?
   g. What is a relative cell reference?
   h. Write a list of function keys on your computer and describe their use.
   i. How do you "undo" entries if you goof?
3. A Sample SuperCalc 5 Spreadsheet
   a. What is the current location of the spreadsheet cursor called?
   b. What key is SuperCalc's GoTo command?
   c. How are formulas shown on your display?
   d. On what line are characters shown that are input from the keyboard?
4. 1-2-3
   a. Can you issue a series of Lotus 1-2-3 commands using 1-2-3?
   b. What command/option allows you to issue a series of 1-2-3 commands?
5. Add-in
   a. How can you determine what programs and functions have been attached to a file?
   b. What can you do to simplify the use of an add-in?

c. How is an add-in removed?
d. You can designate how many add-in programs to automatically execute when SuperCalc 5 is started?

6. Arrange
a. What is the primary purpose of the Arrange command?
b. What should you do if you make an entry error?
c. Describe two ways to start commands.
d. What key is pressed to complete a command?
e. What keys are used to move the cursor on the Command menu?
f. When are double quotes used for text entry?

7. Blank
a. Describe the purpose of the Blank command.
b. How many cells can be simultaneously blanked? Explain.
c. Write a Blank cells reference that uses the range and union operators.
d. How can SuperCalc 5 be used as a desktop calculator?

8. Copy
a. Describe the use of the Copy command.
b. What is the difference between copy + and copy – ?
c. What does transpose accomplish?
d. Write the keystrokes and results for copying cells C2:D5 to cells H1:G3.
e. Describe three benefits offered by the Copy command.

9. Data
a. What are two main purposes of the Data command?
b. How is the data selected that is to be analyzed?
c. How many variables are allowed for solution of simultaneous equations by the Matrix operation?
d. Can data strings be split and put into individual fields? How?
e. Which option searches for data to match your requests?
f. Is every matching record in a search automatically written to an output range by the Select option?

10. Delete
a. Describe the purpose of the Delete command.
b. How large an area may be deleted?
c. Write the keystrokes and results for deleting rows 5 and 6.
d. Write the keystrokes and results for deleting column 8.

e. Write the keystrokes and results to delete a square cell area in rows 2 and 3 and columns B and C.

f. What happens to relative and absolute cell references within formulas when cell positions change as a result of deletion?

11. Edit

a. Describe the purpose of the Edit command.

b. How might you change a cell's contents without using the Edit command?

c. List the keys used for cursor control and deletion during Edit.

12. Export

a. In what formats can Export save files?

b. How are files saved to these formats identified?

c. What additional format can Import convert for use by SuperCalc?

d. Can all formats use the Consolidate option?

e. What is the character limit per cell in the Text option?

13. File

a. What key is pressed to display a file list?

b. How is the default directory changed?

c. How can the displayed file list of a directory be limited?

d. Does an incomplete filename (not qualified) stop a file search?

14. Format

a. Describe the main function of the Format command.

b. What are the four selections offered by the Format command?

c. Write the keystrokes and results for centering text in cells R2C3 through R2C6.

d. Write the keystrokes and results for displaying a number in cell R5C4 as dollars and cents.

e. Write the keystrokes and results for displaying the numbers in cells R3C6 through R9C6 as percent to two decimal places.

f. What is the primary purpose of the Format Default command?

g. Write the keystrokes and results to change the width of columns R through AH to five spaces.

15. Global

a. Describe the main function of the Global command.

b. What is the purpose of the Cartridges option of the Spreadsheet command?

c. How can you operate on Lotus 1-2-3 files that you have imported?

d. When the Evaluation option is in the manual mode, how is a spreadsheet re-calculation started?
e. What option is used to set the display characteristics for your monitor?
f. Can you change the page orientation of a chart? How?

16. Graphics
    a. How are charts and graphs previewed before output?
    b. What does the Type option allow you to do?
    c. What input is made to the Chart Data and Options menu?
    d. How many colors can SuperCalc support?
    e. What does the Global option allow you to do?

17. Import
    a. How many different file formats can be converted to SuperCalc by the Import command?
    b. Can files be converted and consolidated with a SuperCalc file by the Import command?
    c. What is the limit for each SuperCalc cell when converting a NUMBERS format file?

18. Insert
    a. Describe the purpose of the Insert command.
    b. Write the keystrokes and results for inserting a row above row 3.
    c. Write the keystrokes and results for inserting a column to the right of column S.
    d. Write the keystrokes and results for inserting two cells in row 3 between columns J and K.
    e. What happens to absolute and relative cell references within formulas that are affected by cell insertion?

19. Justify
    a. Describe the purpose of the Justify command.
    b. What options are available under the Justify command?
    c. What does the Word-wrap option do?

20. Load
    a. What is consolidation arithmetic?
    b. Can a partial file be loaded? How?
    c. How does the Values option affect the spreadsheet it loads?
    d. What does the Single option do?
    e. If during loading of a file created by a previous version of SuperCalc a Memory Full message is displayed, what might the problem be?

21. Macro
    a. Define the term macro.
    b. Describe the advantage of a macro.
    c. What function is used to type a macro?
    d. Write the three steps in macro creation.
    e. Make a list of six macro control functions and their meaning.

22. Move
    a. How does the Move command differ from the Copy command?
    b. What may be moved?
    c. Write the keystrokes and results for moving row 5 to before row 11.
    d. Write the keystrokes and results for moving columns 2 and 3 to the left of column 6.
    e. What happens to absolute and relative cell references within formulas that are affected by moving rows or columns?

23. Name
    a. What is the purpose of the Name command?
    b. Why would you want to name a series of cells?
    c. What is used between words in a name?
    d. Write the keystrokes and results for assigning the name "Subtotals" to columns 3 through 6 of row 5.
    e. What happens to a formula that references a named cell when it is relocated by the Insert Row command?

24. Network
    a. How can you prevent access to network files?
    b. Can you change output devices using the Network command? How?
    c. Can you access a file server through SuperCalc? Write a syntax for doing it.
    d. What is the procedure for disconnecting from a file server directory?

25. Output
    a. What two peripherals receive the data when the Output command operates?
    b. The Console option does what with the output data?
    c. What is the purpose of the Borders option?
    d. Which option allows you to design the page format of a printed report?
    e. Can you print parts of a file? How?

26. Protect/Unprotect
    a. What is the purpose of the Protect command?
    b. How can a protected cell be deleted?
    c. How can protection be removed?
    d. What happens if you fail to enter a range and execute the Unprotect command?
    e. What type of error is encountered if you try to unprotect an unprotected cell?
    f. What other command can remove protection from protected cells?
27. Quit
    a. What is the purpose of the Quit command?
    b. What step should be taken prior to quitting?
    c. What does the DOS option do?
    d. How can you protect against losing files?
28. Restrict
    a. What does the Restrict command prohibit?
    b. What mode does Restrict put you into?
    c. How do you exit the Restrict command and operating mode it puts you into?
29. Save
    a. What option is used to save a file in the format of an earlier version of SuperCalc?
    b. To save the unaltered version of a file you have just edited as well as the edited version, how would you save it?
    c. The Values option of the Save command saves what data of a cell's contents?
    d. For what use is the Duplicate option well suited to?
    e. In what format does Save write a file on disk memory?
30. Spreadsheets
    a. What primary operations are done by the Spreadsheets command?
    b. How many spreadsheets can be open at one time?
    c. What key, when pressed, displays a list of open spreadsheets?
    d. How many spreadsheets can be displayed at one time?
    e. What option is used to scroll all displayed spreadsheets in unison?
    f. How do you move to other spreadsheets that are open?

31. Test (Audit Mode)
    a. What mode is entered when you select the Test command?
    b. Which option lets you look for cells that contain only formulas?
    c. What does the Overlap option look for?
    d. How does the Squeeze option save memory?
    e. Are search and replace operations done only when an exact match of an entire cell's contents are found?
    f. Is a search for cells containing only macros possible? How?
    g. Can you search for empty cells or cells that are not referenced by another cell? What options would be used?

32. Title
    a. What is the main purpose of the Title command?
    b. The Horizontal option does what?
    c. What three ways can title locks be removed?

33. Window
    a. What is a window?
    b. What are the five options available in the Window command?
    c. How is the cursor moved from one window to another?
    d. What is the purpose of the Synchronize option?
    e. What is a window border?
    f. How may a window be eliminated?

34. Zap
    a. Are protected cells affected by the Zap command?
    b. Does Zap erase a file from a disk?
    c. When a spreadsheet is erased from memory by Zap, is the file deleted from memory?

Index